The Big Game

The

Edwin H. Cady

Big Game

College Sports and American Life

THE UNIVERSITY OF TENNESSEE PRESS : KNOXVILLE

Quotations from Peter Matthiessen, *Under the Mountain Wall: A Chronical of Two Seasons in the Stone Age* (New York: Viking Press, 1962), are by kind permission of Viking Press.

Clothbound editions of University of Tennessee Press books are printed on paper designed for an effective life of at least 300 years, and binding materials are chosen for strength and durability.

Library of Congress Cataloging in Publication Data

Cady, Edwin Harrison.
  The big game.
  Bibliography: p.
  1. College sports — Social aspects. I. Title.
GV347.C3   796'.0973   78-6794
ISBN 0-87049-254-3

*"Looking with side-curved head curious what will come next,
Both in and out of the game, and watching and wondering at it."*
—WALT WHITMAN

Contents

Preface

This book began in a personal experience of wonderment—as a retired player tried to puzzle out the meaning of what you see and hear in the stands and around the edges of the game. What was all the fuss about? It took years to see that other, however related, games were played on the peripheries and by onlookers. Though the differences between the players' game and the others resemble the differences in wartime experience between fighting men and others, it came clear at last that their games are also real to the "civilians." Therefore *The Big Game* is a book about the games we play in the seats, in the stands or at home, much more than it is about the games the young play on the field or court.

A decade of intense experience with the effort to maintain "faculty control" of intercollegiate athletics at a major institution, in a great conference, and in the NCAA, cast light upon further dimensions of the situation. There is a great deal more, and at levels of much higher moment, than fun and games when the Big Game becomes play for the mortal stakes of the health of a great university—or even the welfare of higher education in the United States. There are recommendations.

Finally, professional experience with the study of "American Civilization" from mainly literary, historical, intellectual, and culturological points of view suggested that no phenomena so widespread in a population or so intense in expression could fail to be of great interest. I understand myself and my country better than I did when I began to write the book. I can only hope my reader (you *have* to believe in readers) will feel the same.

While this book was nearing completion, two of what I suppose the best books on sport appeared. I am glad they did not come earlier, because I might not have been able to free my own perceptions from the power of their fields of force. But I recommend them wholeheartedly. Excellent books, they are very different from each other and from mine—which illustrates the scope and multiplicity of the subject. The first I read was James Michener, *Sport in America*. The second was Michael Novak, *The Joy of Sport*. They seem to me to mark an era, superseding all but the classics of what went before, erecting a new and elevated base for work in the future. Where Michener's is ency-clopedic, analytical, in many ways extraordinarily well informed, Novak's is intense, personal, decidedly poetic, often metaphysical.

Neither, however, deals much with the college game. Both assume that the pro game is the American thing; and Novak inclines to suppose that the pro game on television, or the watcher's experience of it, is it. With deep respect for both, I of course cannot agree. In any case, I was committed to the perceptions of this book before I could read either. Grateful for their many supporting insights and a bit sorry for my necessities silently to disagree, I must hope that my book has its own truths. My debts to many other writers I have listed under "References."

Acknowledging personal debts is much harder to do, for I never learned anything about sports from a book one tenth so important as the major things I learned from people. They have taught me that, like all the most intense human experience, play plumbs too deep for the reach of mere language anyway. The first, least definable personal debt is acknowledged in the dedication. My father's keen thought, like his vivid speech, spoke from sporting analog to corresponding simile and metaphor. He lived *homo ludens* and treasured class, and I cannot remember when I did not plan to be like that too. Norma Woodard Cady not only typed every word of this—again and again—but she lived me into and through it, for many years.

After that my debts rise up beyond reckoning. Shall I try to name all my teammates and coaches—and opponents—who taught me the real thing? Or all my colleagues who taught me the operative truths of academic reality? Or the athletes and coaches I know and have known? Or my Big Ten and ACC and NCAA colleagues? Let me say Tenafly High School, Ohio Wesleyan and the Buckeye Conference, Wisconsin, Syracuse, Indiana and the members of its Athletics Committee, the Joint Group (with its commissioners and their staffs) of the Intercol-legiate Conference of Faculty Representatives, the National Collegiate

Athletic Association and its staff, and now Duke and the Atlantic Coast Conference. I could not guess accurately at how many people, and many vividly remembered, I represent by those collective names.

But I must name the people who have talked to me directly about this book and helpfully read all or parts of it for me. Though of course nobody but the author is responsible for his mistakes, those who have read all or some of the text in one of its several forms include Bill Bradford, Tom Butters, Clark Cahow, Anne Durden, Bill Foster, Fran and Ned Hitchcock, Bobby Knight, Mike McGee, Bill Orwig, Fanny Patton, John Pont, Ken Pye, Dorothy Roberts, Elizabeth and Larry Saler, John and Cathie Seelye, and Tom Wortham. New thanks to all of them and, for painstaking and sympathetic editing, to Ken Cherry.

For a special contribution made by each I must single out Bob Gregg, C.D. Henry, Elroy Hirsch, Jim Maguire, Hershel O'Shaughnessey, Lawrence Rosen, Ed Shaughnessy, Hank Sparapani, Bob Veteto, and George Williams.

And, finally, for many years, in some cases, of suggestions, information, or just good, rich talk, thanks also to William S. Armstrong, Brad Bomba, Ben Boyce, Howard Brown, Walter Byers, Don Canham, Dorothy Collins, Doc Counsilman, Chris Dal Sasso, John Dewey, Bob Dro, Wayne Duke, Oliver Ferguson, John and Jane Fisher, Fritz Foster, Bill George, Bob Hicks, Bob James, Don Kibbey, Don Matheson, Jack Lunn Mowers, Bill Murray, Reynolds Price, Gordon Ray, Bill Reed, Marcus Rhoades, Herm Rohrig, Harald Sandberg, Mary Sanford, Ben Schwartzwalder, Elvis Stahr, William Pearson Tolley, Herman B Wells, and Bill and Ellen Wilson.

Duke University made a special adjustment to provide a sabbatical year, and the John Simon Guggenheim Foundation renewed my fellowship—failing either, I could not have finished this book.

EDWIN H. CADY

Hillsborough, North Carolina
31 August 1977

Book 1.

The American Big Game

CHAPTER ONE

Givens

Though nobody in the modern world holds a monopoly on sports frenzy, the Big Game happens only in America. Except perhaps in China, sports madness is almost everywhere. Olympic competition is now a vicarious form of global war. Central American nations breaking diplomatic relations over soccer matches tell us the same thing as the moats and barbed wire around European soccer pitches or British fans trashing their trains and the shop windows of one another's towns.

But the American Big Game, repeated annually and often simultaneously on dozens of fields and floors, is a college game. Not, of course, that college sports monopolize American frenzy. Mets or Celtics or Cubs fans, Pittsburghers blowing the municipal mind over the Pirates or the Steelers, or mass downtown beer-busts in Cincinnati for the Reds merely illustrate the intensity of athletic passion in the common life. Participation active and spectatorial in sport occupies a mjor portion of the national attention. Newspapers often assign more space to sports than any other segment of the "news." Television networks scramble for ever increasing shares of the action, and there is still radio. Sports clothing crowds other styles to the wall. The manufacture and sale of sports equipment create significant industries. As enterprise as well as entertainment, sport in the United States is a massive cultural phenomenon. And yet it is hardly ever considered seriously.

Nevertheless, the collegiate Big Game is different. Nothing elsewhere resembles it. Nothing in professional sport captures, for all the flackery money can buy, the same glamor or intensity or significance. "I'm filled with wonder every Saturday," says John Pont, one of the more imaginative coaches. The difference arises from the unique involvement of major institutions of higher education and learning. It locks in symbolic combat the peoples of "sovereign states": Texas-Oklahoma; Tennessee-Kentucky; Wisconsin-Minnesota. It confronts massive regional and cultural differences: Notre Dame-UCLA; Penn State-Alabama; Virginia-DePaul. It pits life-styles and social convictions: Stanford-USC; Duke-Carolina; Rice-Arkansas. It is symbolically fratricidal: Grambling-Florida A.&M; Yale-Harvard; Providence-Marquette. Whole spectra of the national life clash fraternally in the Big Game.

"It was such an *American* experience," a Swedish boy cried after he had lucked into a classic. But what did he mean? The pageantry and hoopla have been raised to levels of artistry among us—the bands, the twirlers, the card sections, the cheerleaders, the stunts. Huge crowds pack the stadia all over the country at once, and their absorption has often been observed to resemble religion. We are used to the fact that millions watch the Big Game televised, while crime and accident rates plummet. But perhaps we should remember that before television there was, and now is, an immense radio audience; and before radio the telegraph wires clacked the play-by-play across the nation, and in Western Union offices, at railway stations, on the streets, and in the pool halls men chalked up the scores on blackboards for eager crowds. It is beyond doubt that something huge, intense, and meaningful to American life happens in the Big Game. If our appetite for it can be satisfied, we have not yet approached the limit. We are willing to put up with innumerable moments of the lesser try, the near-miss, the foregone failure, even the mendacious imitation, for a few moments of the real thing. The century past has been rich, as the present is eager, in the invention, evolution, and multiplication of new games, new modes, bigger and better facilities, improved methods, more opportunities, heightened communication. But what is this thing? It is a major form of public art.

As a topic of popular grocery store, filling station, cocktail party conversation—or of media discussion—collegiate sport is a subject without a temperate zone. Scratch a citizen and you find a zealot. Pro or con, everybody is interested, prejudiced, passionate, single-minded—of course. The net mood resembles that of the marine drill instructor of whom the boys said, "He has a very even disposition: fightin' mad all the time."

To come at a subject like that from a middling standpoint can be dangerous. No one ought to play God, and I am too simply a product of the same culture to pretend to be objective. The possible ploy may be to take an idea from Erasmus and write in praise of folly. Mine is the foolishness of the man in the middle, the American Innocent, the seer of multiple views and variant perspectives. I praise the folly of commitment by men and women to the best their bodies, hearts, minds, and spirits can imagine and attain in youth. I praise the folly of "fandom": of a passionate, communal, theatrical, Dionysian madness confined to the wild people in the stands. But I praise the folly too of honor, the impossible, necessary dream of control, a rational, sensitive, Apollonian reconciliation of athletic frenzy with the intellectual missions of a community of scholars. The wisdom against which I praise folly is every sagacity of easy, stark, monocular, exasperated, commercial, corrupt, ideological, or managerial simplicity.

Erasmian views, if that is what these are, generally prove unpopular, partly because they call off all the fights, but partly also because, being easily misunderstood, they often start new fights. Intending to help myself a little as well as the reader, therefore, I propose a set of principles for understanding American intercollegiate athletics, secure in a knowledge based on many conversations that I shall end in making everybody more or less unhappy.

Propositions

I. The two extreme positions familiarly taken with regard to the Big Game are both wrong. One party rallies around an aphorism, often attributed to the late Vince Lombardi, which achieved the force of a folk-saying: "Winning isn't everything—it's the only thing!" The other party holds to the proposition often advanced by the late Robert M. Hutchins: the Big Game has no legitimate place in the life of a community of scholars and must be abolished.

Both the Lombardi and Hutchins positions seem to me to lack connection to an adequate reality principle. Lombardi's fails for want of integrity. And Hutchins's position fails for want of authenticity. After roughly half a century of not catching the ear of the American university, the good Doctor seemed never to grasp the point that perhaps he had not understood the nature of the whole community of scholars; or the nature of the culture which nurtures that community.

II. The games we play and care most about (particularly football and basketball) were evolutionary inventions of the American universities, their students and faculties. The games evolved simultaneously with the institutions. They express organically the character and ethos of those communities. They possess, in essence, extraordinary authenticity.

Corollary 1: Our games began as boys' games. They belong to youth, not adults. They belong to the colleges and keep their true, best character only as college games.

Corollary 2: The professionals are in show business, like rock bands. What they really do belongs to the mass entertainment industry, which is notoriously corrupt, and they and their games are corrupted by it.

Corollary 3: Intercollegiate athletics must keep vigilant, even militant, to guard against being swept into show business corruptness.

III. Because time does make ancient good uncouth, integrity and authenticity in our athletics, faithfulness to their nature as expressions of the total academic community, not some genteel notion of "amateurism," must be the criteria for honor.

IV. The American university has become unique in the world. One aspect of that uniqueness is the existence, to say nothing of the character and effect, of our Big Game. These are facts: they are among the "givens" of our situation and can neither be wished away nor ignored with impunity. They demand to be understood more exactly and broadly than we have managed hitherto.

Corollary: Not only one of the givens of our culture, sport may be regarded as given to the human condition. Therefore our duty and necessity are to learn how best to deal with it—on the principle that the givens of the human condition may be transcendent goods if treated wisely but deadly evils if treated ill.

But this is not a book devoted to the question whether people would behave the way we do in the best of all possible worlds. It is too modest for that. "One world at a time," as Thoreau is said to have remarked on his deathbed. It is a book concerned with certain questions about how we do in fact behave: What happens? And what do those events mean? What can we learn about the nature of American culture nowadays? And, do all those things taken together look toward certain moral implications for American "good citizens"? Folly like the foregoing would challenge the powers of an Erasmus, and it is a shame that we have no Erasmus to take up the challenge.

Nevertheless, when everything had been said, it would remain true that the issues which matter in college sports also matter in American life: authenticity, community, democracy, honor, and redemption or renewal. Those words really are different names for the same thing and cannot be segregated. In the American grain the thirst for renewal is as old as the senses of failure, guilt, and sin. Really, again, they are the same thing—older than Western culture on this continent, yet in the American grain, at the heart of the matter. And the matter, the substance of the topic and so of this book, is finally moral.

"DOES IT HAVE TO BE THIS HARD?"

In half a century of watching athletics I have often felt that some of the finest achievements went almost without recognition. The same holds true in war, where medals too seldom go to the right people. Of course it holds true in human life. But there does exist a silent complex of recognition and respect which moves between men and women who have "been there" and suffered and come away with honor. It is most often a quiet tribute to that style of achieved personality which the athletes call "class."

There is a poem about all that by Emily Dickinson which would be psychically obscene on any set of terms but one. It begins: "I like a look of Agony, / Because I know it's true—." The saving circumstance is that the poem, typically of her best work, carries convictions to the reader that it really knows the truth it is talking about. It is that truth known to every veteran of agony—in military combat, crucial medical care, disaster fighting, personal crisis, or in athletic devotion at the extreme.

A black athlete phrased the question which provided the title for this portion of the book. It seems to me to stand near the heart of value judgments which have to be made in every aspect of the Big Game and in American life, to say nothing of the life of the race globally. It relates as a question to the impulse academic commentators call Faustian. It came "true," in Dickinson's sense, from the lips of Max Walker. Until he was a senior, Max rode the bench while some great basketball players fought, often staggering with exhaustion, magnificently—and just missed winning the championships one basket here or two there would have won. "They" never gave Max a fair chance. When he was a senior and the great ones were all gone, there was a new coach struggling to rebuild. Then Max proved himself.

Everything depended on Max. He ran the offense, led the scoring, provided leadership, played hurt and exhausted before scornful crowds mourning departed greatness. His team lost, narrowly and desperately, the hardest way. Max always came back. He had nothing to say about what might have been, and he never quit. And when it was over and a social occasion offered, full of admiration, I asked him, "Max, you had one of the greatest seasons I ever saw a man put on. How does it look to you now it's over?" "Well," said Max, "I have been wondering. Does it have to be this hard?" From many a failed athlete—or person—that question might seem disgraceful. But from Max Walker it came, in exactly Dickinson's sense, "true."

It is also hauntingly apropos, applicable to things far more important than basketball but illustrating the symbolic relevance of serious sport. Does it have to be this hard? Does there have to be just as much demand on human resources of body, mind, and spirit, just as much "pressure" as can be? Yes and no. Yes because man's fate, the human condition, the opportunity for a life with joy and truth in it, demand that. No because it does not have to be that way all the time, rhythm and balance and periodicity are essential, too. They require limits, and the name for those limits rightly understood is civilization. I like to think it allowable to translate what the oracle at Delphi proclaimed to a superb and tragic people as, "Not too much."

Yes, but what is enough? The point, I suppose, of Greek tragedy is that nobody, including the immortal gods themselves, can tell. As a personal experience, I found Dr. James Counsilman and his swimming teams a stunner. They revolutionized their ancient, beautiful sport—not alone, of course, but centrally. Repeatedly they smashed records which had represented the same sort of barrier as the four-minute mile. They have won every Big Ten championship since 1961 and more Olympic medals than most nations. Amid all his inventions in technique, equipment, training methods, openly shared with all the world, Counsilman proclaimed a personal formula for his people: "Hurt. Pain. Agony." If you wish to win, you must do it through real pain. If you wish to perform at the peak of your potential and break records and be the best in the world, you must learn to practice and train for long hours and compete, unerringly, in agony so great most people would think it unbearable. You must even do it gladly. It does have to be this hard.

Observation and academic records showed that, though of course not universally, Counsilman's paragons were charming, relaxed, well-humored young men. Their team grade-point averages not only topped those of all the varsity teams but ran well above the all-men's averages. Some of the best swimmers carried perfect or near-perfect "A" records while majoring in "hard" sciences. They trained eleven months a year, during the academic terms working, under Counsilman's formula, in the pool from six to eight o'clock in the morning and again from four to six o'clock at night. They were the best in the world. Could it be supposed that what they did was somehow wrong? out of keeping with the character and missions of a true university?

The accusations came to seem absurd to me. The real scholars and artists, like the real administrative servants of a university, live no less Spartan, devoted, productive lives than Counsilman and his swimmers. As prospective professional men and citizens, the swimmers—or the students at large—could carry away with them nothing more valuable than such experience can teach. No agony, no truth.

But of course it has to be agony in a form which does not destroy. It has to be an agony you cannot only survive but surmount, agony that educates. To teach by experience that such things can be and can be limited and brought to balance is one of the things for which a university exists.

The years during which this book gestated span the period, roughly, from the advent of *Hair* to the victory of Jimmy Carter. I suspect that you would speak the largely real but mute mind of the nation at Bicentennial if you said that in it a condition of moral fight, of ethical civil war, prevails. The country appears to yearn in some dim sense to ratify Emerson's faith "in the moral sentiment, which never forfeits its supremacy." He set forth the essence of his perception in "Montaigne; or, The Skeptic," saying:

> Things seem to tend downward, to justify despondency, to promote rogues, to defeat the just; and by knaves as by martyrs the just cause is carried forward. Although knaves win in every political struggle, although society seems to be delivered over from the hands of one set of criminals into the hands of another set of criminals, as fast as the government is changed, and the march of civilization is a train of felonies—yet. . . . Through the years and the centuries, through evil agents, through toys and atoms, a great and beneficent tendency irresistibly streams.

Without arguing about this famous "optimism," I think it is clear that the critical Emerson, as usual, threw his spotlight into the heart of one of the human—and American—dramas on which the curtain never rings down. And we are at a moment in it of William Blake's "mental fight," when "the moral sentiment" is awake in the aftermath of a double discovery from the events of the past decade in the national experience: that there have to be limits because there really are consequences for behavior; that our institutions are not invulnerable but

9

fragile and they need to be supported because the price for losing them is fatally high. Is there a state of war in American ethical sentiment between the moral and the amoral in business, professional, service, and public life? I think so.

I suppose the main evidence lies in the steadily rising heft of the national sense of scandal over the consequences of the moralities of exploitation, peculation, and "rip-offs" in general, of indulgence, affluence, and "trips," but especially of power and its abuse, "ego trips." It adds up to the horrors of Herbert Hendin's *The Age of Sensation*. And that problem, all worked out, arrives at one of two results: "moral fight," which is hard; or despair, which is at last harder. Said Emerson, "the world-spirit is a good swimmer, and storms and waves cannot drown him." Even if they might drown us, had we better not swim? To keep moralities of personal integrity and sensitivity and of service and sacrifice in being requires a good, tough, competitive fight. It has to be that hard—but it doesn't have to be so hard as despair.

I find myself inclined not to cite the daily juicier evidences of the M.D.'s and Ph.D.'s and Honorables of every description caught out in rip-offs and ego trips, or the evidence of the countless millions of "little guys" who can no longer morally manage a day's work for a day's pay. The hell with it. Given the fact of the Moral War, there exists no other way in which the Big Game stands symbolically and dramatically closer to the heart of the condition of American culture in our time than it stands in the moral relation. When such a war rages, should the culture's institutions of higher education, the real colleges, real universities, take sides? To say no is to capitulate to the amoral side; and in athletics that means that anything goes and the names of the games are *Win* and *Burn*. Personally, I cannot believe that the answer can be no; and if it is yes, I think the nature of a university requires it to fight on the moral side. What that means for athletics is control, internal and intrinsic to academe, to protect the Big Game and preserve it to perform its positive functions.

As we shall see, the esthetics of the Big Game loom so large, carry such intensity of charge, that people bodaciously lose their heads. Everybody wants a piece of that great, gorgeous thing, everybody wants to coach, everybody develops a yen for a piece of the action. And the roots of much of the trouble with the Big Game spring from the fact that, though the players enact their art on the field or floor, performing as serious artists, in the stands, just as in the audience at a play or concert, six or seven entirely different games are played in response. The same point holds for media consumers. It is a point observed since ancient times but never, perhaps, better than by Stephen Crane.

In 1896 Crane was sent to report the Princeton at Harvard football game for the *New York Journal*. Crane, just turned twenty-five, had won a varsity baseball letter at Syracuse and quarterbacked a town football team somewhere. He described the game crisply, unmistakably; but the crowd, ritualizing, celebrating, drew his uncanny eye. If you send a literary genius to a game, he will tell you something uncommon, of course. Crane wrote:

> Boston, Mass., Nov. 7.—Before the game and before the crowd the huge new wooden stands resembled monstrous constructions of the Northwestern lumber region, but soon black clumps of people began to dot these great slanting expanses, and the crimson flags of Harvard flashed here and everywhere. The silhouette of the vast crowd against the blue sky was a moving and tremendous thing . . . . In the certain section of the eastward stand, where yellow chrysanthemums bloomed profusely, there was a general and expectant silence. The orange and black flags rustled quietly and without emotion.
>
> Suddenly . . . Princeton's cheers rolled over the field, and the orange and black team trotted into the field. The gorgeous shocks of hair bobbed around after the ball, and the great orange capitals colored the dull November grass.
>
> They were grouped and consulting solemnly when the Harvard cheers pealed, crimson flags flamed out from the black crowds and the Cambridge team came on at a fast run. There seemed enough of them to make a batallion of infantry.

The colors, typically, served Crane as symbols, images, narrative motifs. He reported the first half as fairly even: "Then the Crimson came to defend the walls of its city of success, and the chrysanthemums in the stand threw a series of convulsions." At halftime, "the Harvard elation developed in songs and cheers, the great living hillsides flared with crimson, and the college band played the triumphant march of Sousa." (And at least two philosophers sat, reflecting, in the bleachers. Professor George Santayana, the bitter foe of American barbarism, who had published his essay in praise of football, "Philosophy on the Bleachers," not two years before, was almost surely there. Crane, master of ironies still deeper than Santayana's, was studying American life at every level from Bowery outlawry to Park Avenue plutocracy.)

After the half, Princeton gaining the wind, things changed. At a good Princeton punt, "the thousands of Harvard adherents broke forth a long and doleful groan." Eventually, Princeton scored on a broken-field run:

The Harvard flags were dead; the Harvard throats were silent. Everyone in the crimson stands might have been undergoing a surgical operation. But the Princeton crowd, minute proportionately, made havoc of the ears of the people across the bay in Boston. They howled and roared and raged. The enthusiasm of the orange and black for their team and their Bannard went to that acute stage which is almost the verge of tears.

A shadow of dusk came over the field at this moment to cover a grim time for Harvard . . . .

And after that, in spite of Harvard play "with the energy of a final despair," it was all Princeton:

The jubilant din increased as the day faded slowly to the twilight hour . . . . For the last ten minutes Harvard continued her same furious and desperate opposition, but the sublime Church, the illustrious Baird and the inspiring Brokaw were too numerous and too present, and so at sunset the Harvard fortunes concluded in defeat and three hundred maniacal chrysanthemums danced weird joy in the gloom.

Crane's story underlined the point that the crowd's game was played in a world different from that of the players. As counterpoint to the intense tone of his mass themes, he contrasted the silliness of spectators with the competency of the players. The climax of the action he framed in a little scene as aristocratic as a moment of Shakespeare:

Cabot, the Harvard end, went out of the game, and Arthur Brewer took his place.

A messenger boy said:

"Say is that Arthur?"

"Yes," said another messenger boy.

"Well, you just watch Arthur," said the first one. "Just watch Arthur."

The messenger boy had but concluded this encomium when the ball went into play, and Bannard, the Princeton quarterback, went through Harvard like a skyrocket, swept Brewer heels over head and swung through and around Harvard's backs. After a long and gallant run, aided by faithful interference, he went over the line to secure a touchdown for Princeton.

The aristocratic irony had nothing to do with "Cabot" but everything with Stephen Crane, whose gift of ironic insight had been sharpened by an athlete's astonishment at the incongruity between his order of reality and those of fans and the media. Crane's eye registered strata of experience at the Princeton-Harvard game, not fewer than six games going on simultaneously and without much if any necessary connection from one to the other. The variant games were those, first of the players and, second, of the student communities from which they came, which they represented. Also at the game were the "in" participants—they of the crimson flags or the "maniacal" yellow chrysanthemums in the stands. They represented a collegiate and upper social class of a prosperity which, in coming from Princeton or New York, could afford the Pullman jump or the night boat or the parlor car trips with two nights of hotel bills—all glamorous ways to party in transit. The messenger boys represented the "out" participants, those at the game but never part of the college community or those (the media audience) for whose pleasure Crane (the media) was paid to write from Cambridge. It was an oddly matched set with emotional and imaginative responses bound to flow in often conflicting currents. It was then, as in many ways it remains, a social, a cultural mystery: so much involvement, so broad, so intense, so extrarational.

Intrinsically nonrational play or hobby behavior seems natural, rather universally human. Kept clear of power considerations, it seems a harmless, probably healthy way of escaping from the cruxes of illusion and fact, appearance and reality, which afflict us cruelly in real life. Literature, for instance, can become one of the greatest of games; and I once was told at an alcoholic two o'clock in the morning by a *Moby-Dick* cultist, "For the past three years I have been living aboard the *Pequod*." Among the most amiable and best organized of such folk are the Baker Street Irregulars—devoted to playing a game of "Sherlock Holmes Lives" and entering fancifully into the reconstituted life of Conan Doyle's entrancing genius.

The trouble with the situation in college sport is that the equivalent hobbyists insist on a piece of the ongoing action. They insist on mucking into the lives of players, coaches, and colleges. And in spite of every experiment in control, some people are always rich or powerful or persistent enough to buy, bludgeon, or worm their way in. They become Baker Street Irregulars of college athletic life; but where there may be a few hundred balmy Sherlock Holmes fans, there turn out to be tens of thousands for the Big Game.

They dote on turning intercollegiate athletics into soap opera. They infest the recruitment process, scrambling to convert it into black bag operations, cops and robbers, cowboys and Indians. Left uncontrolled, they might not stop at anything. I do not know of a murder committed by any, but I know of serious warnings about the danger thereof. If the scholastic superstar is a little wise, or a little lucky in his parents, his coach, or an adult friend who has a little class, he will start to college the right way—which means keeping frenzy out of his college selection process. Perhaps at no other point in his career will an adequate reality principle serve him better. Players have been kidnapped in some cases, hidden out in others, even falsely arrested to sequester them from rival recruiters. No few youths have shipped a trunk on a ticket bought for Magnolia, Dixie, but found themselves housed, matriculated, and practicing at Athabasca, Montana, before they quite knew how it happened. Who did it? "The alumni"—if, indeed, they were so. Really, it was the Baker Street Irregulars, who may in person be actual alumni, or may not.

These are mainly the people designated in the NCAA rules as "representatives of the athletic interests" of a given college. In the arts as in all games, there always stand two fine lines: that between the player and the game, that between the vicarious player (spectator) and the actual player. Though there is an important sense in which, as Yeats suggested, you cannot tell the dancer from the dance, there is another, still more important, in which it is essential to sanity to be able instantly and perfectly to distinguish dancer from dance, artist from work, player from game, spectator from doer. The commonest test for the difference between psychopathology and neuroticism is customarily said to be whether one has the ability to distinguish between orders of inner and outer reality. Some of the Baker Street Irregulars of intercollegiate athletics get transported over the sidelines of sanity. They become wild, rigid literalists of games and arts. If you don't learn to expect them to do nutty things, you don't understand the situation.

Though the Irregulars are prone to be nuts, the significant issue looks to the moral war. On which side are they nutty? Are they good ones, our nuts? Or are they power crazy and ego trippers? The baddies are, in my observation, not "evil people." It's mostly not difficult with them to hate the sin but love the sinner. And the problem of the state of the bad guy's soul can be left to whatever issues there may be between him and himself or him and God. What will not do are the effects of his sins toward corrupting and at last achieving the moral disorientation of students, coaches, and academic communities, not to mention the public. He is, however, really sinister only when organized into a "program." Such a scheme to dominate Big Game competition by corrupt means often has two separable, though interrelated, lines of organization: an underground of coaches, scouts, alumni, subway alumni, paid recruiters and two-bit seekers of glory whose table of organization peaks at a senior assistant coach; a Fifth Column of trustees, high administrators, leading citizens (doctors, bankers), and professors whose line runs loosely to the office of the director of athletics.

Where the coaches' underground exists, its impulses toward horse-play and moral defiance are perhaps easier to understand. It comes readily to the members of such a group to think of the logistics of personnel replacement in their team as a *cosa nostra*, with three main sources of psychic energy to fuel their motives for spending life and treasure in the program. One source, always present in college life, is an adolescent hangover of identity-seeking defiance of authority and constraint. It splices neatly with the ancient connection between athletics and that masculine, sublegal "sporting life" often defined as vice, and they two join again with the antiprofessorial, antigenteel, antiacademic grudge many a student and ex-student carries from kindergarten to the grave. Hackles thus raised, the underground Irregular feels challenged by proposals to control him or his game by "the profs" or "the prexy": whose university is this, anyway? Defeated, he fights on, *homo agonistes* underground. Try to write a rule in which he can find no loophole!

Join to those impulses the relatively new ones rising from "the youth culture" and almost weirdly dominant in the life of American towns this decade past, and you will find that in the effort to control the Big Game you have a formidable competitor on your hands in the underground. For one thing, it has a moral sentiment, however misguided, of its own; and its fighting morale is superb. It sees that it has much of the firepower in the culture, no matter whether the alliances are quite conscious or not, on its side and it means to win.

Not quite so easy to understand, partly because its existence and operations are in some ways so implausible you have to see them repeatedly to believe in them, are, where they exist, the Fifth Columnists. On evidence direct as well as hearsay and evidence powerfully inferential, I have come to believe that almost no scandalous situation in major intercollegiate athletics occurs without the active complicity of some trustees. That is a fact which makes hay of the 1929 Carnegie Foundation report's simple faith that the college president can personally control the Big Game, be he only "possessed of the requisite ability and courage." If some of his trustees, some of his potent donors, some of the power centers in the politics that matter, and some of his key administrative officers and faculty are not only Irregulars but Fifth Columnists, he may face a fight so hard, and so costly to other and more important academic enterprises, that he will wish either quietly to join them or acquiesce. Hemingway's idea of "the Fifth Column," of course, was that it consists of enemies already inside the gates of the besieged city who are working actively under cover or lying dormant so as not to blow their cover until the moment comes, or who are fellow travelers and can be used, or who may even be double agents, working for both sides. Applied to the control of intercollegiate athletics, the idea sounds melodramatic. But how better to describe the persons who hold positions of honor and power and trust, whose word is pledged when the university's word to follow principles, comply with rules, honor treaties, is given—yet who actively, eagerly, pay and plan and act to the contrary?

I suppose their motives to be those of the crude fan, the literalist who would like to possess and devour in fact what can only be enjoyed esthetically, symbolically. They are also the motives of power grabbing and the ego trip so dominant among amoralists. No seat is handier to the pastry cart than the chair near the center of the academic—or any other—establishment. It's one thing to fight a coach—a proved, professional competitor. And it's another to fight that hard-nosed, many-handed underground with its closed mind and sealed ears. But if you want a real antagonist, try the Fifth Column, with all its power and all its cover and all its superb serenity—as Mark Twain said of such morale, "Like a Christian with four aces." There's a fight that has to be hard. But I am convinced that it has to be made, unrelentingly and all over the country, for the reason that the costs of not winning prove to be a great deal higher than the cost of fighting, even the cost if you fight and lose.

CHAPTER TWO

Beginnings

"HOW DID WE GET THIS WAY?"

So, in a burst of chagrin at the shame and confusion of his university after the exposure of cheating in its athletics program, a famous historian wrote me to demand not long ago, "How did we get this way, anyhow?" If a simple answer existed, of course there need be no angry question. But you can learn some useful things from a look at the historical paths along which Americans came to get this way.

As the present fact of the Big Game is peculiarly American, so of course is the story of the experience behind it. The early history of play, games, and sport in America is roughly known and, like much early history, satisfactory enough except that it tells us almost nothing about what we most need to know. For practical purposes there are no documents to illustrate what obviously happened. The rough, competitive team and communal games of Old England were, like the rest of its popular culture, imported to the American colonies. William Bradford tells us that, when they were hard at work trying to build and fortify Plymouth at Christmas, 1621, some of the non-Pilgrims of his company rebelled against labor "and said it went against their consciences to work on that day."

Accepting conscientious objection, Bradford excused them until, coming in to dinner at noon, he found Old English Christmas games in full swing, the men "in the street at play, openly." Bradford was shocked, called the games on account of blasphemy, confiscated the "implements of play," and told the men they might keep their holy day, if they thought it such, as a matter of devotion indoors: "But there should be no gaming or revelling in the streets."

It was of course a cardinal point of Puritan conscience to object to the sacramental symbolism of the Church calendar with its feast and holy days. Certainly it was the Christmas celebration not the games themselves—"some pitching the bar, and some at stool-ball, and such like sports"—which offended Bradford's conscience. It is true that various Puritans variously preached against games for grown-ups as lazy, good-for-nothing wastes of lives God meant to be productive. And Bradford had what was from his point of view an airtight case; they were playing childish games in the village street when the community had every sinew under stress to palisade its walls against the threat of Indian massacre.

The problem of the Puritans and what they called "temporals"— God's good gifts of the cheering pleasures and restoratives of this present, physical world—has been misunderstood, as scholars have pointed out for many years. The Puritans' documentable consumption of alcohol speaks the same thing about certain qualities in their lives as their bountiful production of babies in lawful wedlock. "Temporals" were, to Puritans, to be enjoyed richly—but properly—as God's gifts. That such was their attitude toward games and sports in themselves suggests itself in the extraordinary poetry of Edward Taylor, much of it "Preparatory Meditations" written as a Puritan minister readied himself to administer the Eucharist. Taylor's poetry is rich in imagery taken from the games and sports of Old England.

It will not do to say, as most sports histories do, that Puritanism suppressed sport in early America. There are the contrary hints; for one thing, effective preachers do not thunder from the pulpit against behavior nobody is doing anyway. Even in New England there was from the beginning, as W.D. Howells shrewdly observed, "that anti-Puritan quality which was always vexing the heart of Puritanism." The rest of the colonies were mainly, often decidedly, not Puritan.

Yet in the history of all the colonies stands a bothersome blank in testimony about the mere evidence of games. They were rooted so deep in the culture of the folk that they could no more have been lost than the Child ballads. Why is there no record, then, for two subsequent centuries of American behavior like the following instance of English folk culture noted at the historic threshold of American colonization?

In 1602 a Cornish "antiquary," or folklorist, recorded a game, obviously well established, called "Hurling . . . from throwing of the ball." In eastern Cornwall they hurled "to goals" but in the west "to the country." Its mere existence knocks the traditions about the founding of rugger into a sentimental cocked hat. Still more fascinatingly, Cornish hurling had in its rules and practice elements prominent in early college football in America which came from neither soccer nor "the Boston game." Underground connections must have existed.

For "hurling to goals," the eastern game, a shrewd evolution of bounds and limits had evolved, the better to test and display skill and hardihood. They paced off a field of a hundred or so yards in length and set bushes eight or ten feet apart at either end for goals. Then, said the observer, "there are 15, 20 or 30 players, more or less, chosen out on each side, who strip themselves into their slightest apparel, and then join hands in ranks one against another. Out of these ranks they match themselves by pairs, one embracing another, and so pass away: every of which couple are specially to watch one another during the play." At the goals each side "assigned for their guard a couple of their best stopping Hurlers." The rest went to midfield for the toss-up.

To start the game, "some indifferent person" threw out "a ball, the which whosoever can catch and carry through his adversaries goal hath won the game." But far easier said than done. Winning to the goal was a man's game, said Richard Carew, "therein consisteth one of Hercules his labours":

> For he that is once possessed of the ball hath his contrary mate waiting at inches and assaying to lay hold upon him. The other thrusteth him in the breast, with his closed fist, to keep him off; which they call Butting and place in well-doing the same no small point of manhood.
>
> If he escape the first, another taketh him in hand, and so a third, neither is he left, until . . . he either touch the ground with some part of his body in wrestling, or cry, "Hold," which is the word of yielding. Then he must cast the ball (named "Dealing") to some one of his fellows, who catching the same in his hand, maketh away withal as before. . . .

Since not many goals were usually scored, that side carried away "best reputation" which gave "most falls" or kept "the ball longest" or moved the action nearest the other goal. The closeness and roughness of play kept down the scoring, but so did the rules, the "many laws" of hurling:

> as that they must hurl man to man, and not two set upon one man at once: that the Hurler against the ball must not *butt*, nor handfast under the girdle: that he who hath the ball must *butt* only in the others breast: that he must deal no "Fore-ball," *viz.* he may not throw it to any of his mates standing nearer the goal than himself. Lastly, in dealing the ball, if any of the other part can catch it flying, between, or before the other have it fast, he thereby winneth the same to his side. . . .

Without referees the hurlers interpreted rules "by going together by the ears"—fighting. But "with their fists only," Carew hastened to add; and he thought it important to note that "neither doth any among them seek revenge for such wrongs or hurts but at the like play again." In an age when knife and swordplay were common, they left the game on the field. Finally, Carew noted, hurling tended to be a party game, "mostly used at weddings, where commonly the guests undertake to encounter all comers." Yes, sir!

"Hurling to the Country," however, played as a mass, cross-country brawl, comparable only to the Native American lacrosse matches of village against village or tribe against tribe. The country hurlings were matches made by "two or more Gentlemen" and pitted the players of "two, three, or more parishes" to a side. The goals were usually somebody's house on either side, "three or four miles asunder." Rules were few. "The ball in this play may be compared to an infernal spirit," said Carew: "for whosoever catcheth it, fareth straightways like a mad man, struggling and fighting with those that go about to hold him." Brought down, the carrier could throw it, and forward, to a team mate, chancing interception.

Country hurling led to mass scrimmages, "through bushes, briers, mires, plashes and rivers whatsoever so as you shall sometimes see 20 or 30 lie tugging together in the water, scrambling and scratching for the ball." Military strategies came into play, with ingenious end runs "seven or eight miles out of the way." Cavalry even were used, though a horseman with the ball could never feel safe, "for gallop any one of them never so fast, yet he shall surely be met at some hedge corner, crosslane, bridge, or deep water. . . . and if his good fortune guard him not the better, he is likely to pay the price of his theft, with his own and his horses overthrow to the ground."

Customarily, however, somebody won at hurling to the country, for the winning gentleman got the ball ("for a *Trophy*," said Carew, who did not mention the bets) and the surviving players devoted themselves to "the drinking out of his Beer to boot." In the last analysis, Carew concluded, "I cannot well resolve whether I should more commend this game for the manhood and exercise or condemn it for the boisterousness and harms which it begetteth." Players came home from hurling to the country as from battle, "with bloody pates, bones broken and out of joint, and such bruises as serve to shorten their days; yet all is good play, and never Attorney nor Crowner troubled for the matter." In a bitterly revengeful and litigious age, sport was sport.

For all the records seem to tell us, however, it was not the violence of "folk football" which disappeared from colonial American culture. The communal dimensions of team and village competition vanished. Nothing was more characteristic of early American behavior than personal or, to be truthful, mob violence. And the personal violence, at least, had a sporting side to it. You whipped or got whipped, maimed or got maimed, and no more hard feelings than were customary after hurling. But ritualized and symbolic war seem, at a folk level, to have been absent unless they found some thin expression in horse racing.

What, meanwhile, had happened to the ball games, the rudimentary team sports of Old England? Were they eradicated in America? Did they have to be imported again? Apparently not. They surfaced again in the early nineteenth century, well-rooted in American behavior, as in the famous plate of 1806 which shows top-hatted, tail-coated Yale gentlemen at rough play with a football. Where had the games been, then? What generally happened to patterns of adult behavior when, "in the old days," they lost their couth? They were absorbed into children's culture and preserved there like paleolithic bees in amber. Though evidence can be adduced to support the idea, it cannot be established beyond a reasonable doubt; but I believe that many of the forms and much of the spirit of Old English sport survived in American boy-life through the five or six generations during which they disappeared from historical perception in American colonial culture.

Here is testimony from the boy-life of what was then a "western" and had not long since been a frontier town in Ohio of the early 1840s:

> In the Boy's Town, they had regular games and plays, which came and went in a stated order. . . .
> There were many games of ball. Two-cornered cat was played by four boys: two to bat, and two behind the batters to catch and pitch. Three-cornered cat was, I believe, the game which has since grown into base-ball, and was even then sometimes called so. But soak-about was the favorite game at school, and it simply consisted of hitting any other boy you could with the ball when you could get it. Foot-ball was always played with a bladder, and it came in season with the cold weather when the putting up of beef began: the business was practically regarded by the boys as one undertaken to supply them with bladders for foot-balls.

It should not surprise that nobody much earlier thought to record what the kids were doing. The official invisibility of children's culture preserved it for centuries before our intrusively "child-centered" age destroyed it. For snobbish reasons, records like Richard Carew's observations on hurling have always been rare. Folk culture, much less that of children, has largely seemed beneath serious notice. Not until after the middle of the last century did Child collect the ballads most people took for granted. We knew that American college football evolved differently from soccer because of the decisive influence of "the Boston game"—brought up to Harvard from the secondary schools of that town. The fact illustrates a significant point: the games which grew into American college sports were indigenous to the student populations because the boys were people in transit, through the colleges, from boy-life to adult-life and brought the games to college with them.

In American life at large the games, especially baseball, moved back into adult life with the growth of cities. As the original "boy-books" of Aldrich and Mark Twain and Howells show, classic American boy-life was neither rural nor urban but a phase of village culture. A fair guess might be that putting increasingly large groups of boys into city schools, even private schools, stimulated organization and codification of the games and tended to increase school rivalries, which required control and institutionalization of the riotous results. On that base, perhaps, were built the fraternal and military and, after the Civil War with its demand for something for the boys to do in camp, the professional teams and clubs which become "organized baseball" and all that followed. The collegiate evolution was to pursue its own paths. But how did it come to be?

Thanks in part to Robert Merton, we are now fairly agreed that where a culture ceases to perform its office anomie afflicts the people. In American terms what is often wrong about our handling of that good idea is the accompanying notion that before modern urban-industrial times culture never failed and anomie was never social, only an individual aberration, a symptom of the sickness of a soul. It is one of our myths of romantic pastoralism about the Old Green Age. Culture was always fragile, subject to breakdown, seldom sufficient, always vulnerable to one of many forms of devastation. And never more vulnerable, obviously, than in such transits of culture as the creation of American life. The true wonder is how any form of American culture lived to survive its transits.

The major American cultural resource during the generations of the Atlantic transit was, unmistakably, religion. And the religion was "Judeo-Christianity" pluralistically expressed in Protestant forms. The colleges in their foundation and governance and continuing support were instruments of that religion, and their prevalence saved the turbulent new nation from its threatened relapse into barbarism. The national sense that they were important was correct. That all this has changed radically is one way of saying that we do not know yet whether we and the culture can survive the transit across the ongoing Industrial Revolution. But the Atlantic transit and the frontier transit of culture succeeded; and the colleges, with their foundations, faculties, and student bodies all religious, were prime instruments of survival.

It is as easy as it is sometimes desirable to forget all that; but I think it is necessary to remember and understand the religious circumstances if we are to understand the Big Game by its origins. It is about equally untrue that American sport was the child of Weber and Tawney's "Protestant ethic" as that "Puritanism" and "Protestantism" hated sport and suppressed it. To say nothing of Notre Dame, the elegant and penetrating work of theorists like Santayana, Huizinga, and Father Rahner speaks for the Catholic point of view. And no matter how many sermons were volleyed or how many denominational boards of education adopted resolutions of censure, the sports won out. George Santayana, in *The Middle Span*, spoke autobiographically to the heart of the matter. He went in the '90s to a Harvard game at New Haven as the houseguest of William Lyon Phelps, the Browning man:

> Yale, seen under the enthusiastic guidance of my *cicerone*, seemed a most living, organic, distinctive, fortunate place, a toy Sparta to match our toy Athens at Harvard. I liked it very much: what is more, I *believed* in it. That was the direction in which the anonymous, gregarious mind of America could be sympathetically brought to become distinct and integral. Harvard liberalism tended, on the contrary, to encourage dissolution, intellectual and moral, under a thin veneer of miscellaneous knowledge. Phelps was naturally pleased at seeing me so sympathetic. Not considering that I was fundamentally a Spaniard and a Catholic, he thought he had converted me to muscular Christianity; and in fact he had converted me to something Christian, namely, to charity even towards muscular Americanism.

Everybody talks about "muscular Christianity" but nobody studies it; it is not even a topic in standard religious histories. Its purported English founders, Thomas Hughes and Charles Kingsley, seem to have been willing to say little more than that they thought physical fitness and a readiness to compete appropriate for Christians: the subject cries out for a good book. Perhaps "muscular Christianity" expressed itself in the college sports, but I suspect that the effective impulse ran the other way. Religion was vital, though threatened, in the colleges. The athletic impulse, created by the students, was obviously powerful, authentic. People interested in religion brought them together as "muscular Christianity."

But the religion itself, "Judeo-Christian" through all its variants, was always agonic (strenuously competitive) and fraternal. Trying to cope with the present human condition, we have preferred to forget that Biblical realism is often militant. It may sometimes be a grave hindrance to our imperative search for the peaceable kingdom that our myths of the pastoral forbid us to recall that before Pasteur the world held human life cheap. What we keep having tragically to relearn as "military morality"—that in combat everybody is "expendable"—was once the universal rule of life and of the essence of Biblical realism. In its histories, in the Psalms, and in the prophets the Old Testament is agonic as only the literature of a cause defeated but not lost can be. In many of the parables of Jesus, in the history of the early church, and in the epistles of the New Testament a militant, even imperial imagery echoes again. Yet God's Israel, the righteous, the saving remnant, the elect, His Chosen, the company of believers, the congregation of the faithful, the Church—all these and more are fraternal: the families, and the brothers and the sisters, the children of God, the collective bride of Christ.

The Judeo-Christian scenario for universal history and man's fate was the same. Whether universal, national, confessional, or personal the script was apocalyptic and probationary. It was agonic and aimed at victory: God, making all things, began history, maintains it as the drama of His covenants, and will end it as He chooses, in humanly inscrutable wisdom with total victory for His People. It was all war and drama, but as macro-history it was a fixed fight. And for early college men in the midst of micro-history, it was absurd not, at the last, to avail oneself of Pascal's Wager and enlist as a child of God. Then all the trials and dangers of man's life became mere probation. Play but a man's part on God's stage and fit yourself for Heaven: "The Trial by Existence." So "manliness" in the soul was godliness.

The imagery in which St. Paul found it useful to talk to his Greek households of faith spoke directly to the condition of American undergraduates a century ago and speaks to athletes now. Not, he told the Philippians, to talk as if he were already a winner or perfect, "this one thing I do: forgetting what's behind me and reaching toward what's ahead, I press forward for the finish-line for the prize." Or, as he explained to the Corinthians: "Don't you know that of all who compete in a race only one wins the prize? Run to win. And every man that competes in the games pays the price, he trains hard. Now they do it to win a prize that will fade away; but we for one that lasts forever. So I run hard. When I fight, I don't shadow-box. I punish my body to get it under control." And so he told Timothy at the end: "I have fought the good fight; I have run the distance; I have kept the faith."

Standing with those who do not believe that there can ever be one key to unlock all the mysteries of what Walt Whitman liked to call "This America," I do not offer the formula of agonism and fraternity as the one true rule. But it was and it remains basic to the American experience. In preindustrial America, through religion and agriculture, through marriage, the family and child-rearing, through business and law and politics and social groupings, through the arts, crafts, and modes of fun, through the sense of national destiny and significance ran impulses agonic and impulses fraternal. It was not that some were the one thing and others the other, either. All were both, all ambivalent and therefore laden with tension and conflict.

It is notorious that from their contradictions and multivalences the Americans got mixed results—results so mixed as to tend toward polar opposites. Great energies were released with fateful consequences; and new hopes for the future of the human race seemed to spring from the virgin soil of a new world tilled by the world's new man, the American freeholder. "What then is the American, this new man?" inquired St. Jean de Crèvecoeur in famous words, and replied: "The American is a new man, who acts upon new principles"; therefore "we are the most perfect society now existing in the world." But he was poignantly aware of contradictions. In the too great freedom of the long hunter's wilderness conditions, Crèvecoeur saw people take on the character of "the surrounding hostility" and become "ferocious, gloomy, and unsociable," degenerate and worse than Indians, lazy, rapacious, vicious, and violent.

Fenimore Cooper, who really knew his frontier better than almost any other American writer, saw the contradictions differently from Crèvecoeur; probably both were right. In the wilderness, "at the commencement of a settlement," he observed, generalizing from the experience of his father's foundation of Cooperstown, the fraternal reigns in "that sort of kind feeling and mutual interest which men are apt to manifest toward each other when they are embarked in an enterprise of common hazards." Here, "Good-will abounds . . . and life has much of the reckless gaiety, careless association, and buoyant merriment of childhood." It is a period, once outgrown, the pioneers

25

remember affectionately and regret the more because what comes next is an era sheerly agonic "in which society begins to marshall itself, and the ordinary passions have sway."

His middle, agonic period of American social evolution Cooper thought "perhaps the least inviting condition of society that belongs to any country that can claim to be free, and removed from barbarism." He saw in it a condition of total war for wealth and status, a time coarse, vulgar, tasteless, a time civilization could only hope to outlive until the struggles had been concluded and the issues settled by the victorious emergence of the American country gentleman.

Long awaited, often announced, eloquently mourned, Cooper's settled society never emerged, of course. But those themes of the fraternal and agonic with which all his writings work became the themes of Emerson and Hawthorne, of Melville and Whitman, of Mark Twain and Henry James and Howells, of Stephen Crane and Robert Frost and William Faulkner—of American expression from the beginnings to the nows of John Updike and Saul Bellow. They are not in the least exclusively American themes; on the contrary, they perhaps characterize more variant cultures than not. But that there is an American blend and force in our variants and that these found expression which brought peculiar verve and satisfaction to the popular culture—not only in literature, the heart of highbrow culture, but in the Big Game—seems so patent it is almost embarrassing to have to say it. It all dawned with the second century of the Republic and the coincident rise of the Age of Sport.

In the early colleges, of course, far more than religion supported the agonic and fraternal values of Western culture in their American and then current conditions. They taught the classical rudiments of a gentleman's education and "political economy" until they began to add serious scientific subjects as the nineteenth century wore on. But it all came to the same things. To Americans the classics spoke the language of romantic individualism: "Produce great persons, all the rest follows." And George Washington, if not Ben Franklin, was as good as the heroes of Plutarch. When the sciences came they were baptized; and then they were romanticized; and when they had outgrown that they were Darwinized.

"Political Economy" was sometimes the course the college president gave the seniors. It justified the ways of mercantile capitalism to the children of privilege, supplying them with reasons for the propriety of the class structure and its advantages to them. When economic, the arguments were mainly agonic. When political, they were often fraternal. Hardly anybody noticed any hint of difficulty about this or about the facts of social class in the colleges. They had been created, on the British model, by clergy and gentry to perpetuate those classes and, incidentally, to serve as social ladders for "natural gentlemen," the gifted sons of the lower middle classes.

At any rate, the official and intellectual side of the college encouraged the student to suppose that agonic and rather limitedly fraternal ideas answer to the nature of reality. As he brought it with him and as it struck upon the collegiate consciousness, the world outside academe taught the same lessons. One of its prominent features was violence— often said to be as American as apple pie, it is also as Indian as curry, as British as beer, as Chinese as chopsticks. American folk fought with fists or rough-and-tumble, adding sticks and sometimes stones upon occasion. The gentry traveled armed and got into cutting and shooting affrays, sometimes duels. Mob actions and prosecutions by Judge Lynch were nowhere unimaginable. On the frontiers the arts of biting, gouging, bushwhacking, and "the quick draw" embellished the violence.

With whatever regional differences, the American had to demonstrate his "sand" and vindicate his "honor" or grow accustomed to humiliation. Quite naturally, violence was endemic in student life. The eternal wars of town and gown raged unabated, and at Yale they had a college bully for defense against the New Haven toughs. He was the formidablest fighter in the student body, carried as his mace of office the hereditary Bully Club, led and rallied student forces to the defense of the dormitories and the rescue of waylaid comrades, and was relied upon as the "stopper" in any serious fray.

From certain points of view a college can be described as a four-year initiation ceremony marked at regular intervals by successive *rites de passage*. The student body is a community, a subculture which functions to help adolescents move, step by step, toward citizenship and adulthood. Internally, the relatively senior members of the community train up the relatively junior until, at the end of the process, the faculty and other adults must step in to administer something like terminal rites to the finalists. From "freshman days/daze" to "Commencement" the initiates' problems are adolescent and fundamentally defined by Freud's *Civilization and Its Discontents*. And ritual violence works as well for colleges as it works for adult military and fraternal organizations or other primitive societies.

Ritualized as fagging, hazing, flag rushes, pole rushes, cane rushes, "class football," and the like in a hundred local variants, college violence "cured" the "green" out of newcomers, knocked and ground rough corners off too abrasive young egos, discovered and defined identities, and, in the odd way of such things, promoted group solidarity. It was of course a safety valve. But insufficiently binding and satisfying in those inchoate forms, it left too much energy and discontent over for hell-raising and vice.

My grandfather admired basketball and gymnasia because his recollected experience of the ennui and stress of mudtime in Schenectady during his years at Union College in the 1890s had left him appalled. With nothing active to do for gray, soggy weeks, the boys on his landing had one traditional resource. They would steal their traditionary cannonball from the tutor's room down by the entry and at just the right moment of an unbearable evening send it booming and smashing down the stairs to be confiscated. After the compelling need of youth, however, they destroyed the game and tradition—and very nearly their collegiate careers—one night. Wondering what would happen, a bemused lad put the cannonball on the stove for a good while before he sent it down the stairs. Then they clustered solemnly at the top to watch what came next after the tutor tried to pick it up.

But the Union jape is easily capped from the treasures of history. Samuel Eliot Morison cited in *Three Centuries of Harvard* a student notebook from 1671 preserving the story "of a dirty trick played on President Dunster." Having daubed the bannister with "sir reverence," the boys kicked up a fuss at the top landing which tolled the President into the trap: " 'Who did this foul deed?' Dunster demanded. 'Whoever did it, it seems you had a hand in it,' answered a voice from the dark at the top of the stairs."

Of course the evidence could be multiplied. At Yale even Timothy Dwight found that religious revivals and student riot went hand in hand. At Princeton the student riots and defiance threatened the life of the college. *In loco parentis* for more than three rugged centuries, the presidents and faculties struggled to inculcate morality and maintain order while, over and over again, for twenty-five college generations to the century, and in ever-growing tens and hundreds of institutions, the students wined and wenched and gambled on the waterfront or "on the levee" or in the taverns. Rackets and riots boomed through the quads, and bells were silenced by having their ropes cut, clappers stolen, or their mouths stopped with water left to freeze in upturned forms.

Outhouses were turned over, and gunpowder banged in corridors. Professorial buggies bloomed mysteriously on steeple-tops, and presidential cows were tenderly led up the narrow steps of belfries. In the long run, student inventiveness would handle these matters better.

The face the early college turned toward its students was grim, the qualities of life it offered not only disciplinary but penitential. College life grew bleak, even brutal, except as it could be tempered and sweetened by the students. And the students had three resources. They could raise mere adolescent hell. Or they could import into college life the amenities and vices of the world outside. Or they could invent their own amenities which, accumulating through the generations, were to become one of the few American subcultures to take on a genuine glamor for the nation at large—"college life."

WHAT THE STUDENTS CREATED

Though it has been argued that people learned from their play to think in the first place, it is sure that thought about play is ancient. Still, the most useful starting points for discussion of the Big Game were set by George Santayana at Harvard during the Gay Nineties. Subtlest and most austere of philosophers, Santayana was perhaps the least placable of American culture critics. He is even now among the most melancholy of American poets. He scorned our tradition for being that bastardized version of Europe which he called the "genteel tradition," supplying the field of culture criticism with a most treacherous cliché. The bulk of what he thought authentic in the life of the United States he scorned as barbaric.

"My heart rebels against my generation," he said, meaning even such figures as his colleagues William James and Josiah Royce. And as a philosophic naturalist he could believe in no ultimate truth beyond that streaming chaos of inhuman fact and force in the universe which Justice Holmes called "cosmic weather." Knowing for himself, an intensely cultivated, lonely humanist, that in such a universe what realities human beings can bear must be of the sort Wallace Stevens called "supreme fictions," Santayana proclaimed himself "a Catholic who does not believe in God." For such a manifestation of "Americanism" as the art of Walt Whitman, Santayana could find only the praise that it was "the poetry of barbarism." He may not be the most ruthless culture snob in the history of American self-criticism, but he is competitive.

All that being true, no one could expect to find among his poems an "Athletic Ode," done self-consciously in the mode of Pindar, the great Greek Olympic bard. Ignoring baseball—as not Greek?—he began with the sports of spring: track and field, crew. But then he leaped in climax to the game he loved, the one he wrote to justify:

> But the blasts of late October,
> Tempering summer's paling grief
> With a russet glow and sober,
> Bring of these sports the latest and the chief.
> Then bursts the flame from many a smouldering ember,
>   And many an ardent boy
> Woos harsher pleasures sweeter to remember,
> Hugged with a sterner and a tenser joy.
>   Look where the rivals come:
> Each little phalanx on its chosen ground
> Strains for the sudden shock, and all around
>   The multitude is dumb.
>   Come, watch the stubborn fight
>   And doubtful, in the sight
> Of wide-eyed beauty and unstinted love
>   Ay, the wise gods above,
> Attentive to this hot and generous fray,
> Smile on its fortunes and its end prepare,
> For play is also life, and far from care
>   Their own glad life is play.
>
> Ye nymphs and fauns, to Bacchus dear,
> That woke Cithæron with your midnight rout,
>
>   Arise, arise and shout!
> Your day returns, your haunt is here.
> Shake off dull sleep and long despair;
> There is intoxication in this air,
> And frenzy in this yelping cheer.
> How oft of old the enraptured Muses sung
>   Olympian victors' praise.
>   Lo! even in these days
>   The world is young.
>   Life like a torrent flung
>   For ever down
> For ever wears a rainbow for a crown.
> O idle sigh for loveliness outworn,
> When the red flush of each unfailing morn
>   Floods every field and grove,

And no moon wanes but some one is in love.
  O wasted tear,
A new soul wakes with each awakened year.
Beneath these rags, these blood-clots on the face,
The valiant soul is still the same, the same
The strength, the art, the inevitable grace.
  The thirst unquenched for fame
Quenching base passion, the high will severe,
The long obedience, and the knightly flame
Of loyalty to honour and a name.

Give o'er, ye chords, your music ere ye tire,
  Be sweetly mute, O lyre.
Words soon are cold, and life is warm for ever.
One half of honour is the strong endeavour,
Success the other, but when both conspire
Youth has her perfect crown, and age her old desire.

Santayana played a subtle game with his classical "machinery"—
allusions, invocations, quotations—in "Athletic Ode." Precisely the
fake "classicism" of American thought, art, architecture, and education was what he damned as "genteel." How could he wax Pindaric
about college football, then? Because he saw it to be free, unpremedi-
tated, and real—*gentlemanly*, not *genteel*. American freedom, spontaneous and disinterested, as in humor or sports or student life, seemed
to Santayana the best thing in the national manners. At Harvard, a poet
among professors, he aligned himself with Barrett Wendell and "Char-
ley" Copeland in "affection for . . . the College, not for the University."
He sympathized with "the traditional follies there present . . . the
normal, boyish, almost desirable follies of youth," because "the *virtu*
there fostered and admired was genuine *virtu*, not perhaps useful . . .
but good and beautiful in itself." He felt moved to protect and "propa-
gate that *virtu* against the steam-roller of industrial democracy," seeing
that "these were precisely the follies and *virtu* that democracy, if
liberated from the steam-roller, would cultivate of its own accord." He
could not bear "that this spontaneous life of the people should be
frustrated by the machinery of popular government and of incorpo-
rated private interests."

What did he mean? He illustrated his point in a number of places: as
in remarks on American humor, good, for all its banality, because it
genuinely amounts to "an admission that existence is absurd; it is
therefore a liberation of the spirit over against this absurd world; it is a
laughing liberation, because the spirit is glad to be free; and yet it is not

a scornful nor bitter liberation, because a world that lets us laugh at it and be free is after all a friendly world." Or in rejection of owlish remarks on education in the United States: "Freedom—and young America furnishes a proof of this—does not make for enlightenment; it makes for play. A free society would create sports, feasts, religion, poetry, music."

Only in the light of such remarks can "Athletic Ode" be read accurately. And the same is true of that other surprise from the years Santayana called "the high tide of my second College period," with its "recently acquired taste for contemplating athletic contests." In the *Harvard Monthly* for July 1894 appeared an essay by Professor George Santayana entitled "Philosophy on the Bleachers."

Most of the usual explanations and defenses of "the sudden irruption of the sporting spirit" are misplaced, says the philosopher, for "athletics have a higher function than gymnastics and a deeper basis than utility. They are a response to a natural impulse and exist only as an end in themselves." It may be true, he admits, that "athletic enthusiasm" is "irrational"—not "Athenian, not vivacious, sensitive, or intelligent. It is rather Spartan." But, he contends, "this reproach of irrationality ultimately falls upon every human interest, since all in the last analysis rests upon an instinct and not upon a rational necessity." It is now, as it was with the Greeks, not even true that athletics are militarily useful. On the contrary, they flourish in the absence of wars, "only in nations that are young, free, and safe." Athletics stand in the same relation to war as "that of the drama to life," symbolically, by analogy, as a peaceful "liberation of martial energy from the stimulus of necessity, and the expression of it in beautiful and spectacular forms . . . . War can thus become a luxury and flower into artistic forms."

There is the heart of Santayana's philosophy on the bleachers: true athletics are true art, and the bleacherite sits, watching football, experiencing art as well as the consumer of any form of esthetic expression. The argument is worth following. Though "comfort and happiness" might best be equally distributed to every person in the world, the opposite is true of the arts: "The value of talent, the beauty and dignity of positive achievements, depend on the height reached . . . . Enthroned in those best moments, art, religion, love and the other powers of the imagination, govern our character, and silently direct the current of our common thoughts."

Athletic sports, then, stand among "the powers of the imagination." They are "not children's games; they are public spectacles in which young men, carefully trained and disciplined, contend with one another in feats of strength, skill, and courage." Though "spectators are indispensable, since without them the victory, which should be the only reward, would lose half its power," it is only accidental, not necessary, that athletics have a "relation to colleges." It is natural, since they have "a necessary relation to youth" and "those of our youth who unite leisure with spirit are generally at some university." Still, as Plato knew, who assigned "seven years to the teacher of the arts and seven to the athletic trainer," competitive sports are inseparable from a liberal education.

The true reason for that may be grasped in the distinction between "athletics and private sport." The difference between football and angling "is that between an art and an amusement," says the philosopher on the bleachers:

> The possibility of vicarious interest in the one and its impossibility in the other are grounded on the meaning which athletics have on their appeal to the imagination. There is in them a great and continuous endeavour, a representation of all the primitive virtues and fundamental gifts of man. The conditions alone are artificial, and when well combined are even better than any natural conditions for the enacting of this sort of physical drama, a drama in which all moral and emotional interests are in a manner involved . . . . Therefore, when some well-conceived contest, like our football, displays the dramatic essence of physical conflict . . . the whole soul is stirred by a spectacle that represents the basis of its life.

Therefore "athletic games," as "physical dramas," are capable "like other tragedies, of a great aesthetic development" not yet seen, Santayana perceived, in his time. "Our own games," he added, "in which no attention is paid to the aesthetic side, are themselves full of unconscious effects, which a practised eye watches with delight." And so to a philosopher's peroration:

> When I hear, therefore, the cheering at our great games, when I watch, at Springfield or at New London, the frenzy of joy of the thousands upon one side and the grim and pathetic silence of the thousands upon the other, I cannot feel that the passion is excessive. It might seem so if we think only of what occurs at the moment. But would the game or the race as such be capable of arousing that enthusiasm? Is there not some pent-up energy in us, some thirst for enjoyment and for self-expression, some inward rebellion against a sordid environment, which here finds inarticulate expression? Is not the same force ready to bring us into other arenas, in which, as in those of Greece, honour should come not only to strength, swiftness, and beauty, but to every high gift and inspiration? Such a hope is almost justified by my athletic philosophy.

Though it was all prescient, penetrating, permanent into our own era as only the insights of genius can be, there was one trouble with Santayana as he helplessly knew. Like Pindar's, his mind and taste were aristocratic. And the world has grown not to permit the aristocratic to govern, perhaps not to permit the aristocratic, as such, to retain vital meaning in it any more.

Considering the poet's concern for "fame" and "success" as ingredients of "honour" and the philosopher's recognition that "spectators are indispensable," there is a small temptation to smile at the philosopher's insistence on "disinterestedness." How far really have the poet and philosopher come from certain worlds of primitive culture? To be sure, "essences" only concerned Santayana. It was all so Hellenic and chivalric: was it a bit romantic? Still, Santayana had put his alienated fingertip on a crucial point. As the American problem has always been to democratize the feudal culture of Western Europe without sacrificing its best values, so the global parallel has become a problem of the whole world in our times with regard to the total past. Nowhere is that truer than in the one activity, sport, around which all the world can unite—at least to compete.

In the immediate context of American intercollegiate athletics, Santayana had seen into the stone deeper than any critic, reading the true nature of a new phenomenon with a precision not matched in his time and seldom since. The very type of "modernism," Santayana personally was what the French call *déraciné*, a rootless plant, a Spaniard and Catholic in Protestant America, an atheist and American in Catholic Spain. To redouble his alienation, at Harvard he was a poet and a live, creative philosopher among scholars, historians, scientists—what seemed to him the anesthetic and second hand. His heart went out to the students, whom in certain ways he understood.

His best insight was the perception that, flouting the "rationality" of the faculties, student activities, for all they might be "the follies of youth," deserved the name of *virtu*. For *virtu* is an Italian term sacred to the tradition of Baldassare Castiglione's *Il Cortegiano*, or *The Book of the Courtier*, the greatest of classics among the courtesy books. On those books, in all the polite languages of Europe, were trained the gentlemen of Europe for centuries. And *virtu*, untranslatable, was their name for an essential quality of the Renaissance gentleman. It meant that he was not merely acquainted but "accomplished" in the arts so that he could not merely enjoy but practice them, could not merely perform but adapt them to triumph esthetically over the troubles and boredoms of life. *Virtu* was, as a word, in itself one of the achievements of European high culture.

To have said in a meeting of the Harvard faculty that undergraduate behavior and activities represented *virtu* in the United States would have got Santayana consumedly laughed at in adult Cambridge. Chief among the mockers would have been Charles Eliot Norton, the great, kindly, mournful authority on the Medieval and Renaissance who regularly told the students, "None of you has ever seen a gentleman." And the silvery laughter of the town would largely have echoed from that audience for Norton's sorrows who taught Santayana that culture in the United States belonged to "the genteel tradition."

The problem of an American culture, as Emerson said, is to be alive and furnish the American soul authentically. Without much liking Emerson, Santayana saw that student "follies" responded creatively to Emerson's charge and therefore deserved the name *virtu*. Another way, historically accurate, to say much the same thing is to observe that the circumstances and conditions of early American college life demanded creative response from the students. They could not have adopted the traditions of English or European student life, itself confused and bewildered by recent developments, had they known them well. Theirs was a perfectly American situation, and they responded.

You have to be monocular not to notice that at least since the time of Abélard the lives of universities have had two sides. The faculties and their facilities constitute the intellectual side, official and indispensable, of an institution of the higher learning. But the students constitute the university, now and in its particular being. If the university be a community of scholars, the students, existentially and vitally, so dominate that they *are* the community and that community has, in the present, little other life than theirs. Every wise professor knows that he can as professor represent but half. He remembers that he was (and is) a student; and he remembers from experience that at least half, and perhaps the better half, of education comes from what the students and their collective life teach. He sees the energy and wit and creativity of the students blazing among their adolescent griefs and disabilities; and as teacher he begs, not always tacitly, "Just give me an even break. All I ask is half of it."

The other half belongs to student life. It fuels follies: as what human energy does not? But some of them are Erasmianly sophomoric. They are follies wise because, responsive, at their best, to personal need, they call forth *virtu*. In a university, personal, human, student need is communal and a challenge. For the collegiate subculture it is, in Arnold Toynbee's sense, a challenge of the sort to which the culture must rise or suffer diminution. Insofar as the university is a living organ in the body of the culture at large, the health of the culture rides with its fate.

The inventions which created college life, then, are obviously significant—both important and meaningful, that is. But if they represent *virtu*, what were and are the challenges to which they arose? The answer is, challenges which came from the conflicts and deprivations of the culture at large. Of that culture at large, a lumpy mix of institutions and patterns of behavior, the colleges were both instrument and expression. The culture was at once, and with pungent ambivalence, agonic and fraternal. If, in collegiate games, student *virtu*, with its roots in the larger culture, could invent something, a major public art form, which spoke to the condition and met part of the needs at large of that hugely convulsed culture, that would be a contribution indeed. And it is what, in the Big Game forms of intercollegiate athletics, the students actually did.

The instrument which came handiest to student invention was so richly available in the larger culture that some observers have thought it typically American: voluntary association. The late Bradford Smith was fruitful in sharp analysis of that favorite device for reconciling the agonic with the fraternal. Though American expertise with association had sprung from Protestant and frontier roots, he thought, it had proved especially serviceable to the mature, pluralistic nation:

> There are functional groups like labor unions, occupational groups like the medical societies and farmers' organizations, philanthropic or reformist like the associations to stamp out disease or improve education, religious groups, nationality groups which depend on the Old World ties of immigrants, groups which perpetuate shared experiences such as the Daughters of the American Revolution, college alumni or war veterans, symbolic groups like the totem lodges or the Masons, and recreational, political and feminist organizations. . . . Our society, in short, is competitive in its social and civic groupings as in its economy.

Politically, religiously, communally, the nineteenth century teemed with organizations, loving nothing so much as an occasion to parade their solidarities and replete with the uniforms and bands and paraphernalia, often totemic, calculated to make the gaudiest impression. Though student communities were specialized, masculine, and under tutelage, from the middle decades of the eighteenth century forward they grasped the creative potential of voluntary association and organized "activities." Beginning with "literary" and "elocutionary" societies which gloried in idealistic constitutions and odd-sounding Hellenic names ("Philomusarian," "Zetagathean," "Cliosophic"), they progressed to the secret, Greek-letter fraternity (Phi Beta Kappa). From there it was a short step to organizations for music, theatricals, publications, fields of intellectual interest, conviviality, hoaxes, or simple snobbery. "Success" came quickly to be equated with acceptance or election, as the agonic moved into the fraternal bed once more. Rather oddly, it took almost a century until the advantages of association for sport were gradually perceived. Nothing could be more perfectly agonic and fraternal than a team in the newly dawning Age of Sports.

The French, who admire without having quite understood, still call it *le sport*. Competitive sports of all sorts, building on momentum slowly accumulated since the Restoration, "took off" in Great Britain during the second half of the nineteenth century. Not cricket, soccer, and rugger alone, but almost everything now in the program of the Olympic Games together with sports that are not, like tennis, became more than pastimes—virtual ways of life. The rest of the English-speaking world, including the United States, followed eagerly, inventing games of their own as they ran. Europe and the rest of the world tagged along behind. Competitively, their time would come in the next century.

It is now just about a hundred years since the full storm of athletic enthusiasm burst on the English-speaking societies. In broadest terms there were three obvious factors in the British and American situations which energized the rise of sport. A true triad, mutually reinforcing, they were at once institutional and cultural; and as culture they were at once overt and covert. No matter what the prices of which we are now deeply conscious, accelerating industrial and technological success brought rising mass prosperity: the nations became "developed." Coincidentally, there arose, on the base of the sharply increasing populations, larger and more diversified strata of middle classes with steadily increasing margins of leisure and income available to spend on it. It was not the aristocracies, obviously, which "manned" the sports boom—they had always been at it after their fashion. It was the new and now relatively numerous members of what Veblen would teach the world to call the "leisure class": except that they were "leisure classes" of many intermediate grades from the farm boy playing ball after chores to the banker with a boat.

American intercollegiate athletics began with boat clubs. If that fact seems surprising now, the reason for our surprise is partly ecological. American water sports were delightful, during the ages when you could drink the water unless it was salt, in ways lost to the age of the swimming pool. And among the ordinary attributes of manliness, in the ages before the internal combustion engine, were the skill and strength to propel a boat swiftly and efficiently—and if necessary all day—with oars. In the harbors strong men made their livings as boatmen, doing a little better what every fisherman or sailor or duck hunter had to be able to do well. It was as traditional as it was natural for oarsmen to compete.

Add to all that the joys of getting away, and boating was a perfect collegiate sport. The catch was that to own boats and fit them out acceptably, house, maintain, and have them available cost money. The ideal solution was the club with its boathouse and amenities. Competition among boats and clubs became as inevitable as challenge from the watermen. Races grew formal, and the idea of the college interclub all-star boat was obvious. "Varsity" for "university" was a word ready to hand from Oxford and Cambridge (whose ideas of training, technique, and design taught the colleges how to whip the professionals). Anyone could have foretold the outbreak of intercollegiate competition.

Perhaps as good an event as any other from which to date the beginnings of intercollegiate athletics in the United States is the set of races between Harvard and Yale boats on Lake Winnepesaukee, August 3, 1852. Although Harvard can claim that it had already named a "university crew," perhaps it did not compete as such (or perhaps it did). By 1856 senior oarsmen were selecting the varsity crew, *pace* the clubs. In May 1858 the *Harvard Magazine* issued a call for a general intercollegiate regatta, and at the Worcester regatta with Yale the next year side-matches were played at billiards and chess by champions from each college.

I cannot, incidentally, feel that claims to college priorities or priority by sport matter much. It should cause no consternation if it turned out that baseball teams, representing Williams and Wesleyan or, alternatively, Princeton and Pennsylvania, played first. The colleges and their sports passed a point of critical mass about 1850; the readiness was all.

Athletics belonged to the "sporting element" in the colleges at the start. The participants represented money and "family" and "society"—or, in American terms, success. At Harvard, for instance, they represented not the great tradition of "the Brahmin caste of New England," a "race of scholars" and ministers, but its latter tradition of "Proper Boston"—wealth, power, position, and exclusiveness. In part for those reasons, small doubt, the faculties stood alert to put down athletics as another manifestation of resistance and the Old Harry in the boys. Races led to parties, parties led to riot; and the faculty officially censured the Harvard boat clubs as early as 1850. So King Canute held back the tides.

For the students were inventing an instrument of a glamor so potent historians agree that it altered the character of American college life after the Civil War. The appeal of collegiate athletics from the beginning split the faculties, of course. The Rev. Mr. J.F.W. Ware, presiding over a Harvard Chapel service the day after the big crew race of 1857, for instance, proclaimed College solidarity by slyly giving out hymns with reference after reference to races and oars: "the students smiled audibly." The faculty tried again, in 1860, but probably not so effectively as the War, to stop crew: "on account of the disturbances which the students made at Worcester in 1859, and especially in 1860. These exuberances were seized upon eagerly by enemies of the colleges, and made up into very highly colored accounts, and created a great deal of scandal." After the war it began again, with fresh exuberance, and was joined at once by other sports, especially baseball.

After the Civil War, "to the old-timers," said Morison, "the spontaneous growth of athletics was the most astonishing phenomenon of student life." It is too easy to say, in retrospect, that a brief attention to the achievement of student *virtu* in the 1850s might have dampened that astonishment. The students had hit upon a device for leavening college life, a device of real puissance. The astonishment now is how sharply and early the public reacted to intercollegiate athletics. If some of the clerisy and moralists were put off, the nation as a whole, no matter what it said, was positively polarized, trance-struck. It almost instantly became the greatest problem of intercollegiate athletics that no way could be found (though few enough were tried) to keep the American public out. The student invention must have been a drama, in many forms, which, accidentally from the student point of view, spoke profoundly to the condition of the national culture.

No doubt Reuel Denney was right in feeling that football was once "lyric"—crude but fresh, naive but inspired—before it moved to levels of development more sophisticated. But I should add that football was, sometimes still is, "lyric" when circumstances permit spectators to move up and down the sidelines with the ball. At a guess, the largest crowd who can do that and see the game and not riot numbers fewer than five hundred. After that there must be stands and the lyric condition withers. The lyric age had gone when Stephen Crane saw Princeton at Harvard in 1896. Historically, the first Big Games were played at Cambridge, New Haven, and, because Princeton scheduled its big home games there, New York. In those centers the lyric period began to fade during the late 1880s.

The steps by which the public took over college football present no mysteries, however enigmatic its motives. Play in itself attracted student athletes passionately. The game attracted passionate community participation, which became ritualized war when colleges competed. It was the heyday of the age of "the strenuous life." The occasions, communal and symbolic and dramatic and orgiastic, drew collegiately oriented people and became "in" affairs, socially glamorous. The "in" events fixed the attention of American journalism, always as tropic toward snobbery as a plant toward sunlight. And the media—at this point newspapers, magazines, books—romanced the public. Perhaps the public grabbed at the Big Game because the students had created American versions of something human life, even life itself, craves: games, dances, parties, communal busts with the final esthetic pleasures of form, celebrations of life, its bonds and bounds and outbreaks. Something new had obscurely passed a critical point in cultural expression and evolution when, as the *Targum*, the Rutgers student newspaper, reported, "On Saturday, November 6, 1869, Princeton sent twenty-five picked men to play our twenty-five a match game of football."

CHAPTER THREE

The Big Game and Human Nature

LANGUAGE PROBLEMS

Do we act like that—as we act at the Big Game and about it—because we are Americans or just people? Both. Though merely American factors have entered in, it may be true that many if not most groups of human beings would, in fact do, behave much like that about games and gambling, about what is at once agonic and fraternal, whenever they got the chance. Everything about the Big Game is "natural," in part expressing what we are and the ways we are so. Mainly we act like that because in so doing we enact a kind of art; and it is of the nature of "human nature" to play, to create art, and to play art games. But all too obviously, by this point, a great many difficulties in understanding the Big Game have been exposed as language problems. The vocabulary of the subject is poverty stricken. Too much discussed while too little thought about, the phenomenon lies surrounded by the debris of exploded ideas like "game theory" and "amateurism." Still worse, some essential concepts, with their essential language, are, though growing, at best half-formed and less than half-known.

Aside from the fact that games and athletic exercise (as any active baby will show you) speak body languages, it has been shown that culturally games work like language. The perception that games are "expressive models" was taken forward by a challenge from Robert E. Gahringer to the fad of tagging every kind of enquiry "a game." Does that help linguistics? he asked: "Can Games Explain Language?" Though his answer was negative, he reacted triumphantly to its opposite: "a game in play is a kind of community, and as such is an occasion of communication among players." Therefore "the game has to be understood . . . as a *language*." And his conclusive generalization is worthy of a philosopher: "Thus, while a game may be regarded as play (and that goes deeper than one might think when we consider it as a disinterested concern for action in principle), a game is first of all a real language between players (or spectators) . . . . Games are, as much as more adequate verbal expressions, fulfillments of the fundamental will to communicate which is at bottom a will to be."

However, at the game of finding language and ideas for understanding play the grand master remains the Dutch Catholic medievalist who flourished forty years ago, Johan Huizinga. His mere title educated the world—*Homo Ludens: A Study of the Play Element of Culture*. Play, he insisted, is humanly ultimate, an irreducible idea. Though "irrational," it always "means something." Language and myth and ritual stand on the same footing: "The great archetypal activities of human society are all permeated with play from the start," he said. And he drove the nail home with his conclusion: "Now in myth and ritual the great instinctive forces of civilized life have their origin: law and order, commerce and profit, craft and art, poetry, wisdom and science. All are rooted in the primeval soil of play." From that ground he proposed to show that "culture itself bears the character of play" and that "civilization arises in and as play." Commentators on sport of late have been a shade zealous to finesse their debts to Huizinga.

In the last analysis, his book seems built around two ideas doubtfully reconciled: that play is sacred and the ground of religion; that play, being "agonistic," is the ground of aristocratic virtues. One of the best-poached footnotes in the literature of any subject must be Huizinga's observation that Plato in his *Laws* had said something of the first importance:

> God alone is worthy of supreme seriousness, but man is made God's plaything, and that is the best part of him. Therefore every man and woman should live accordingly, and play the noblest games and be of another mind from what they are at present. . . . What then is the right way of living? Life must be lived as play, playing certain games, making sacrifices, singing and dancing, and then a man will be able to propitiate the gods, and defend himself against his enemies, and win in the contest.

Developing the thesis that playing "the noblest games" is in fact "the right way of living" brought Huizinga to propose that "the two ever recurrent forms in which civilization grows in and as play are the sacred performance and the festal contest." In tracing the sacred performance lifted to rite, thence to ritual, thence to sacrament, he laid the ground for the "theology of play" developed by Father Hugo Rahner. But his more daring concepts sprang from perceptions about "agonistic" play.

42

In primitive cultures, Huizinga thought, it appears that competition, ritual conflict, antagonism as play, are universal. He generalized from Boas's Kwakiutl, from Malinowski's Trobriand Islanders, and, of course, from primitive Greece: "The Greeks used to stage contests in anything that offered the bare possibility of a fight." From the Greek *athlon* for "prize" and *athlaetaes* for "prize winner" he derived the ideas of risk, suffering, success, superiority, honor, glory, excellence, and perfection. With another step he arrived at the constellation of heroic, aristocratic virtues, as in the "man of quality. . . . the whole semantic complex of strength, valor, wealth, right, good management, morality, urbanity, fine manners, magnanimity, liberality and moral perfection." Thus equating "play" with "agon," he proceeded to locate the sources of law, morality, knowledge, philosophy, poetry and the arts, and so circle back to the sacred. The good history of civilization, he concluded, owed everything to the *ludus*: "Medieval life was full of play" and "the whole mental attitude of the Renaissance was one of play. . . .a gorgeous and solemn masquerade in the accoutrements of an idealized past." After that, of course, everything ran down hill to the squalors of the present.

Though the jargon of "play" and "games" has become an intellectually chic *lingua franca*, psychiatrists and psychoanalysts appear to have found it especially useful. Two books which appeared in 1967, Arnold Beisser, *The Madness in Sports* (fine book, vile title), and Ralph Slovenko and James R. Knight, editors, *Motivations in Play, Games and Sports*, were notably worthwhile. In the preface to Slovenko, Menninger himself wrote:

> These are crucial and important questions. For if play is truly a method of self-expression, a communication of goodwill in an inhibited aggression, an important piece in the mosaic of a well-rounded life, then it is, indeed, a *preventive* device and a necessity, not a luxury. This many of us believe, though we have no proof. We know people who play too much, to be sure; but we also know people who do not play enough. We lean to the belief that people should play more—not less, and this is in the interests of mental health and the furthering of social good.

If in humanity as the psychiatrist knows it, "intrapersonally," play is *egosyntonic*, strengthening personality, in humanity as the ethnologist knows it, "interpersonally," play is *enculturative*. It draws people into communal relations, educates them about the nature of their culture, reconciles them with and to culture. There are now many different guesses about what that means. Sutton-Smith and Roberts, to whom I

43

owe "enculturative," speculate that "games are, among other things, models of power." Roberts, again, with Arth and Bush, trying to survey all of ethnographical literature, suggests that "games occur so widely that it is an easy inference that they meet general human needs" and that all games have "two general characteristics . . . the expressive and the model characteristics." Games express the nature, aims, and dominant motifs of the culture in which they are played. In this way they are like "folk tales, dramatic productions, music, and paintings." Thus they become "models of various cultural activities" and may be "related to problems in abstract thought and cognitive mapping."

After Huizinga, then, not only do we begin to accumulate useful terminology and at least the fragments of a network of concepts behind it, a suspicion begins to dawn which matches recent insights into genetics and linguistics. Lewis Thomas, for instance, a most sophisticated biologist, discovered surprising things to say about play and the instinctual ground for language. I have no way of telling whether he knew how close he came to Huizinga on agonic behavior as the source of civilization when Thomas wrote:

> Scientists at work . . . seem to be under the influence of a deeply placed human instinct. They are . . . rather like young animals engaged in savage play. When they are near to an answer their hair stands on end, they sweat, they are awash in their own adrenalin. To grab the answer, and grab it first, is for them a more powerful drive than feeding or breeding or protecting themselves against the elements.

Though this is "something like aggression," he confessed, he would argue apologetically that it is different "in having no sort of destruction as the objective." It looks and feels "like aggression, . . . like a primitive running hunt, but there is nothing at the end to be injured." Very well, intellectual pursuits may be said to be aggressive, agonic, but not violent; and the distinction—which applies also to the Big Game—is important. But is it true that nobody gets hurt in the intellectual agon? Not quite. Are there not Old Men, predecessors, to be superseded? Are there not opponents, heretics, to be corrected, put down, stripped of prestige? Are there not companions on the trail to be outstripped, anticipated, left behind, set back in the professional pecking order? The hurts may be civilized and psychic, but they seem real to the losers. And when the losers take the practical professional consequences to the bank, the differences become painful objectively.

Less predictable in the "Notes of a Biology Watcher," as Thomas called his superb familiar essays, are his insights into language "among other biologic systems for communication." In one root sense he is Chomskian, accepting the probability that "the gift of language" is genetic, "the universal and biologically specific activity of human beings. . . . We are born knowing how to use language." And he guesses "it may be safe to say that art and music are functions of the same, universal, genetically determined mechanism." So, I think a great deal of evidence suggests, are play and games. "The human mind is preset, in some primary sense, to generate more than just the parts of speech," Thomas continues: "the same sets of genes are at least indirectly responsible for governing such astonishing behavior as in the concert hall . . . or in the art gallery."

I agree. Those sets of genes put the musical symbols on the scores, the performers in their places, the instruments in their hands and the audience in their seats. And they evolved the games in the colleges, put the players on the field, and drew the spectators to their seats at the Big Game. The arts and speech, Thomas says, suggest a "view of things compatible with the very old notion that a framework for meaning is somehow built into minds at birth." But only a poetic scientist would have noticed that in the human structure uniquely "ambiguity seems to be an essential, indispensable element. . . . If it were not for the capacity for ambiguity, for the sensing of strangeness, . . . we would have no way of recognizing the layers of counterpoint in meaning." Just so: for language and other arts, among them games.

If all the dreamers of fancies about the prehistoric human psyche were laid end to end, it would become all but impossible not to conclude that we need multiple explanations for the origins and development of that many-natured creature, humankind. William James rejected unitary generalizations, holding that mind arose from the "random images, fancies, accidental out-births of spontaneous variation in the functional activity of the excessively instable human brain." Multiple explanations we possess in plenty, and others crowd in on us every season. Yet, running through that multiplicity since the primal moments in American thought, go two great themes and patterns, both contending for our belief about how we got this way.

At present bitter argument resounds among intellectuals about whether human beings behave aggressively by nature or from bad habit. Though actually it is true that the controversy has raged continuously in America since early Colonial times, at present it may be defined within structures of concern which rest on the fathers of what Herbert W. Schneider called "genetic social philosophy." The two great foundations of American disagreement in this matter have been for a century the works of William Graham Sumner and his now too much forgotten antagonist, Lester Ward.

Rather caricatured in his role as the Bad Old Man of Social Darwinism, Sumner preached the gospel of the rugged individual to Yale and the world. The founder of American sociology, he proclaimed that "the survival of the fittest" was "the law of civilization," that uncompromising individualism bound to granitic rules of aggressiveness conformed to the laws of life: "It's root, hog, or die!" The social classes, he argued, owe nothing to one another but honest competition: "The world owes no one a living." The species is, Sumner thought, by nature what might be called *homo agonistes*, the triumphant aggressor.

In a book called *The Psychic Factors of Civilization*, Ward perfected in 1893 his retort against Sumner. Human dominance in nature, he replied, depended obviously not on formidable natural armament like that of the great cats or incredible ferocity like that of the shrew or the shark. It rose from "cooperation." The power of human survival lay in "group selection." Superior "cooperation within the group" promoted "The growth of mind"—and with the growth of the group mind developed teamwork, thence group identification and loyalty, and at last in-group altruism. The more the more powerful—and on the rungs of that ladder humanity rose to the top. The species is, Ward thought, rather *homo fraternalis*, the triumphant altruist.

Which is right? Are people naturally aggressive, competitive—to put it frankly, murderous and domineering? Or are they, on the contrary, naturally cooperative, altruistic—to put it nicely, loving and friendly, even self-sacrificial? Or do you really have to choose one or the other conclusion? May not both, together with perhaps other things, be right?

A deal of the current hullabaloo about the issue may be stimulated by partisan readings of what I think a book as intellectually elegant and important as it is oft-misrepresented: *On Aggression* by Konrad Lorenz. Though Lorenz is a Nobel Laureate in the relatively new science of ethology, animal behavior, it has to be said at once that now he and we are talking metabiology, not biology, "scientism," not science. I take it for granted that the state of the art in no science permits anybody to make generalizations about "human nature." But "scientism" is an art of metaphor. The difference is that where a science is an intellectual discipline addressed to a scrupulously delimited field of natural phenomena, scientism is an extradisciplinary game of applying ideas drawn from a science to a nonscientific realm like theology or metaphysics, history, literary criticism, or cultural analysis.

Searching through the realms of animal behavior, Lorenz found aggression everywhere, urgent and basic as hunger, thirst or sex, and marvelously diverse in outlets. He thought it self-evident that aggression is instinctual, built into the human genes; and the essential point is not fecklessly to deny but seriously to consider what those facts mean and what we need to do about them. Writing just before World War II for a happy nation which preserved its neutrality during World War I, Huizinga felt a confidence in the *agon,* that good, Greek fight, not so easy for a thinker sensitive to reality after 1945 and its aftermath of terrible revelations. Lorenz, insisting on the facts as he perceived them, was properly afraid. One of his most interesting ideas concerns "the spontaneity of irresistible outbreaks," as he called it. The grand fallacy of the humanitarian mind, one may interpret Lorenz to say, has been to suppose that aggression can be forgotten, denied, repressed, frustrated, somehow fenced out of life. Not so. To suppose that is to repeat the mistakes of pre-Freudian gentility about sex. But even more disastrously, for if, like sex, aggression repressed explodes (often in perversions), in mass human expression it explodes into mass or mob violence, the most dreadful variety of human behavior.

These are not pretty ideas; and both some of the Lorenz enthusiasts and some of his opponents have been too quick to ignore the long, elegant, and at least half-hopeful development of his further but still essential theories. None but a somehow puritanical mind ever supposed the positions of Sumner and Ward, for instance, to be irreconcilable. Sumner, who named "folkways" and "mores" for sociology, thought the supremacy of "the mores" over the individual indispensable to humanity, culture, and civilization; and he engaged himself in fighting for them as an active reformer. Ward saw that highly advanced group development can lead to wars. Perhaps what is too infrequently observed of Lorenz is that, though he is Baconian and behavioristic in his ethology and Freudian in his psychology, in scientist vision he is Hegelian and a wishful partisan of the party of hope. His ideas will, in at least significant part, dance in partnership with those of, for instance, Lewis Thomas as Sumner's dance with Ward's.

One of Lorenz's startling observations concerns "the process of ritualization and . . . its effects in inhibiting aggression . . . what mechanisms evolution has invented in order to channel aggression along harmless paths." He saw good reason to reverse certain ancient misunderstandings fossilized in language. In formidably armed species, for example, critically disarming inhibitions arise. Wolves turn out really to be nice guys. Let one fight another, and the loser has only to make an instinctive gesture of submission, presenting his jugular to the teeth of the victor, to be safe. The power to strike is frozen by instinctive inhibition. The fight is over, the loser goes in peace. Doves on the other hand, are mean. Not equipped for quick killing and used to room permitting a loser to fly away, they possess no ritualized defenses. A caged dove who has lost a fight will be pecked and beaten to slow death. Men "naturally" (that is to say, until recently) were armed like doves. Given weapons, we enjoy the morals of doves with the powers of wolves.

A still more fundamental Lorenzian insight is that all we most cherish as humane in values—love, friendship, comradeship, loyalty, creativity—rise from aggressiveness. The rest of nature has learned how to profit from it, and human beings have evolved unique and wonderful gifts from it. But the human mind and its arrogance now combine to place us above but apart from nature, including our own. Human aggressiveness has become perverse. Having escaped old natural controls, it cannot gain time enough for the slow, evolutionary growth of new ones. What then? What can we do? We must depend upon our best resources of reason, laughter, and altruism to win the race between self-control and catastrophe.

How to do this? By creative development of the impulses toward ritualization and safe instinctual outlet already opened by experience. Among those outlets may be games. Lorenz said, "All the culturally evolved forms of 'fair fighting' . . . are functionally analogous to phylogenetically ritualized combat in animals." In that context, sport "can be defined as a specifically human form of nonhostile combat, governed by the strictest of culturally developed rules." Therefore, though "the main function of sport today lies in the cathartic discharge of aggressive urge," it has a value "much greater than that of a simple outlet of aggression. . . . It educates man to a conscious and responsible control of his own fighting behavior." To develop such ideas is to recast William James's famous essay, "The Moral Equivalent of War."

It may then be true and important that aggression is not the same as violence, can even be used to work against it. It may be, as Lorenz said quietly to an English symposium, that, if "phyletic" (that is, animal) ritualization works "in the interests of a species' survival," then, "It is to be hoped that cultural ritualization will be able to do the same with that kind of intraspecific aggression in Man which threatens him with extinction." The Lorenzian hope lies in a dialectical working out to higher and liberating forms of deep, terrible antagonisms. Whether you take such observations to be grounds for hope or despair may depend on your temperamental capacity for belief in one or the other conclusion.

I suspect, for instance, that careful analysis might show that those two apparently mutually exclusive masterpieces of modern scientism, *On Aggression* and *The Lives of a Cell*, somewhere toward the end of the ends may be reconciled. Lorenz's way is to move by Hegelian thesis, antithesis, and higher synthesis: aggression versus death leads to agonic competition; agonism versus estrangement leads to fraternity, and so forth. Thomas's vision of an aggregative, infinitely mutual and altruistic cellular universe looks and sounds, at first blush, wholly otherwise. As he says, "If you were looking for something like natural law to take the place of the 'social Darwinism' of a century ago, you would have a hard time drawing lessons from the sense of life alluded to by chloroplasts and mitochondria, but there it is."

Helped wonderfully by his transparent, rhythmic, yet familiar English, Thomas is kidding about the "hard time." For, as he had just been saying, "There is something intrinsically good-natured about all symbiotic relations, necessarily, but this one, which is probably the most ancient and firmly established of all, seems especially equable. There is nothing resembling predation, and no pretense of an adversary stance on either side." Indeed, Thomas inclines to wonder whether "all reflexive responses of aggression and defense" were not, at the levels of cellular reality, devices to keep a rather entropic uniformity in hand in order to promote differentiation, even evolution itself.

Could you say then that aggregativeness versus nothing leads to insignificance; but aggregativeness versus agonism leads to differentiation; and numbers versus difference leads to federated, larger units and so to macrobiologic life? If so, reality in the world of Thomas could be said to match reality in the world of Lorenz at last—and perhaps both match reality in the worlds of human culture, too. No doubt, again, much depends on your capacity for belief.

Speaking of faith, William James liked to urge that the only belief which is real or matters is the one we are willing to bet on when the stakes are high, when, as Robert Frost once put it, "the work is play for mortal stakes." Taken that way, I incline to believe that we may be the creatures of a long experience which could be expressed in tensional sets, perhaps pairs, of factors in life full of pull and haul, which in their final product tend, as Emerson and Whitman thought, to achieve advancing results. Against any such advance fights entropy, the crushing weight of the falling waters of time. Everything fails; the cost of every life is death; the whole may some day run down like an unwinding clock, or blow up, or plunge into the nameless fate of an astronomical "black hole": but whose business is that? Where we live, it is necessary to play the game and possible, perhaps advisable, to play the big game.

I suppose the ethnologists have taught us that nothing is more essential to human culture than the patterns in which shared emotions, including aggressions and frustrations, are displaced upon group activities and by which the resultant games and rituals are transformed, of course symbolically, into artifacts which bring individual and group satisfaction, even joy, because they work. By such processes games and rituals become transpersonal—they belong to the culture and become givens for children, for instance. And they become reified—that is, they become, for all practical, cultural, and personal purposes, real things. As such they can become works of art or art forms, and then their great good office becomes that of cultural reconciliation and concentration—perhaps even to trigger that cultural transcendence which provides mere human beings, however temporarily, triumph over entropy and death. In some such terms as these it can be argued that games may indeed be thought to possess the potential to fulfill Lorenz's hopes for them.

Though to the best of my perception no such idea ever crossed Lorenz's mind, it is possible to see structural parallels between his ideas and familiar Christian themes. The Christian thematic is that of the *felix culpa*, the fortunate fall. In Adam's sin the potential for redeeming grace abounded. It suggests that the divine love works by overwhelming ironies: out of sin comes death; but out of death come resurrection and redemption. In Lorenzian parallel, out of aggression comes violence; but out of violence come ritualization, bonding, community, and love. And so aggression is redeemed. It may not make terribly much difference whether aggression is "in the genes"; nobody denies that it lies deep in human psychic and culture patterns, if not universally, still powerfully and globally. Nobody denies that the race confronts an imperative to deal with gigantic threats from aggression and personal as well as mass violence. The last truth might be pluralistic: that there is some aggression in the genes together, as thinkers from

Lester Ward to Lewis Thomas have supposed, with some altruism in the genes. It could be argued that Lorenz and a number of commentators, not engaged in sinister ideological machinations, are trying to tell us that the terrible issue really is there and that the right way to handle it is not to shriek "Beast! Beast!" so it will go away. The right things to do are to canalize it and redeem it.

The homely fact about religious wars is that they begin in logomachy, the war of words. And much of the militant concern regarding "aggression" pivots upon definition. If you define "aggression" as emotion or action which leads to "violence," that is one thing. For "violence" means maliciously hurting or wounding, maiming or killing somebody. It is usual, among other factors, to posit "love" as an opposite of "violence"—and "aggression." Yet, whether it be true or not, as Lorenz says, that love takes its rise from aggression, can it be said that love is not aggressive? Hardly. In fact, if the motion of the heart, the intent, and the act be not aggressive for the good of the other, it is not love.

How do you practice it? asks Eric Fromm in *The Art of Loving*. By active discipline, concentration, patience, and supreme concern, he replies. Then he proceeds to wise admonitions about how, intensely, to do these things. Does love not seek action and change and growth, to make something happen, to reach out toward affect and effect? So does aggression. These truths equally hold for eros, philos, and agape. They hold true for works of love like child-rearing, healing, teaching, service to the community or State, or reform. The careers of Jane Addams and John Woolman, like those of St. Francis or Socrates or any great Hebrew prophet were centered on loving aggression. Whether all violence is bad, in short, not all aggression is violence. From that difference much good might flow.

Nevertheless, as Addams or Francis or Socrates could testify, the world we live in is haunted by Woolman's "Spirit of Fierceness." You can call the dark, hog-wild forces in the human mind and its cultures bad nurture or misguided impulse or the devil—or, as the Greeks did for some of them, Dionysus. After Freud and modern history we are learning that you have to give the devil his due—by the moral holiday or by sublimation. If you try not to recognize Dionysus, said the Greeks, he will break out and drive you crazy. But you cannot let him take over, either. He has to be limited, purged, governed, or he will drive you to suicide. Through dance and rite, however, he can be purged and appeased.

Such may be, celebrated properly, one function of the Big Game with us, in our culture. The liberal imagination, as Lionel Trilling described it, has far less to fear from the Big Game than it thinks. There are terrible truths of the human condition to which our college games hold symbolic relations: aggression, competition, exploitation, violence psychic and physical, torture, murder, cannibalism, and war. But, unlike much in the rest of the popular culture, the Big Game does not celebrate, nor teach, nor nourish such. It deals at the remove of symbolic drama. It ritualizes, limits, sublimates, and diverts aggression and violence into play and art and holiday. Through it the aggression grown in the grain of American culture is shown to be redeemable. Its powers are illustrative, momentary, partial—not sovereign. But why should its symbolic drama not speak what has always been the root conviction of the nation: it can be, we can be redeemed even from our worst selves?

PEOPLE PROBLEMS

To try to use the language of Huizinga and Gahringer, of Lorenz and Thomas and Beisser, to think about the Big Game is to realize that "language" has here become a thing of many natures—almost as many as the variants of human nature. Body languages, kinesthetic and gesticulative, make two. The nature of play counts for several more, and the philosophical, psychological, and ethnographical variants multiply the number. Still, however, we have not talked much about behavior, the languages of culture patterns—although our whole enquiry began from the question: "Not, 'What are the players doing out there?' But, 'What are all the wild or bemused people doing in the stands? in front of the tube? behind the sports section at breakfast?' " Everything about the Big Game, including the applicable language, resolves at last into people problems.

We have seen that, for our purposes with the Big Game, anthropology—the theory of human nature—might usefully consider humankind as *homo agonistes*, the aggressor and competitor, but simultaneously as *homo fraternalis*, the team worker and altruist, and *homo ludens*, the player: worshipful and agonic. But I think there is yet another, too little discussed in the literature (though glanced at by Caillois), *homo aleator*, the gambler, a devotee of the raptures of risk.

It is not easy to set forth exact, comprehensive definitions of *homo aleator*. One of my favorites fleets past in a remark made by a character in a tale by Henry Wallace Phillips, one of the pioneers of cowboy fiction. He has one Old Western tough remark of another, "for a man who takes no kind of interest in what comes afterward, give me Pioche Bill." It is in some sense that one who takes relatively little "interest in what comes afterward" who is accommodated in gambling cultures. However unconventionally, *homo aleator* draws a line of honor: he or she must play and will not be shamed. He will have action which requires him to challenge the world and be a rogue or hooligan, if he must, to get it. In a culture adapted to him he may be a hero. Though not all cultures are well adapted to his needs and some not at all, most find outlets for *aleator*. Many are "gambling cultures," few more than ours.

I can put my sense of a gambling culture briefly in two stories. The first was told by an anthropologist who said he knew a primitive jungle tribe whose folk were swift of foot. They loved to run races for fun; but they did not care who won because the culture did not include the notions of winning and losing; it was not a gambling culture. I have no way of checking on those Indians; but the point is that the impossibility to us of conceiving of races run without an ego-investment in winning registers how profoundly gambling a culture we have. The other is a favorite golf story, which seems to me a parable of forces dominant in American life. Two golfers stood on the tee of a par three hole, and the first sent his shot arching high and deep to the limits of vision at the sun-dazzled green. His opponent stood at the markers and peered until he asked, "Is that my good old buddy in the trap? Or is the sorry son of a bitch on the green?"

Perhaps one reason for a certain shyness in thinking about *homo aleator* and the Big Game arises from the conviction, powerfully presented by Dr. Edmund Bergler, a psychiatrist, that gamblers are sick. On his proper therapeutic ground, treating neuroses, Dr. Bergler may well be right. Beyond that, after the scientistic fashion of his brand of conviction, he seems too reductive, too cocksure. His *aleator* gambles disastrously to enjoy the ambivalent pleasures of childish megalomania (I can do anything, I own the world) resulting in ruin so one can enjoy the self-hating pleasure of inflicting retribution on the bad child who will not grow up and face reality. Bergler's gambler is a "born loser" avidly seeking masochistic satisfactions in self-destruction.

As a conceptual ground for effective therapeutic encounter, Bergler's ideas may well be right; but there is much in *homo aleator* not dreamt of in his philosophy. Not counting casual, peripheral punters, there seem in fact to be four general types of gamblers: Bergler's pathological cases; simple losers; simple winners; and adepts. They pop up at Balinese cockfights, in California cardrooms, and all over this country playing, among other games of chance, what Larry Merchant calls *The National Football Lottery*—betting on professional football. Merchant, writing a personal testament, dramatized the tension between two ways in gambling. The winning way asserts life in defiance of death; it is synergistic, explosive, a way of joy subject to limitation and control. Losing asserts death; it is an agonizing way of self-hating, punitive suicide (like alcoholism) for the possessed; or it is a way to expiate guilt for the self-loathing who crave penance, not extinction.

Martinez and LaFranchi, studying habitual poker players for several years from an inside position, "found it useful to distinguish four types . . . the consistent winners . . . the break evens . . . the losers, those who try to win but don't. . . . Finally, . . . the action players, those who compulsively try to lose." Winners and break-evens, they found, have sportsmanly manners, calm and pleasant in triumph or loss. Losers, and especially action players who have come to lose, act out rage. Investigating the personalities involved, Martinez and LaFranchi found that their winners and break-evens "usually have good social relationships" in life beyond the cardroom. They play for the thrill of mastery and pride themselves on coolness under stress: "at poker they have a fateful situation for highlighting and reinforcing this much-admired quality."

The losers at poker, however, tended to be losers in life, not sexually so much as socially. They lived "on the periphery of social life" and seemed "to use gambling as a substitute for satisfactory primary relationships"—the more pathetically in that they did not know how (or were afraid?) to win. They bought relationships by "making the game" for the house and the winners. The action players, however, purchased catharsis: their "poker game is a social situation that allows a release of tensions . . . not provided by their normal social relations."

You can say that risk players always lose only by observing that all life loses: at which level, of course, all bets are off, at least for this world. But to say, therefore, that all risk-taking, all gambling are irrational and wrong is to say the same for life, a view which may be tragic but is life-denying. Not money to spend or hoard but money as a symbol of luck and potency, pride, power, and success, the ground of exultation, draws the gambler. *Aleator* at his best dices for life not cash;

he may find cash, in fact, too feeble a symbol for what he craves. He thirsts for pure action. Creative people of every sort are gamblers. And since it is only in the arts that even the illusion of action can be found, he thirsts for art which presents to him the right figure of relations to struggle, fate, and death. Money, career, or life itself the mortal stakes, his stance is almost universal.

Much of the thrust of the gambler as winner or adept, much of the force of the gambling culture as the way of would-be winners, I think, originates in what might be called the rapture of risk. Dr. Roy Rosenthal tried to study it as what he called the "RE effect"—searching for a psychopharmacological substance secreted by the body to produce the experience of euphoria and power, "a sensation . . . at the far horizon of human elation: following success in risk exercise." Whether that substance exists or not, however, the rapture of risk—of defying fate, defeat, humiliation, loss, injury, or death—does exist. Young Robert Frost, lately an exultant high school end and at the moment of writing a young man preparing to risk everything on decades of agony to become a poet, said it well in "The Trial By Existence":

> Even the bravest that are slain
> Shall not dissemble their surprise
> On Waking to find valor reign,
> Even as on earth in paradise. . . .
> To find that the utmost reward
> Of daring should be still to dare.

Could it be said that somehow young Frost stood closer to Freud than Dr. Bergler and closer to St. Paul than Father Rahner?

The *aleator* sensibility was and remains the source of that mainly masculine, ironic humor often called "frontier" but everywhere belonging to the military, men who work in the open air, sportsmen and athletes: the rough, horse-playing, deflating humor of the barracks, the bull pen, the locker room. Herman Melville, not surprisingly, picked it up to illustrate life in the world of the *Pequod*. Ishmael's initiator into whaling in *Moby-Dick*, Starbuck, the most prudent of hunters, struck a whale in the midst of a howling, blinding white squall and nearly killed himself and his boat's crew. Saved, Ishmael reflected:

There are certain queer times and occasions in this strange mixed affair we call life when a man takes this whole universe for a vast practical joke. . . . That odd sort of wayward mood I am speaking of, comes over a man only in some time of extreme tribulation; it comes in the very midst of his earnestness, so that what just before might have seemed to him a thing most

55

momentous, now seems but a part of the general joke. There is nothing like the perils of whaling to breed this free and easy sort of genial, desperado philosophy; and with it I now regarded this whole voyage of the Pequod, and the great White Whale its object. . . .

Now then, thought I, unconsciously rolling up the sleeves of my frock, here goes for a cool, collected dive at death and destruction, and the devil fetch the hindmost.

It is in fact the mood of experienced combat types, daredevils, athletes—*homo aleator* matured. That he saw a tragic side to that mood's Dionysian qualities Melville suggested subtly. He entitled the chapter "The Hyena." Perhaps that tragic sense, older than Euripides' *Bacchae*, accounts also in part for the general suspicion that in *homo aleator* there lurks something beneath or outside, something hostile to and outlawed from positive, organized civilization. But I think that at best a half-truth, probably in the long run an error. It may, on the contrary, be that the risk rapture, together with other gambling motives, fuels human achievements without which civilization is not. Certainly what communicates at the Big Game, from the ritualized risks of the games the athletes play to the vicarious, wholly symbolic games we play in the stands, creating the possibility of the game as culture, are many variant forms of the rapture of risk, the elations of gambling. It is among the ways of the world.

A real danger to sport as culture, as art, as life, however, comes from the "business" side of gambling, which has been and sometimes is, of course, criminal. As with most forms of crime, power and value in a good thing create its criminal abuse: no banks, no heists; no sex, no rapes. But culturally more threatening to sports than mere crime is casual public cynicism. Only Dr. Bergler's types want to be suckered. For the rest, a certain faith in the authenticity of the *agon* is essential. Suspicion that "the dump is on," even if it is only that the points are being shaved, destroys the culture.

That it need not be destroyed, however, is food for reflection. The finest of British sports historians, Dennis Brailsford had an insight of prime importance—that the rules of sport "grew up not from motives of 'fair play' . . . but to protect the investments of gamblers." They were, he said, following Thorstein Veblen, "proof of the fraud and chicanery endemic in games." Certainly in British history, he concluded, "The years following the Restoration were, therefore, years of development and formulation for a number of sophisticated, 'modern' sports, owing their development to aristocratic participating and encouragement and to their utility and attraction as media for gaming." If not only our games structurally but "sportsmanship" could take their rise from some of the sinister ways of a gambling culture's world, perhaps there are still grounds for hope in the future.

In the global intellectual life of the present century some of our most enlightening insights have seemed to come from cultural anthropologists, and among their contributions are a number especially suggestive regarding our gambling culture and the place in it of the Big Game. "It is not wisdom only to be wise," said Santayana, quoting from the *Bacchae*, where Euripides had taught him that, together with the Apollonian, "the Dionysiac inspiration" was "also divine." It comes, he continued, "from the chaotic but fertile bosom of nature, . . . the frenzy represents the wild soul, not at home in the world, not settled in itself, and merging again with the elements, half in helplessness and half in self-transcendence and mystic triumph."

In *Patterns of Culture*, Ruth Benedict sketched a perfect example of the gambling culture in her portrait of some famous Native Americans, the superbly theatrical Kwakiutl potlatchers of the Pacific Northwest first studied by Franz Boas. Marvelous artists at costume, masks, dances, and sensational dramatic performance, the old Kwakiutl "fought with property" to establish rights to play certain roles, dance certain dances, hold posts of honor. Their methods of "combat" were conspicuous consumption, the overwhelming, humiliating "gift" of property, or, at the extreme, conspicuous waste of goods in a madly agonic destruction of treasure to crush less wealthy opponents.

At heart, Benedict pointed out, Kwakiutl behavior suggested a culture so Dionysian as to resemble megalomaniac paranoia: "They recognized only one gamut of emotion, that which swings between victory and shame." Every misfortune became an insult, exposing one to ridicule, and it had to be "wiped out." The worst insult was death, which must be affronted "by distribution and destruction of property, by headhunting, and by suicide"—whichever came best to hand:

> There are many stories of this behavior at death. A chief's sister and her daughter had gone up to Victoria, and either because they drank bad whiskey or because their boat capsized they never came back. The chief called together his warriors. "Now I ask you, tribes, who shall wail? Shall I do it or shall another?" The spokesman answered, of course: "Not you, chief. Let some other of the tribes." Immediately they set up the war pole to announce their intention of wiping out the injury and gathered a war party. They set out and found seven men and two children asleep and killed them. "Then they felt good when they arrived at Sebaa in the evening."

So much for a Kwakiutl "away game." Their special game at home, an expressive mode raised to a form so striking it lent a new word to English, was the potlatch. A game of economics reminiscent of "Monopoly" with more or less real counters, it melodramatized that great spring of human conduct which Thorstein Veblen called "conspicuous consumption." They piled blankets, the units of currency, by the hundreds and thousands to match mystically precious "coppers." The essence of the game was challenge: A "gave" to B, who must take or be shamed but must return the "gifts" with one hundred percent interest after a year. *Superbia*, vainglory, then demanded going him one better, inviting the poker techniques of "raising" and retaliation until Dionysian fury brought on the conspicuous destruction of wealth. Precious oil was poured into fires until they set the house aflame and scorched the opponent in his cold contempt. Blankets were heaped up to "put out the fire" and the mystic coppers were burned or broken or thrown into the fjords. Canoes were cut up and burned, slaves were sacrificed: almost anything went (though all had to be "repaid") to shame the opponent and vindicate the glory of one's name, one's family or tribe or totem society—above all, one's brag.

Restudy of the Kwakiutl has suggested that they had a sense of humor and knew that potlatching really was a game. But those facts take nothing away from its value as a figure of speech, a metaphor representing parallel tendencies in our behavior and feeling. As the ideal drama of *homo aleator*, it represented the acme of ritualized fighting emotions; and it provides the perfect figure for what John Woolman understood to be the root of developing racial evil in the American colonies more than two hundred years ago, when our black and our Native American sins were aborning. It dramatized the essence of the "Spirit of Fierceness." It is merely notorious that the same spirit characterizes every business, occupation, or profession, every political, organizational, or social relation in American life. Why argue what everyone knows?

The last portrait of a simple people I should like to use to illustrate our language problems and the force of ideas like agonic, ludic, aleatic, and fraternal is pictured in Peter Matthiessen's masterpiece of creative ethnology, *Under the Mountain Wall: A Chronicle of Two Seasons in the Stone Age* (1962). Matthiessen's book is a work of art. Living with the scientists who studied in New Guinea one of the last Stone Age cultures to come under ethnographical scrutiny before civilization blasted it, Matthiessen pictured "the Kurelu." Their patterns of life revolved about war and agriculture, with the gardening, largely woman's business, subordinate. Like the still more subordinate crafts, it supplied logistically the ritual, festal, theatrical, bloody games on which the shared life of the people centered. With the powers of a novelist, Matthiessen used his art to present what any fine eye might see. He wrote dramatic combat studies of the Kurelu, who had chosen up sides with their neighbors, the Wittaia, so as to make the conduct of life possible. As *akuni* ("people") the two sides perfectly shared language and the rest of the culture, of course:

> The sun had climbed over the valley, and its light flashed on breastplates of white shells, on white headdresses, on ivory boars' tusks inserted through nostrils, on wands of white egret feathers twirled like batons. The alarums and excursions fluttered and died while warriors came in across the fields. The shouted war was increasing in ferocity, and several men from each side would dance out and feign attacks, whirling and prancing to display their splendor. They were jeered and admired by both sides and were not shot at, for display and panoply were part of war, which was less war than ceremonial sport, a wild, fierce festival. Territorial conquest was unknown to the akuni; there was land enough for all, and at the end of the day the warriors would go home across the fields to supper. Should rain come to chill them, spoil their feathers, both sides would retire. A day of war was dangerous and splendid, regardless of its outcome; it was a war of individuals and gallantry, quite innocent of tactics and cold slaughter. A single death on either side would mean victory or defeat. And yet that death—or two or three—was the end purpose of the war.

Colorful as could be, however, formal combat was only the theatrical side of the common life of that war culture. Individual insult, injury, rape, and murder were common and casual within the community. Between the communities foray and bushwhacking were daily threats against which the men had always to mount guard:

> Unlike the wars, with their fanfare and heroics, the raid has as its sole purpose the stalking and killing of any smaller party or unwary individual. No distinction is made between man, woman, or child: the spearing of a little girl or an old woman is ample reason for a victory singing. The kaios are the consequences of such raids, for without these sentry towers and the squads of armed men which, during the day, are always in the thatched shelters below, the women working in the fields would be defenseless.

The women's rewards in the culture were emotional and came in the rites of mourning and triumph. In rituals of mourning, individuals occupied the center of the stage in their roles of bereaved mothers and wives, each with a supporting chorus of sexual solidarity chanting and keening behind her. But it was centrally for the victory celebration that all the patterns of the culture were arranged. There everybody had an ecstatic role, cultural solidarity was, for the moment, perfect, and joy reigned supreme. The *etai* was celebrated for any enemy death, however achieved; but here it was when the Kurelu had actually won on the field, spearing Huwai the Wittaia:

> The Wittaia rose out of their silence, filed away. . . . At this the shouting was renewed, more strongly than before. The wild dancing of etai began, a whirling and prancing in which the men leapt high in the air or in a circle, driving both heels against the ground, or performed an odd taunting shuffle in which the feet are still, the knees pushed in and out, the hips and shoulders cocked in turn, and the arms darted snakily forward; the effect is one of lewd, jeering enticement, though it is a joyful dance, performed out of the wild high spirits brought about by a death among the enemy and the knowledge that no further risk will come that day. . . .
>
> A few women had collected from the fields, and these had begun their own slow sensual dropping of alternate knees, a swaying of the shoulders, while their arms shivered in and out, palms upward. One tall woman danced alone, far out in front of the rest, wearing a mikak shell above her breasts; in her splendor, she dominated a grassy hillside between the men and the women. This was the wife of Wereklowe's son, who had killed Huwai.

But that was only the impromptu after the game. The *etai* proper demanded preparation, including costuming, and took all the next day:

> The sun had already reached its crest when a large company of women came, led by the tall young wife. . . . In a small circle on the grass of the etai meadow she moved slowly, as if feeling for her rhythm, and as she did so she began to call *We-Re-A-Re-WAY! We-Re-A-Re-WAH!* Another woman answered with the high pure hoot of chorus, and the rest joined them, moving forward. Most of the women had confined their decoration to a thick coat of yellow ocher or gray clay, but a few had feather crowns or shell bibs or inferior small or shell bibs or inferior small mikaks. From the masks of clay their dark eyes glared, depthless and spectral. Led by the girl, they moved back and forth in a massed body, wheeling sharply at the end of each phrase, *We-Re-A-Re-WAY!* the turn being made on the *WAY* or the *WAH*. Periodically they would screech, breaking into a heavy run, breasts flying faster and faster and faster in a tight, driven circle, like creatures fleeing pain. Small girls in their reed skirts pattered hopelessly along the fringe of the bodies, until exhaustion spun them away from their mothers; they sank in little heaps into the grass.

The men waited an hour or two, then charged onto the fields,

> spears held high against the clouds and long plumes tossing. Immediately they turned and thundered back again, *AY-A-Wo-AI*, then broke to form a roaring circle. Some women rushed in from the side to mingle with the fringes of the men; as the speed increased, they ran more like men than women, the sulphurous colors of their bodies blotting out without obscuring

the female breasts and hips. *Au-HOO, ay-HOO*, the women wailed, their voices remote in the men's tumult. Just as their grief was deeper at the funerals, their joy was fiercer in etai, as if all of their emotions, accumulating in their long brown days, must find release in this abandon.

There is of course a great deal more to Matthiessen's book than appears here. But I do not think the materials quoted misrepresent the heart of the matter. Indeed, one of the themes not generalized but persistently suggested is that, emotional and psychic life aside, Kurelu war culture was ecologically functional. It kept the population stable to permit the culture to survive in a remote valley with limited resources.

Certainly theirs was the war team life of *homo agonistes* synergized by the wild, intensely colorful and Dionysian creativity of *homo ludens*, who transformed ritualized combat into games, theatricals and ecstasy. Can it be argued, then, that such are human nature, the human condition, and man's fate?

No. Primitive cultures as we know them, expressing the experience of small groups relatively isolated over long periods of time, tend to show dominant motifs. Of course none, any better than all of them together, supplies indubitable evidence about the whole content of human nature, the whole history of its experience, nor its whole potential. Many primitive cultures present patterns of behavior and motifs different from those of the Kurelu, sometimes radically so.

Nevertheless the Kurelu, which is why Matthiessen pictured them so well, can but haunt us. It could not be denied that they have appeared often before and elsewhere, and often enough in our past. The conjectural prehistory of man is usually imagined in Kurelu-like forms. Historically, the Greeks were much like that, and the Vikings. The native cultures of North America were often rather like that. And it is simply true that we ourselves in all our "civilization" are often like that. We meet the Kurelu on Matthiessen's living page, and, say what you will of what more we are than they, they are we.

Whatever God may know that we cannot about the nature of human-kind and human cultures, nothing is more obvious than that most mightily common among the varieties of behavior patterns is the con-figuration linking *homo agonistes* to *homo ludens* and both to *homo aleator*. From press reports, Dr. Napoleon Chagnon may have discov-ered a striking new variation among the Yãnomanö of the Amazon Basin. As between them and the old Kurelu or the old Kwakiutl on their side, the struggle-play-gamble pattern characteristic of our Big Game culture seems preferable (insofar as we stick to it) to their fight-murder-war patterns. We are not so far, and what withholds us is not so indestructible, from relapsing that we can afford to rip up the fabric of custom and consolations which holds us to the possibility of our pattern. And we need urgently to promote *homo fraternalis*, the citizen of the world.

The way things are now is public beyond all previous imagining. As in the life of the university at large, in college sport you have to be insignificant or eccentric not to live with the nation and the public looking over your shoulder and stepping on your feet. At the instant of this writing, what to make of theoretical literature about "popular culture" would vex the child of five generations of Philadelphia esthetes. But the Big Game did long ago become part of American popular culture. No matter what anybody wishes, American collegiate football and basketball belong to the people, are flesh and bone members of the family of popular arts. What characterizes the way things are now is the fact that the national culture and the Big Game may be said to be not only married and interbred but still passionately in love.

Why? What is all the excitement about? For one thing it is about something for which we seem not to have an adequate English word: the Big Game is a *fiesta*, a communal and ritual party, a blowout at which you are authorized to take a moral holiday from work, worry, and responsibility. A French artist sent by a national magazine a few years ago to paint his impressions of an Ohio State football game found it exhilirating: such an explosion of energy! It has often been noted that the Big Game fiesta shares qualities with religious drama. D.W. Brogan found it comparable in communal attention and concern to the great Greek celebrations of the drama—and the Games. George Stoddard is said to have maintained that Americans need the football weekend because we have no other equivalent of the feast days lost with the old religion. Perhaps there are deep reasons for the placement of the football season at harvest time. At any rate, there is a lot more going on here than meets the incurious or untrained eye.

Nothing reveals more about the Big Game than the fact Stephen Crane noticed. In connection with it a number of different games go on simultaneously, inside the stadium and out. Though all focus on and take symbolic cues from the game the athletes play, each plays to its own ends. There are now so many no participant could hope to keep them all in mind at once, so many I am not sure I can count them up without missing some. Everything starts, of course, from "givens" provided by the past. Now a mature part of American culture, the Big Game is massive, spectacular, magnetic, dynamic—and arrived from its longish evolution. Tradition, the practical expectation, means much. The game itself, as a pattern of culture and form of art, as a set of skills, conventions, and rules, comes to the field or floor and the stands as a given. The players have grown up within the game in communities where it "always" was. The professionals who serve to present the game, the coaches and administrators, live and work within received patterns. The stadium and other support facilities represent accumulated investment which could be duplicated only with grave difficulty.

With occasional exceptions the American intercollegiate Big Game presents football or basketball, but the significant differences between those games I must sink for the moment (in the interest of sanity) to concentrate on football. By "game week" of a Big Game the long preparation of players and coaches, including the season to date, has become only foreground, another set of givens. The schedule the then director of athletics hammered out a dozen years ago, consulting perhaps with his conference, with his coach, perhaps with a committee including faculty, student and alumni members, perhaps with his president or certain trustees, spending hours on the long distance telephone, has been a given recognized and prepared for—perhaps even when the coaches undertook to recruit their present players.

But now it is game week. Not to complicate the situation by subdividing, the vital points of view at the event will number not fewer than ten. The Big Game will be different to the watchers posted at each of these points of vantage: those of the players, the coaches, the auxiliaries, the students, the faculty and staff, the administrators (including trustees), the alumni, the fans present, the media, the fans latent who consume the media product. Though folk with other points of view are sure to be affected by what transpires, they will not be "present" in an equal sense. During game week, all who are to be involved have to get ready.

Early Sunday morning the coaches will be at work on the films of Saturday's game. Every player earns a numerical grade for what he did on every play and a "game grade" for net performance. Honors will be awarded for outstanding contributions. At the same time the trainers will be readying supplies and equipment; and by mid-morning players will be in for treatment of bruises, strains, injuries from the day before. The team physician will attend. After dinner coaches will meet with their special charges to review and discuss film; and, when that is over, last week becomes history and, perhaps at four o'clock, game week begins. Coaches will sit as late as seems productive, studying the latest films of the Big Game opponent. By one o'clock Monday afternoon they must have the essentials of a game plan from which to assign every precious minute of the perhaps one hundred they will have for that day's practice.

Meanwhile every other part of the support apparatus works hard. The "game face" shows commonly all week. The athletic establishment must cope every week in the season either with travel plans or crowd preparation. For travel the business manager, a professional, has long since reserved transportation and meals and housing and scheduled it all, going and coming, down to the last minute and room key. The equipment manager, a professional, has purchased supplies and equipment and planned what to take, how to get it there, and how to handle it at the site of the game. He will coordinate with the trainer. They will both have to cope with changes and vicissitudes before they go and portal to portal. The business and equipment managers will deal, firmly but tactfully, with student managers.

Everybody will keep checking and clearing with the director and the coach. The difficult they will perform routinely. The impossible will take a little time, but they will do that too if they get the time. "Every day," they say, "we have a crisis. But every once in a while we have a JEEZ-us Crisis!"

It's easier to take team and team party two thousand miles than prepare for a home crowd of fifty to a hundred thousand people. Then the director and his staff earn their pay. He has to have staffs, housing, and equipment to plan and care for: physical facilities; ticket sales and money handling; media representatives; special guests, especially the president's party; crowd control; parking and concessions; the auxiliaries; medical first aid. Preparing a field impeccably for play is a science, "dressing" a stadium an art. And so it goes—from architecture to police work to popcorn. Everything left to chance will go wrong. Hard work, informed planning, and good morale in performance count as much in the support apparatus as on the field. In magnitude it is big business.

The reason why it is big business is, of course, that at least imaginatively the majority of the male and a considerable fraction of the female population connect to the Big Game through the media. Though the capacity to survive as a media worker perhaps requires you to think that without you the world would pop and disappear like a big soap bubble, the media exist because the culture creates and sustains them. They stand on the same footing as the Big Game. Do they create it or does it sustain sports commentators? It is not really the same as the rooster who crowed the sun up. Because the relation is symbiotic, the institutional support apparatus maintains a Sports Information Director and provides funds and facilities for him to supply media workers with such means of hospitality and functional convenience as may induce in the naive among them delusions of grandeur.

The SID has long since circulated a brochure so colorful and replete with fact you could almost write your "story" before coming to the game if you left room for the score. He has periodically written and mailed out "rushes" in advance of the Big Game. Every day during game week he will memorialize sports desks and the wire services with bits of prose and film. No few of these pieces, including film clips, will be calmly plagiarized into columns or appear as "news" on sports pages or shows as if the media worker had originated them. But the SID will not feel robbed. During game time, amid the refreshments, there will be a terse, accurate announcement in the press box of just what happened after every play. At halftime statistics will be circulated to every occupant of the press box, and after the game the full statistical sheet will be supplemented by a careful play-by-play account. The SID's staff works well and true at build-up, ballyhoo, and follow-up.

Meanwhile, back at what are now called "living centers," the students have not been loafing. They have a lot to do, much of which is somehow folkloristic and relates to the Big Game as a fiesta. With a return to the traditions of student life now in full swing, a bewildering network of student organizations and committees presides over the festivals. It is a world which enacts life for its own sake. Chronologically before it lies the American adult fishnet of voluntary associations. Behind it lie years of student experience with the shadow world of American children schooled to belonging—as when a six-year-old comes wide-eyed home to confide that they have elected class officers and all year refers reverentially to her playmate as "Hibby, Our President."

For a Big Game the students may elaborately, expensively, fantastically, sometimes artistically decorate their houses or build floats (or both). In either case their theme will celebrate Siwash and promise to destroy "the Red Raiders" in every variation student ingenuity can devise and sleepless industry execute. Wise professors will muse upon what half of either would contribute to their classes. Yet that will be only part of it. There will be parties to plan for Saturday night and affairs to prepare for returning alumni (at the fraternities and sororities) for Friday night or perhaps Saturday or Sunday brunch. Organized living center groups will attend the game together, and hundreds of students will be organized to stage the card-section displays.

The keynote throughout this burst of energy and resources expended in preparation for the Big Game is a blend of cooperation and fraternalism on the one hand with competition and antagonism on the other. All their lives, likely enough, Siwash alumni will live joined in business and social and public affairs with Red Raiders in bonds of mutual affection, understanding, and rivalry. The model duplicates the fraternal and agonic relations of parties in the political democracy and reappears in every relation of American life.

The Siwash-Raider relation will surely influence the election of the governor or the conduct of the legislature, affecting the *res publica*, from time to time. It could be what it is in college or in life after college only if it were what it is on the fields of play: sharp competition within bonds of similitude, respect, cooperation. If the fraternal requires bonding, so does the agonic. Bond the two and you must have bounds—limits, rules, decorum—or there can be no game and no fun. But the fraternal and agonic bonded look very much like certain kinds of love.

Therefore the student body of the home team will go all out for the Big Game. There will be prizes for best decoration in as many classes as seem decent, at the least for fraternities and sororities and for coed dormitories. The grand climax of the pregame festivities will be the Friday night pep rally, preceded by a parade and climaxed with the bonfire. Wisely, nothing so formal will be planned for a victory celebration after the Big Game. Its issue is always in doubt, and tradition long ago adjusted to that fact. How deep into the recesses of the folk-mind, into the evolution of human emotion and symbolic adjustment to stress, go the bonfire, the parade, and the rally, however? When were they not practiced? or when did they first become satisfying symbolic dramas? For all the purposes even of history so conjectural it is fanciful, they have always been with us. The racial memory of humanity runneth not to the contrary.

The university band will march and strut and blare away in full fig.

The floats will sail majestically or comically through the town, escorted by capering students. The cars with dignitaries, with the stern coach and the players, often ashen-faced, will sweep past cheering crowds lining the sidewalks. At the site of the rally the speaker's platform will be bathed in light, with the crowd, exaggerated in number and emotional mass by darkness, looming around. Songs and music boom under those circumstances and cheers crash. The speeches must be short, their content traditional: oratory or the unconventional would be unthinkable. Then the grand blaze and perhaps dancing, even snake dances, around it. The coach will take the team out of town for the night if he can; and he had better. Sleep will come to the living centers sometime after 2:00 A.M.

Walking back from the field in the gathering darkness after Thursday's practice, coaches are apt to remember an ancient rural remark, "Well, the hay's in the barn!" Their preparation is over; and, no matter what else they do, they are going to have to let the young men play the Big Game. Monday necessarily given to physical recuperation, maybe psychological regrouping, they have had only three, with some key players perhaps two, days of full physical preparation. Perhaps the only students on campus under active disciplinary stress to go to classes, the players have had a busy time. They hardly know at first hand what the campus is doing. They have stared at film, run over and over, individually and in groups. They have mastered the game plan, knowing exactly how the team proposes to do everything. Each has now his accustomed routine for "getting up" psychologically for the game.

During the same days all the auxiliaries were getting ready too. They contribute music, pageantry, spectacle, comedy, and focus to the Big Game. Students with professional directors and consultants, they practice arts peculiarly developed as sections of American popular culture. The football coach will tell you that he recruits as many quarterbacks as he can because on any high school team the quarterback is the "best athlete"—in pure tests of all-around athletic ability, that is, he excels; and if he can't prevail as a quarterback on the college team he can be converted to play another position. I think it a fair guess that traditionally the best athletes among college women became cheerleaders, twirlers, and pompon girls among the auxiliaries. The men and women who pick the performers, often including "guidons" and other relatively immobile girls, will obviously have had an eye to show-girl types, too.

The auxiliaries represent rigorous competitive selection at the level of Big Game talent. They also represent music, dance, and theatrical personality at some of their highest levels of development even in universities where active programs of training in the arts have become major academic concerns, well-funded in facilities, faculties, and activity budgets. Like the players, they came back to the campus early, with practice and conditioning routines well advanced. While the team suffered through its "three-a-day" workouts in the August heat, the band could be heard blaring and thumping its way through quick-step formations and evolutions. A twirler's skills have to be maintained and honed like those of a musician or gymnast. Everybody in a good college band can out-drill most military units. All through game week they have practiced individually, by sections, and en masse for performances which will begin an hour before game time and run more or less continuously for four or five hours—perhaps longer if there is a big victory celebration.

Musicians and coaches knit well together socially. And twice, at widely spaced intervals, I have heard a delighted musician's wife work her way across a crowded room with great news for her distinguished husband: "Just think! The Coach says Waldo could come to basketball rehearsal!"

It took me a while the first time to grasp her logic. But the logic is that in fact musicians work harder than athletes. When the musician *practices*, he is alone. When he prepares a concert with the group which will perform it, that is *rehearsal*. And yet, the two ways of life are much the same. So are the lives of the players and the auxiliaries, all students, who stage the Big Game. They form a community.

One graduated Big Game cheerleader reports that in the spring of his frosh year "better than seven hundred young women and four hundred young men" turned out to compete "for six male and six female positions." They practiced five nights a week for eight weeks, "running a mile at the beginning . . . and another at the end," doing windsprints and calisthenics as well as the drill for cheers in between. By the final two weeks they had dwindled to fifty postulants of each sex and then performed for judges who cut the total to twenty-four. Next to last came exhaustive motivational and personality interviews before the final selections. All through the summer the survivors worked on conditioning and the cheer-drill, and they came back to campus with the football team for preseason "practice, practice as a group."

Only when the season began, he says, did it dawn on him that the

Red Raider U. cheerleader was part of a large Public Relations scheme: "In and out of uniform we had to represent RRU's public image. . . . On the field we had to look as if perspiration was a human trait quite beyond us; at half time we always changed uniforms; and always we entered the alumni stands before the game to chat with the people upon whose contributions RRU's future rested." The night before a home game the Red Raider cheerleaders helped host "a large dinner given for the visitors," and they went to other campuses as an advance party "two or three days before" to drum up good relations and expectations. With Sundays off, they were back at practice by 4:00 every Monday afternoon.

It paid nothing (though he enjoyed an earned academic scholarship) except a place near the heart of the Big Game and the fun of trips, especially a bowl game. But once, after the team trounced Siwash, "a fan jammed an unmarked envelope into my hands and disappeared into the crowd." It "contained a five-hundred dollar cashier's check made out to the RRU cheerleaders and twelve twenty-dollar bills." He turned it over to the athletics scholarship fund. The one substantial personal benefit was a summer job as a counselor in "a summer camp for high school cheerleaders" which was run at pleasant resorts. It is clear that he loved the whole experience.

All this, however, has been preparation for the increasingly electric moments which come when at last the stadium fills up with the nonstudent audience of fans. As they "make the game," they also make most of the trouble. A University president must deal with many constituencies; and they will be so weightily represented in the crowd at a Big Game that he will be compelled to attend and make the best of it whether he likes it or not. Though the sensitivity and urgency of his relationships with one or another of these groups vary according to the public or private status of his institution, the practical differences may be smaller than some observers suppose. At any rate, you can make a useful sort of Big Game crowd classification by university constituencies. They are at least six in number: the students; the faculty and staff; the trustees; the alumni; public officials, legislators, major opinion-makers, etc, etc.; the public—the repository of "public opinion," the general consumers of the media product, perhaps "the subway alumni," who never went to Notre Dame but "own" it.

If seventy thousand make a median attendance for a Big Game, the size of the Siwash student body will sizably affect the gross receipts. If five thousand students, paying little or nothing at the gate, and a thousand faculty and staff at half-price attend the Big Game at Siwash, the take, at the same gross attendance, will be sizably bigger than at State where twenty thousand student and four thousand faculty-staff coupons are honored. Both institutions will hand out some hundreds of "freebies" for reasons of political or financial gratitude or hope, State perhaps surrendering several thousands to legislators and officialdom. The alumni and the public will pay full price, and if there are anything like fifty thousand of them in attendance the Big Game will be a smashing success. When their financial settlement is made, all costs paid and adjusted, the two directors may split a $300,000 melon between them according to conference regulations or provisions of the game contract made ten or more years before.

That figure is of course round, and pretty plump; but it does not begin to represent the investment in his Big Game weekend by a fan. We are talking the American fiesta, partytime, now; and estimating expenses can be a wild affair. The local airports will fill up with private planes flown in for a Big Game. What that cost the sportsman is as hard to guess as what it actually cost to bring in the several hundred big "recreation vehicles" crowding their parking lots or the launches that come to their slips down Lake Loudon at Knoxville. Some parties arrive at the motels as early as Thursday night and are still around for breakfast Monday. More come Friday afternoon and go home on Sunday. A couple of hundred buses full of people and, of course, thousands of cars blacken the parking lots. One hapless state highway patrol got things so snarled before one Big Game that the traffic jam still reached more than twenty miles up the road at half-time. The governor arrived, fighting mad, during the half.

The economic magnitude of such an event is greater than I ever imagined. My best guess had been that a median Big Game crowd of seventy thousand spent "a cool million" on the game, but I turned out a piker. For instance, the Greater Madison, Wisconsin, Chamber of Commerce in its monthly report for January 1976 totted up the expenditures for 1975 in their Dane County by football fans who came to Wisconsin games from out of the county. Excluding the parents of students, who might have come without a game, the Chamber of Commerce thought that

non-parent football visitors spent an estimated $4,680,000 in Dane County in 1975. Eating and drinking places received the greatest immediate benefit from these football patrons who spent $1,862,000 in restaurants and bars over the six football weekends. Receipts to other economic groups were estimated at:

Apparel stores	871,000
Lodging places	677,000
Auto sales and service	519,000
General merchandise stores	387,000
Miscellaneous retail stores	120,000
Local government	97,000
Amusement places	46,000
Transportation services	39,000
Local households	25,000
Personal and business services	23,000
Furniture and appliance stores	12,000

Pursued as soberly conservative economic analysis, the whole table, for crowds just in excess of seventy thousand, looked like this:

IMPACT OF FOOTBALL PATRON EXPENDITURES

Group	Direct impact	Indirect impact	Total impact
Nonparent visitors	$4,680,000	$5,469,000	$10,249,000
Parent visitors	398,000	474,000	872,000
Local patrons	1,237,000	1,472,000	2,709,000
Total	$6,315,000	$7,515,000	$13,830,000

These "direct expenditures," they caution, "do not include any money paid to any University units, such as the Athletic Department, the Memorial Union, etc." They do not include ticket prices, parking fees, programs, or stadium concessions, for instance. More striking, they do not include transportation costs and food, booze, lodging, and other expenditures outside Dane County, though tail-gaters, bus-loads, and recreation vehicle people may have driven a couple of hundred miles round trip and carried their comestibles.

Nothing of course is allowed for anybody's time, for university investments and expenditures, or for the costs of the media, print and electronic. A cool couple of million is, very conservatively indeed, more like it. But it's "just a game," producing nothing, void of intrinsic value, real only while it is in progress, in duration only, as they say, as good as the next game. It is as a phenomenon that it is "big"—of an impressive magnitude both as to intensity and mass.

There is a temptation to suppose that money in such amounts is spent by "the alumni" or even "the rich alumni." But enquiry would seem not to bear that supposition out. Every college has well-to-do alumni, some of whom spend conspicuously on athletic events. But nobody has enough of them to fill a big stadium. Further, there is a temptation to suppose that a certain class exclusiveness selects the Big Game crowd. But that supposition seems only relatively valid. Except as workers, the poor are not among those present. But blue-collar or hard-hat workers, union members, may be as numerous as, say service club members. Not a few of the bus-loads were organized as excursions from local bars and taverns. The public for the Big Game may well represent the classes who mainly vote in American elections. In that degree it may be said to be an affair of the people.

And for all of them, the affair constitutes a party. Between the booze inside the customers passing through the gate and what they smuggle by and consume in the stadium, the supplies would suffice for New Year's Eve. For the party some fans need drink. The plumber said to me one day: "I know you. I sat in front of you at football games for a couple of years. I'm the one that always brought the big family-size thermos full of martinis."

Others need a big bet down, or a dollar each way every Saturday with Big George from Siwash at the office. Some turn on for the mere rhythm of the occasion, others on coming to the site of the event, the walk into the stadium. For some the bands and the flags and the spectacle do it, for some the coach, for some the players. But everybody who is really there gets high on the party somehow.

Of course not everybody among those present is really there, "in the game," or "knows the score." I once sat in the horseshoe curve behind an end zone, with snow driving into everybody's face, watching a classic. Conversation drifted in, with the snow, from beneath a blanket in front: " 'How many quarters in a football game?' 'How many quarters in an apple?' 'Oh, I was afraid maybe it was like polo, or something.' "

But most of those present have invested their money and time in one of the world's best parties. As "theater" in the broad sense, where is its match? On balance, everybody participates; all the participants consume a heady, highly satisfactory brew of party fun and art experience. Art occasions experience in its consumer, experience more intense, more meaningful, more satisfactorily shaped than he can ordinarily provide for himself. Parties license and reinforce fun while they set fear at rest because they are communal. At the Big Game all the emotions of war run wild with the frenzy of the most terrible of human actions—

mass violence. Hate, hostility, scorn, contempt, and derision for "them" dance hand in hand with love, loyalty, admiration, devotion, and praise for "us." Triumph and joy exult in victory; heartbreak and gloom sink with defeat. And yet all happens within secure walls, redoubts, of symbol, ritual, decorum, vicariousness, community, and "make-believe"—in short, play.

Those fine intensities for which it all exists rise from the simultaneous diversity and unity of the communal factors. The final unity joins the Raider and Siwash competitors in a community of festal, fraternal, and agonic esthetic experience. From that last point of view winning and losing are only the halves, divided by the curve which unites as it divides them, of the famous Chinese circle encompassing the eternal Yin and Yang. Neither could exist without the other. Indeed, part of the force of the true event generates from the ebb and flow of the tides of fortune on the field. The whole stadium experiences the esthetics of winning and the esthetics of losing alternately, often simultaneously, until on great occasions something like a derangement of sensibility occurs. I have heard elements of a home crowd boo a victory out of sheer emotional confusion. Everybody has seen thousands of people sit motionless for many minutes after the final gun, trying to sort out their emotions, trying to realize.

Much of the intensity communicates throughout the stadium along the network of communities present. Each constituency (and one of each for either "side") forms a community, joined by various bonds and tending toward certain varieties of experience. As their variations enrich the mix, they are unified, promoting intensity, by the sharp focus of everything upon the game. But they are embraced into community and, more than community, family by those sentiments of attachment to college or university which seem stronger and more complex in Americans than in other people. We designate them by totemic signs, sacred names and colors, and the untranslatable idea of "alma mater." To see and hear a hard-hat who never finished high school and a hard-hearted scientist with degrees from three other institutions stand side by side and sing the foolish words and vulgar tune of an "alma mater" with a fervor and unction fit for a Bach chorale sung by believers can become a pure amazement. Why are they doing that? Because it is halftime at the Big Game and they have lent their hearts to a moment of secular religion?

Whatever the exaggerations and insincerities, whatever sentimental misplacement of irresponsible emotion may occur, these intensities mount up, then, to more than entertainment, party, art, even community. A sort of sacred festival, maybe the Big Game celebrates a secular religion. It dramatizes symbolically that identity of the American people which is a puzzle and scandal to the world. It speaks to the psychic condition of individual Americans with a generality as well as an intensity matched by few other events and those of relatively rare recurrence. From somewhere out of the psychic depths of American culture it seems to cry meaning. But just what does it say? A game, says Robert Gahringer, "is first of all a real language between players (or spectators)." Like a work of great literature, says Clifford Geertz, a game is a "cultural text." To understand either, you have to learn to experience it; and the capacity to experience, which comes before understanding, requires you to master the art of close reading.

CHAPTER FOUR

The Public Art Form

POP ART AND THE AMERICAN DREAM

But no matter what Huizinga and all his followers declare, I cannot feel, cannot intellectually perceive, that the Big Game really is religious. I think I do not believe in the real existence of what is sometimes called "the secular religion." The Big Game is not in fact sacramental. It only feels that way at some of its highest moments—as every successful art does. It is not at last even "ritual" in a final sense—only, in the pop phrase which catches the situation just right, "sort of" ritual. It is, simply, one of the best, most potent popular art forms.

The best party in American life, the Big Game enacts itself as the most vitally folkloristic event in our culture. Nothing about it, then, seems more extraordinary than the fact that it is also an academic festival, organic to institutions of higher education and learning. It expresses their character and the qualities of their accumulated experience. Perhaps sharing in the lives of colleges and universities permits the people who celebrate it to feel free, licensed, protected. The Big Game is franchised by its place near the heart of alma mater. Who will condemn it? Who would reduce it by hostile analysis to dead components? Only perhaps that fraction of the faculties who happen to hate it. Some of them also despise modern, postindustrial culture for having cut its roots to myth, the rituals of earth's rhythms, the naturalness of the folk. Might it be true that, while folkloristic ways celebrate themselves, alive and well in the stadium, some of the faculty sit sequestered in their library carrels, weeping anew the century-old tears of William Morris?

At what point of complexity organized human behavior crosses the line between "primitive culture" and "civilization"—like ours—it is fortunately no part of my responsibility to define. But it would seem to me that in a brilliant essay by Clifford Geertz called "Deep Play: Notes on the Balinese Cockfight" he had crossed the line and provided a drama of insights both bridging our condition with that of the Kurelu or Kwakiutl and indispensably balancing what their "primitive" gambling cultures appear to say. Dominantly, the culture of Bali is Apollonian as can be. Poise and balance, harmony, detachment, and coolness are everything. Yet Balinese men are obsessive breeders, petters, and trainers, experts about, and gamblers upon fighting cocks. Investigating, Geertz found that the fights and betting functioned as "a dramatization of status concerns" central to the culture. "Fighting cocks," the Balinese peasants in sum told Geertz, "is like playing with fire only not getting burned. You activate village and kingroup rivalries and hostilities, but in 'play' form." The theme runs deep in folktale: "Along with everything else that the Balinese see in fighting cocks—themselves, their social order, abstract hatred, masculinity, demonic power—they also see the archetype of status virtue, the arrogant, resolute, humor-mad player with real fire, the Ksatria prince."

Somewhere, then, at the core of that Apollonian culture lies hidden a Kwakiutl with a Dionysian myth celebrated by participant gamblers "allegorically humiliated by one another, day after day." We are dealing, Geertz says, with an art form.

> The cockfight renders ordinary, everyday experience comprehensible by presenting it in terms of acts and objects which have had their practical consequences removed and have been reduced (or, if you prefer, raised) to the level of sheer appearances, where their meaning can be more powerfully articulated and more exactly perceived. The cockfight is "really real" only to the cocks—it does not kill anyone, castrate anyone, reduce anyone to animal status, alter the hierarchical relations among people, nor refashion the hierarchy; it does not even redistribute income in any significant way. What it does is what, for other peoples with other temperaments and other conventions, *Lear* and *Crime and Punishment* do; it catches up these themes—death, masculinity, rage, pride, loss, beneficence, chance—and, ordering them into an encompassing structure, presents them in such a way as to throw into relief a particular view of their essential nature.

Making an important effort to carry esthetic insights into culturally expressive modes, Geertz pointed out that, essentially, what their cockfight presents to the Balinese imagination and sensibility is tragic, "life as the Balinese most do not want it." Using "emotion for cognitive ends," the cockfight talks "in a vocabulary of sentiment—the thrill of risk, the despair of loss, the pleasure of triumph." It provides for the

Balinese a "sentimental education" in "what his culture's ethos and his private sensibility (or, anyway, certain aspects of them) look like when spelled out externally in a collective text." Geertz has made a brilliant advance over difficult terrain:

> Every people, the proverb has it, loves its own form of violence. The cockfight is the Balinese reflection on theirs: on its look, its uses, its force, its fascination. . . . If, to quote Northrop Frye again, we go to see *Macbeth* to learn what a man feels like after he has gained a kingdom and lost his soul, Balinese go to cockfights to find out what a man, usually composed, aloof, almost obsessively self-absorbed, a kind of moral autocosm, feels like when attacked, tormented, challenged, insulted, and driven in result to the extremes of fury, he has totally triumphed or been brought totally low.

The very fact, Geertz concluded, that "the cockfight is not the master key to Balinese life" but only one among many "cultural texts" and not even one pitched in an affirmative key, suggests that a "culture is an ensemble of texts" (dare you say an anthology?) which only "close" and wary reading can make available to the reader. So it is with our Big Game.

Though it is often argued from the example of Shakespeare that high art may be found in undeniably popular culture, popular art tends to make up in breadth for what it lacks in height or depth. Its appeal is actuarial, so to speak; like the true odds in life or fire insurance, it can be relied upon to cover the majority of cases. It is "Coke," not caviar, to the general. Whether its effects resonate or endure is not so important as immediacy. Nevertheless, when there is art in pop it works like the rest of the arts.

Daniel Boorstin includes an interesting analysis of the broad problem in *Democracy and Its Discontents*. Looking to the "distinction between the great tradition and the little tradition, between the high culture and the folk culture," he says, you see odd discontinuities between the European and the American ways of treating them. European custom generalized the folk culture but kept it powerless; it centralized the high culture and associated it with power and privilege. But with us "high culture is one of the least centralized" aspects of the national life. "And our universities express the atomistic, diffused, chaotic, and individualistic aspect." Our popular culture, on the other hand, comes to us from powerfully centralized advertising agencies. Because it is in business, "the advertising folk culture" is subject to constant "self-liquidation and erasure"; it is "discontinuous, ephem-

77

eral, and self-destructive"; it "attenuates and is always dissolving before our very eyes."

These truths hold for most pop art and culture but not football and basketball. Though the games change, they neither dissolve nor erase. Their continuities are striking, and Wallace Wade and Clair Bee remain trenchant analysts of sports they have not played nor even coached for decades. The games unfold in patterns of repetition, variation, and novelty rich in fascination. And the Big Game—party within party from the pep rally through the Monday Quarterback Club Luncheon—reveals the Americans, stripped of feasts by modern history, strenuous at reinventing the folk-festive heritage of the human race.

Arguably, there may be a linked progression in which materials, themes, ideas, impulses move from folk art to popular art, thence to public "high" art and in turn to high "private" art—and thence back to folk art again. At the Big Game festivities the folkloristic elements have become pop; perhaps they sometimes wash up the beaches of public "high" art. At any rate, the continuities of tradition and forms in student life and the institutions supportive of the Big Game lend the college festivities immense affective advantage. You have only to contrast the dull pathos of halftime activities at a professional game or the stale, faintly sordid activities of the professional auxiliaries recruited from the night club circuit to lend color and cheer to their sidelines. Without forms or vital tradition, the fan at the pro game remains pathetic even when some promotion makes him seem creative. An Associated Press story in 1975 tells it all: "A new fad is sweeping through Baltimore. . . . Thousands of kazoos will toot the Colt fight song when Baltimore takes on the Miami Dolphins Sunday." The mass fad was started by "Hymie the Kazoo Guru," said the account, and "Hymie estimates more than 1,500 kazoos are in circulation for Sunday's game." Fifteen hundred?

On the other hand, the vitality and color of the Big Game are such that everybody wants a piece of that action. Though it can and does profit from shrewd promotion, it is so far from being a creature of the advertising industry that the industry is always alert and vigorous to hook on to Big Game popular momentum. Promoters and politicians tirelessly angle to get the band, get a picture with the quarterback or the coach, use the stadium or arena for a backdrop. Whole media professions live on it.

No small part of the common academic rejection of the Big Game stems from an understandable rejection of its emotional prominence. It takes its rise from resentment of the festival, the party, and can reflect feelings like those Macaulay named when he said that the Puritans abolished bear-baiting in England not because it gave pain to the bear but because it gave pleasure to the spectators. Another fount of resentment is the applause, the attention, that communal and public enthusiasm which indeed create the Big Game. The difficulty is not unreal, as a master of the violin told me once:

> "I find myself really concerned," he said, "about something which is both wrong and right. I can't help it. I never had to worry about it before I joined the University. And it upsets me."
>
> "What do you mean?"
>
> "It's the applause at concerts. I look out at the audience, and there sit Roe, who won a Nobel Prize, and Doe who wrote the best book in his field. I'm surrounded by first-class minds and very gifted people who work hard at really important things, and nobody ever claps for them. And I come out and play a little music and there are storms of applause every time. It's not right."

And so, comparatively, it is not. In the best of all possible worlds the emotional, psychic support of applause, cheers, festival would uplift intellectual achievement even more powerfully than it rewards acting or music or athletic success. But it does not, partly because the natures of the cases differ so radically: the musician plays to a rapt and ardent community what the composer imagined in a loneliness which only fortitude prevented from crushing him. Nothing is more competitive than intellectual work. You fight the self with all its defects and limitations. You fight the discipline, with all its accumulations of genius, famous or forgotten. You fight the other practitioners, to get ahead and beat them out, to impress them and force not only them but their and your successors to dance a measure to your tune. No good professor dare think himself not a competitor, not a gambler. It is hazardous duty, and you have to risk laying yourself on the line and risk humiliation, even crippling injury to those most precious powers of spirit and ego which must be spent in the service of creativity.

And you have to know that in the common life nobody will care. Personally I cannot believe that these facts of life are tragic. But if they were, why not take the loss with good grace? As Loren Eiseley says of man's fate as all our past reveals it, the best response is to know and accept it. "Only so can we learn our limitations and come in time to suffer life with compassion."

Why might the professors not much better settle gladly for the community available to them in academe, with all its constituencies?

Should they think to look, they would find them, communally festive, at the Big Game as nowhere else.

Not to repeat what the cultural anthropologists say, a chorus of impressive voices joins in what really are our times to urge us toward community. Democracy, says Boorstin, "depends on the communication which is sharing, not on that which is purely self-expressive, explosive, or vituperative." Aidan Kavanaugh, Professor of Liturgics at Yale, sets as one of the footings for a strong essay the point that "a people whose festivals atrophy will not long remain a people, much less a culture." And Beisser, in his sober but incisive way, sums them up. "The masses of Americans" in the stands or on the fields or floors of sport are not to be thought psychiatrically disordered. On the contrary, they are engaged in "performing rituals which in every respect constitute an integral part of American life and are in no way deviant. In fact, . . . one might conclude that the non-participant in sports is more likely to be disordered than is the participant." Analysis of "life processes," he continues, has often fatally changed them; and it has killed most of the festivals on which our culture once depended, leaving the skulls to be inhabited by advertising.

For whatever reasons, Beisser concludes, cultural vitality survives in athletics: "Sports events . . . have defied analysis and have retained the appeal of excitement and commitment formerly associated with holiday rituals. The magnitude of sports interest has grown in proportion to the loss of involvement by Americans in other rituals." He hopes, as a last word, that "America's intense interest in games may . . . represent a transition from the vestiges of the past to the birth of a new vitality." Academe need not raise its sights to levels at which the fate of nations is decided to see that the virtues of identity, loyalty, and communitas available in the Big Game ought to be cherished. The advantages of "exposure" and identification from the academic community to the populace at large ought to be exploited, if only for the good of all those, from freshmen to distinguished professors, for whom no applause will ever ring out.

Games might even be thought the true business of the university. And what is there in a democratic culture which might arrogate to itself the condemnation of mass dreams and of those dreams which connect the professional and apprentice professional dreamers to the common? The realities of the situation have turned the seeking mind not back but beneath the crust of fatal appearances toward the sources of human vitality. With something like a practical infinity of resounding titles, prerational and extrarational ways of thinking have become "intellectually" popular in the academy. Though definitionally elusive, they provide instruments for locating and explaining ranges of human experience not available to other means. What is centrally human but rationally inexplicable demands to be studied with postrational as well as rational tools. How striking that, emerging through the debris on the other side of "analysis," the almost necessarily nonreligious psychiatrists and ethnologists should find themselves nearly at one with, for instance, Roman Catholic scholars like Kavanaugh.

> Of all the American games that small boys play and adults take seriously, football has been the most heavily romanticized in print. There is always the suspicion that this is because no one—except coaches, scouts and intellectually gifted players—really understands the game; that those who write about it are forced to lean on fancy rather than fact. But granted the complexities of modern football and the average person's inability to understand them, there is much in the nature of the game that has a distinctly romantic appeal.

So says Jack Newcombe in the best of football anthologies. Take "in print" from that first sentence and it covers most photography, painting, print-making, and sculpture concerned with football, leaving only the cartoon. And football cartooning, mostly devoted to satire on romantic themes, presents only the other side of the one coin. Basketball, too, like football, is "heavily romanticized."

On the other hand, people will insist on taking popular culture into their own hands, letting one man's lie be another man's authentic experience and leaving the recorder of folly to shake his puzzled head. Back to culture theory and its new frontier where ethnology and esthetics, as in Clifford Geertz, interface. Where Geertz found illumination in the esthetic ideas of Northrop Frye, a different light dawned on Gertrude Jaeger and Philip Selznick. Working the standard line from the ethnography of Emil Durkheim to the philosophy of Emil Cassirer and the esthetics of Susanne Langer, they arrived at a definition: "Culture consists of everything that is produced by, and is capable of sustaining, shared experience." Then they turned to the ideas of an esthetician of another stripe: John Dewey.

Dewey's point, American as can be, speaks from his title, *Art As Experience*. He erased the lines between "art" and "life," between "high" and "popular" culture, asking of them all only one question: how authentic is the experience it arouses in persons, whether taken individually or in groups? He thought common experience esthetic and esthetic experience common when either was real. He could not be more democratic. Jaeger and Selznick noted that in proportion as culture is authentic and vital, then, it "strains toward the esthetic." Not quarreling in the last analysis with Geertz, that approach through Dewey makes it easy to see how the Big Game is art.

Though all work and no play will indeed make Jack and Jill dull types, the distinction rigidly applied tends to fog in the topic. Sport and play are not "recreation" conducted during "leisure" from "work." All really productive work is play. Persons successful within themselves play at work and play at life. They turn life and work into art by playing at them and winning. Full creativity expresses life, but it achieves, too. Sport is art, as Santayana said (following Friedrich Schiller); and art, as Picasso said, is the lie that tells the truth about life. But it is a prime truism of esthetics that art comes from struggle. Freedom, inspiration, innocence, love and frenzy fight against convention, medium, craft, discipline, and knowledge to produce form. No fight, no art. No victory, no art. But, no victory being perfect, defeat counts too.

A great deal of true and eloquent testimony shows that his game is art and a life of art to the athlete. But, though they would make a shelf of first-rate books, the formal esthetics of the sports themselves have been little treated. Football and basketball in particular cry out for study as American arts. Though any one of those temptations represents another of the books this one cannot be, however, I think it may be necessary in fairness to say something about the esthetic assumptions upon which this book cannot help proceeding.

As applied to any kind of art, the esthetics which make sense to me are transactional. I can understand the human experience of art best as a series of transactions. The first is a deal made inside the artist between his conscious and preconscious minds.

Watching a painter at work one day, I saw that he worked out a powerful design by combining in one perspective three radically different views, photographically impossible, of his big scene. I could understand that, but I wondered,

> "We have travelled hundreds of miles in the landscape and seen thousands of views. How do you know which ones to make a picture of?"
> "All I know," he answered, "is that every once in a while I see a picture."

Transactional translation: as an artist of forty years' practice, he had, preconsciously, a reservoir of creative impulse which, not controllably, boiled up like a geyser from the depths with its "vision of a picture." He stoked the geyser, so to speak, with incessant stimulation from his trained eye and appreciating mind. But when the impulse rose, the process became reversed. Now his powers, long trained, to capture and fix and meditate upon his "vision" were tested, especially by the challenge: "Can you make a picture of me?" His power to respond depended on his capacity to transact the necessary subjective business, transferring his vision to a craftsman's conception without losing it. The next transaction would be expressive—getting the vision on paper.

> "How do you know how to start?"
> "I am a professional. But as soon as I make the first dot on the paper a struggle begins among my vision, my power to express it, and the laws of art."

Transactionally, all of this went into the production of the work of art. The art experience, which is not at all the experience of the artist in producing the work, can only be a transaction, or a series of transactions, between the work of art, the object, and its consumer—be he hearer, viewer, reader, receiver, or whatnot, alone or in a group. Art happens to consumers as experience. It takes place, transactionally, in the imagination of the consumer. Only through the object can the artist communicate to his audience, and the object is what the audience can know esthetically about the artist. All the rest, I am convinced, is folly.

A sports contest provides an unrivaled analog by which to understand all this. To take an example that really happened, I sat at one of the most hotly contested and beautifully realized games I ever saw alongside a man who, as it unfolded, forgot himself and began to root wholeheartedly for the other team. By that I mean that he had come, as usual, to his seat in a section of fervent home team supporters and found himself swept away by the game into unabashed support for the visitors. Perhaps he was a recent graduate of Red Raider U. who had become a graduate student at Siwash. It became a basketball game where Siwash could not stop the Red Raiders inside but the Raiders could do nothing with the brilliant outside shooting of the Siwash guards, particularly one who sank long swisher after heart-stopping bomb, shattering scoring records. Basket matched basket for forty minutes to a tie, and then through one overtime period after another. My neighbor shouted himself hoarse and limp.

Then came the closing second of the fifth overtime, score tied, and one more of those long shots arching through the air as the buzzer sounded. It is worth remarking that until that point my friend (as by then he was) and I had witnessed exactly the same events, seen the same object. Indeed, everything about the situation depended on the events, however controlled by rule and artifice, being objective, the same to us both. And that ball in the air must either, with entire objectivity and as the same event to us both, swish through the cords or not.

It swished. Were our experiences, his and mine, the same? In a sense not in the least. Mine were victorious, ecstatic. His were defeated, frustrated. But the events were exactly the same. What determined the experiences? Orientation, preparation, commitment—many things, but the chief was imagination. The experience was, as Emily Dickinson said of art, "internal difference, / Where the Meanings, are. . . ."

But in another sense the experiences were deeply the same. They rose from the same events, the same frame and form of things, the same assumptions, the same perceptions and preparations. Winning and losing are really only, esthetically, the inevitable outcomes of the one art. And that is one reason the game is only to the player as the poem to the poet. Neither poet nor player is a consumer, and the consumer need never bother to ask either "What is it like?" Let the player live his own life and we ours. Youth's a stuff will not endure. He will join us in the stands soon enough.

The commerce between the player and the game is one thing, belonging to the athlete as person—of whom more later. But the commerce between the game and the congregation, the audience, the constituencies, the fans, is something else and the heart of the matter. Like most performances of music, drama, dance, the Big Game exists only while it is being played to and within its beholders. As art experience it happens "of within" individuals; but the crowd at an artistically successful game achieves a collective life, too. Its responses can be awesome. Ohio Stadium at Columbus talks back to the game like a great, gruff beast. I heard Texas Stadium turn a game around with one long, disgusted growl at what it thought a cheap shot, lifting Texas and depressing the other team visibly, decisively. The great team games are, then, instant and collective art forms. Hence they are, though Walt Whitman never saw one, ideally Whitmanian—democratic, organic.

They are in type arts of time. Along with the aforementioned audience arts, reading is a different art of time; and it can be argued that the demands of perception, moving from one point of view to another, burning up the energy you have available for concentration and realization, turn painting, sculpture, and architecture into arts of time for the consumer.

The time of play for the game itself and the time during which the fans participate, are "in the game," will vary both as to clock time and the intensities of internal response which often carry players in their way and spectators in theirs into ecstatic orbits where time almost has a stop, elongates blissfully. In any case a most important factor is flow. Dancelike the figures flow on the field or floor, weaving their patterns. Symphonically the progressions of play flow, back and forth, in and out, up and down, punctuated by the clock and scoreboard. Dramatic suspense builds as skill and fortune flow to and fro. The forms of fortune which will become, altogether, the ultimate shape of the game flow into architectonics.

Because all seems freedom, choice, and chance, limits mean everything. No bounds of space or play or time, no game. Plan and training, character and giftedness, devotion, discipline, sacrifice, all flow into equations of tension. And then chance takes a hand. "A football is an oblate spheroid. It takes funny bounces." And who has not seen a basketball balance delicately, impossibly on the rim, rotating gently or dead still, seeming to meditate whether it will lazily roll left to victory or right to defeat? Extemporization can become so decisive and so beautiful in the Big Game that you can understand what Lukas Foss is getting at in music.

The arts of time are like a fire, which is a process, not a substance, but achieves substantial results for good or ill. When it is over the fire is out, dead and gone. It leaves the lovers, vows consummated, abed, or the beans baked on the hearth. Or the pride of the House of Priam dead in the ashes of Troy. So with music or dance or the Big Game. When they are all over they leave behind only the experience, which is what we have made of them but can not get any other way. The theme's intrinsically human. As old as poetry, it asks, "*Ubi Sunt?*" Where are they—the snows of yesteryear? the flowers of spring? the golden lads and lasses? Gone to dust.

The wisdom of the human ages has been that the one thing you can do about that is to shine where your candle is lighted. If the theme is transience, life, as Robinson Jeffers wrote, nevertheless "is good, be it stubbornly long or suddenly / A mortal splendor: meteors are not needed less than / mountains." One way to make meteors is in the brief glory of a human performance that burns incandescent, transcendent, and is over forever—in the dance, the song, the play, the game, the festival—in human life. The wisdom of the game is at once the wisdom of the body and of Ecclesiastes, the sage of this present world, mind, and body. It is also the mystery of humanity: how can mere fragile humankind burn so nobly? die so quickly? A fine Eskimo poet, Orpingalik, got at it exactly for artist, player, and common consumer of life or art:

> A wonderful occupation
> Hunting caribou!
> But all too rarely we
> Excel at it
> So that we stand
> Like a bright flame
> Over the plain.

There seems, regrettably, to be no way to escape the ugliness of the language in which esthetics, the theory of beauty, must be discussed. So perhaps it is best to say that, although you can do interesting things with the esthetics of sport by using Aristotle's ideas about imitation and catharsis, the ideas of Susanne Langer about "presentational symbolism" provide a necessary corrective. Her point, which she applies to all art, works beautifully for sport. In brief, it is that the most direct, most powerful, perhaps most original modes of human contact communicate emotion and experience without the use of words. They "present" themselves, nonverbally, not "discursively," requiring only direct apprehension and no translation by sender or receiver. Sports are by nature visible and kinesthetic, at least as immediate and primordial as music.

THE SORT OF SACRED, SOMETIMES RITUAL

If the Big Game is, then, seriously a popular art form is it also, seriously, "ritual?" About half, I think, "sort of." But let's not wax too serious about all that. Kavanaugh, for instance, helps if we see him squarely. "e.e. cumming's line, 'damn everything but the circus,' contains a truth so true as to be scary," he observes. "Ritual, symbol and feasts are scary because of the power they release." Of liturgical worship, he continues, "Sports are an example. Football is largely ritualized combat." Without "its regular discipline, rhythm and formality," it is merely "a riot," no longer "an event which can bring thousands to their feet as one body in a shared experience of enormous psychic and social intensity."

Talking like that, a liturgist has used football as a successful metaphor for ritual. Turning the relationship around brings interesting questions into view. Is the Big Game a ritual? Or is ritual a good metaphor for the game? About half, I should guess, each way: fifty-fifty. And it pays, by the way, in dealing with "ritual" to take some pains to try to be sure you know what you are talking about. That it is easy to get silly has been demonstrated by T.H. Ferril in "Freud on the 50-Yard Line," a bit of humor worthy of Mark Twain. A wild mix of keen, deadpan observation with arbitrary assignment of "Freudian" meanings, Ferril's essay is funny but mordant. It has earned its popularity, its power as a fool-killer, and ought to have sobered up some of us commentators.

Irony aside, the soberest observer would see at the Big Game all the patterned actions of the teams, the auxiliaries, the crowds. He could hardly fail to feel the rapture of the crowd and, if he knew enough, would glimpse something of that of the players. People become rapt, are "carried away," some in a rapture of fierceness, but some sweetly, in a rapture of identification, of love. Many have it both ways. If our observer could not sense these emotions, he would see and hear them dramatized, even liturgically, during typical "halftime ceremonies." Then suddenly the band comes to attention in solemn array, the bouncy, funny, exhibitionistic mood changes, and a hush falls over the crowd as people rise to their feet. Music in sonorities appropriate to a mass announces the "alma mater" and people begin to sing together a "credo," a "confessio," proclaiming their love and loyalty, everlasting devotion. Sometimes they join in united gesture or salute as well. At Wisconsin they sing the last bar to the words of a cheer, thousands of people swaying in unison as far as they can to left together and then right together with each successive syllable: "U! Rah! Rah! Wis! Con! Sin!" It is liturgical to a degree of intensity not exceeded in St. Peter's in Rome when the Pope appears, to say nothing of what happens in most American churches. Is it not somehow, and other things with it at the Big Game, ritual?

But if you say it is ritual you come up against the demand to say what that means without exposing yourself to Mr. Ferril. Perhaps the best way to begin is to say that ritual means a pattern of established behavior repeated in form to serve a symbolic function. Where some process of cultural evolution has produced particular rituals in specific cultures, what happens then? It is helpful to discover a large degree of agreement among analysts of different stripes. To say nothing of thinkers like Father Kavanaugh, the coincidence between an esthetician and literary "myth-critic" like Philip Wheelwright and a behavioristic ethnologist like Roy A. Rappaport suggests that there may really exist middle ground upon which almost any enquirer might safely stand.

In a fine study of primitive gardening ritual in New Guinea, Rappaport argues that ritual may be objectively as well as psychically functional, as when it makes an ecological difference in the relations between a people and their environment. He visualizes ritual metaphorically as a "mechanism" analogous to such technological devices as a thermostat, or a photoelectric cell, converting one kind of energy (religion) into another (agriculture). The sacred aspect of ritual, says Rappaport, not only lends it credibility but authority, the force of "a functional alternative to political power." Finally, he points out that ritual may be understood from the points of view of two realms of discourse: the realm of the culture in which it functions as "a cognized model"; the realm of the observer who sees from the outside that the ritual may function well in ways not perceivable from inside the culture, functioning as an "operational model." He falls at last into the almost inevitable trap of identifying the "operational model" with "the real world," the normal ethnocentric slip from which not even ethnographers are safe. But it permits him to observe that it is desirable, perhaps even essential, that the two models not be identical, that ritual not "conform in all respects to the real world."

From an altogether different angle of approach, Philip Wheelwright undertook "to inquire into the character of both language and existence" and explore "the semantic characteristics which enable the language of religion and myth and poetry, at their best, to speak in a way that truly 'mounts to the dwelling-place of the gods,' and testify to the reality of that dwelling." It was a work of high seriousness, devoted to what seemed to him the best and highest in contemporary civilization and climaxing in explication of T.S. Eliot's *Four Quartets* as "the most fully pertinent single poem of our moment in History." In short, Wheelwright represents the long line of "myth and ritual" critics whose ideas have moved contemporary culture vigorously.

He sees "ceremonies" of "four main types: the coercive, the contractual, the assimilative, and the confrontative." The first two are forms of magic. "Assimilative ritual" affirms and seeks "to intensify man's continuity and partial oneness with nature, or with the mysterious creative force behind nature." It operates, Wheelwright says, according to the principles of primitive logic which Lucien Lévy-Bruhl called "the law of participation." Ignoring the literalness of post-Hellenic logics, the law of participation makes no difficulty over "contradiction." It seeks images and symbolic patterns which speak intensely to the group, not the individual. They are "collective representations" valued for communal effectiveness rather than consistency. "Confrontation" ritual, explicitly religious, seeks the living presence of that which is beyond us.

Since Wheelwright also recognizes the significance of personal ritual and the sorts of group "secular ritual" which provide the fun and solace of a felt "wehood," it would not be difficult to translate his terms into those of Huizinga. In fact, the points about ritual upon which decidedly different students agree seem more striking than their differences. All agree that ritual serves not only to represent something, or to present something esthetically, to affect people inwardly: ritual wields genuine power; it makes a difference; it makes things happen in the ordinary sensible and outward worlds.

If, then, the Big Game is, among other things, sometimes ritual, what does it do? what difference does it make? what does it make happen? That there may be a difference between the way art works affectively and effectively and the way ritual works depends, I suppose, on faith. An extreme way of putting it would be to say that "ritual" is what they do who worship false gods, and its power is esthetic; what we who possess the truth do is "sacrament," and its power is real. Since in the Big Game we are talking not about the primitive but about forms used in a culture complex huge beyond all human imagining past or present, it pays to recognize that classifications taken from the primitive can be supposed to hold only relatively. They are the best we have but not to be presumed upon.

If you could apply Rappaport's distinction between "cognized" and "operational" models of ritual to the Big Game, for instance, it would clear up our perceptions. But I have yet to see a description of the events which seemed to me even to bring all of the Big Game into one field of reference, one mode of discourse sufficiently sophisticated to take it all in. When you cannot describe the "cognized" except by radical misrepresentation, what are you to do with the "operational"? It's a ritual, all right, functional as Rappaport says, coercive and contractual and assimilative as Wheelwright says, potent even to the point of the "scary" as Kavanaugh says. Part of the difficulty the Big

Game presents may rise from the fact that, like everything in its context, it is a specialization. It began and still functions as specialized to the colleges and their constituencies. So far as it reaches out to the great tumultuous galaxy of the larger culture, it performs increasingly tenuous functions.

In theory, I propose, the Big Game as one combined, dramatic whole may be taken for a ritual, "collective representation" of the American Dream. For reasons not always flattering to the reasoners, the American Dream has often been drastically reduced in analytic discourse. It is, however, inherently complex and many valued, always flowing into new forms. At base it rests on two ideas which, united, compose a vital paradox, as Walt Whitman said in a characteristic poem: "One's self I sing, a simple separate person / Yet utter the word Democratic, the word En-Masse." To treat the American Dream as a unitary generalization concerned only with the "isolato," as Melville called him, the separate person in frantic pursuit of Franklin's "The Way to Wealth," is to miss most of the actuality. Not only does it miss the searching irony of Franklin's little masterpiece and ignore the service-minded and religious aspects of American personal ethics, it fails to see the other, global half, the dream of that nation Lincoln called "the last, best hope of earth." It cannot hear "the word Democratic, the word En-Masse."

From the start the American Dream stood on twin hopes: self-realization, national success. The Puritans, with their Bible Commonwealth, need not have come to the wilderness to seek "election," personal salvation. Of those they had achieved conviction in England. They came to light a communal candle in the wilderness, to be "the city set on a hill" as an example to wicked Europe of what God's community should be. Alexis de Tocqueville, that French aristocrat, thought he saw the American democrat walking naked in the world, without institutions. He saw wrong. To him the covert, Protestant institutions of the word—the anti-institutional institutions—stood invisible. *The American Democrat*, as Cooper called him, went warmly clad by faith. He possessed, as young Emerson put it, "a Land without history, . . . A land without nobility or wigs or debt, / No castles no Cathedrals and no kings— / Land of the forest." It was his answer to Tocqueville.

For castle and cathedral expressed as they symbolized and celebrated faith. When the feudal faiths went, where were the princes of the blood and the church? The American believer in the Dream expected to be saved, under Providence, personally and by his own faith and works. But that he equally expected to be saved nationally, by the national faith and works, will appear plainly in the briefest perusal of the national scriptures from the Mayflower Compact forward. Not to know this is not to have read or merely to discount the documents. Had the American democrat been any such cynic there would long since have ceased to be a nation.

It is among the complex functions of the Big Game to serve for what Geertz calls a "cultural text" which, specialized, speaks to the condition of the academic constituencies in their specialized relations and, generalized, speaks to the condition of citizens in their relations to the multiple components of the American Dream, the American Idea. The dream perceives freedom, equality, and community positively, not negatively, as a set of achievements, not immunities. To return to its foundation, it rests on two pillars: the idea of self-realization; the idea of the supremacy of the common. It supposes these two ideas, articles of faith, to be life-enhancing, mutually supporting, thrust meeting and balancing thrust. To realize the self requires struggle—agonism relieved and lubricated by fraternity. To realize the fraternal supremacy of the common requires achieved selves: "Produce great persons," said Whitman. "All the rest follows."

Putting it with stark, necessary brevity, the dream of self-realization assumes pluralism as a condition of individual probation. It assumes that the person proved itself by attaining the prize of competency—economic, political, psychic, moral, spiritual. Poor Richard's proverb goes straight to the point: "It is hard for an empty bag to stand upright." The supremacy of the common, on the other hand, rests as an article of faith on an innate ambiguity of the word, all language, as Emerson said, being "fossil poetry." The "common" is average, ordinary, vulgar. But it is also shared, harmonious, normative, general, universal, perhaps divine. The trick of seeing the common as double made democrats out of both American platonists and American realists.

Those ambiguities permit the supremacy of the common to function like a governor or self-compensating mechanism upon American fierceness. Where pluralism opens the door to competitiveness and where probation ("prove yourself") compels it, the common asserts equality, fraternity, community, and tends to balance winning with losing and check the spirit of fierceness back to the satisfactions of competency. Politically, it can finally bear an LBJ no better than a Nixon. It wants its heroes incidental to common victory and benefit, and it wants them temporary. Cincinnatus and not the Order of the Cincinnati, heroes for whom success is a journey are its style. Its furthest dream conceives a people's culture, where art and ritual and faith have become at once great and common. Said Whitman, concluding "Song of Myself," "I bequeath myself to the dirt to grow from the grass I love, / If you want me again look for me under your boot-soles." Melville had his Ishmael, considering his Polynesian pal Queequeg, who had just plunged into a wintry sea to save the life of a fool, reflect that, silently, Queequeg "seemed to be saying to himself—'It's a mutual, joint-stock world in all meridians. We cannibals must help these Christians.' "

And so the oft-despised cannibals down on the field or floor undertake to help those—Christians or Pharisees—in the stands. They dance ritually round the magic ring of play, weaving the American text. Team against team, individual with team, person against person, person with person, team against individual: unity in diversity, diversity in unity, agonism and fraternity. The new start, the chance for "the hungry"; democracy by competency; self-realization and respect in cooperation, in victory but yet in loss; risk and fierce competition and catharsis, yet decorum—and all surrounded and buoyed up by the atmosphere and communal joy of the great party: this is the Big Game's gift of a ritual text to participants near and far.

What does it make happen? Two things: first, the presentation with esthetic power of community realized, all conflicts and multiplicities reconciled, the ideal of organic unity glimpsed and faith in its possibility restored. Has this the liability of esthetic experience, its being an only momentary stay against confusion? Yes, but so have all rituals, all human acts. And it can be almost indefinitely repeated. In a democracy there can be no authority wielding the powers of sanctity and unchallenged status; everything depends at last on the piety of the people. So the second function of the Big Game as ritual is renewal. It is "assimilative" in Wheelwright's sense, calling up from the depths not of nature but of the people the powers of piety renewed. It enacts democratic roles and fates, the process of the culture with its relative openness, its myths of risk and chance, the joy of the journey, the tragic sense of life, the festival that reassures. It says, much better to the people, what the democratic poet, for instance Carl Sandburg, kept trying all his life to say, "the people, yes."

Supposing such a theory of the Big Game to be true, or potentially true, to what degree it might be actually operative must depend on two sets of variables, one of them being, for practical purposes, the same as infinite. Only the occasion reaching heights of intensity and near perfection in itself and inducing trances of rapture in participants could attain really ritual altitudes. Only the committed, the free and susceptible, the innocent or the believing among those present could be supposed relatively able to rise to the opportunity. And yet—such games occur; such crowds of the participant devout may be seen; there are that hunger, that thirst, that insistent quest: all to testify that, yes, it is sometimes there. The Big Game may so function, when it is successful, just so far as it is in fact a ritual expressing and communicating a secular religion of the American Dream—about half, I say. For the other half, as ritual it is a metaphor. As religion it is altogether a metaphor. For Kavanaugh as for others, the game works better as a metaphor for religion than religion works as a metaphor for the game. The festival is, at best, sort of sacred.

Beyond that the point has, I think, been perfectly put by Father Hugo Rahner: "we cannot truly grasp the secret of *Homo ludens* unless we first, in all reverence, consider the matter of *Deus ludens*." As soon as you begin considerations like that, you run the danger of being shriveled by the terrible ironies of the comparison. Says Rahner:

> Life then . . . has this dual character. It is gay because secure in God, it is tragic because our freedom continually imperils it, and so the man who truly plays must be both gay and serious at the same time; we must find him both smiling and in tears. His portion, if I may here bring in the profound synthesis of the Fathers, will be both joy and perseverance.

With its stronger connection to an Augustinian, if not Calvinistic, feeling, Reinhold Niebuhr's way of handling the same observation is tougher-minded. In a Christian view, he says, "the whole drama of human history is under the scrutiny of a divine judge who laughs at human pretensions without being hostile to human aspirations. . . . The judgment is transmuted into mercy if it results in . . . prompting men to a contrite recognition of the vanity of their imagination." In all seriousness, when you have carried the metaphor to this sort of point, you are out of the ball park whether you believe or not. As Huizinga quietly concluded, "The human mind can only disengage itself from the magic circle of play by turning towards the ultimate."

To keep ourselves only a little deserving of the laughing derision of the *Deus ludens*, then, it is well for us to deal as truly as we can with realities and to keep our realities as clean as we can. In dealing with the Big Game we can, with a little care, set our feet solidly on the realities of the games as art, as American culture, popular culture, student life, and institutions. In all five realms, people, however subject to error and perversion, can keep it clean. "Corruption never has been compulsory," said Robinson Jeffers. And if in our times you should feel compelled to suppose that this ethic too might be situational, in those five situations Jeffers was right about college sport.

It is when you remember that the Big Game is a mass affair, public, a big market, entertainment, and plugged into the industry that high wind warnings begin to fly on your moral halyards. Though everybody feels at least unhappy and many of us feel guilty or even indignant about the facts, it cannot be denied that the Big Game sports define themselves, are defined by circumstances, as two. Not even the slightly patronizing distinction between "revenue" and "nonrevenue" sports represents the realities. College hockey makes money, occasionally as much as basketball, where they play it. But as a national phenomenon it is as peripheral as lacrosse—though both are great and greatly deserving games. The relations of Olympic sports in general to the colleges have become a perplex.

Football makes and spends for NCAA Division I athletic programs in general. Its one rival, which often talks as if it felt like a younger brother, is basketball. Born just as football emerged from its lyric period, basketball swept the country with striking speed. It quenched the thirst for a first-rate game to play indoors, out of the mud and sleet, when baseball was impossible and football not much fun. Exactly why it triumphed over its rivals and became queen of the games played on boards it would not be easy to say. But that it recapitulated the evolution of football, swiftly overtook it, and in some ways surpassed it could not be denied.

Everything true about football as an expression of student life, as a form of culture and popular culture, as entertainment, and as art, holds for basketball. Though it makes less money because it does not lift people to the same ecstatic heights as football, its peaks are surpassed only by those of football. And what basketball lacks in height it makes up in breadth. Where once little boys played baseball and football in the fallow fields, the pastures, the vacant lots, now they play basketball, indoors or out. Anywhere there is a wall or a post and a bit of paved surface and a boy appear a backboard and a hoop. On city playgrounds basketball is the game supreme, but so it is in farmyards where the hoop may be nailed to the barn and the floor be nothing but smooth-trampled dirt. Where do the best players come from? Ah, to decide that, at least for one year, is the good excuse for playing the far-flung national tournaments.

No game surpasses basketball in beauty, and no fan is crazier than its *aficionado*. As its public base spreads wider than football's into the pool of potential participants, it has a far greater number of school, college, industrial league, and club teams competing. Year by year its players' skills grow, and it spreads internationally with a power of appeal outdistancing other new games. It bids fair to become a substantial American contribution to world culture.

Though television cannot in fact capture anything like the experience of being at the basketball game and near the physical, three-dimensional action with its true rhythms, basketball lends itself better to the tube than football. Pursuing football, the lens never comes close to registering the essential action, and the fabled "instant replay" is a snare and a delusion. Why, then, the continued supremacy of football? The height of its appeal rests on its reach into preconscious and culturally primitive associations deep among the roots of American experience. It is these which entice and romanticize. Basketball is of course not devoid of such associations. Both create the "Big Game." Both supply their participants, active and spectatorial, with intense esthetic experience: the esthetics of winning; the equal and opposite, but finally reconciled, esthetics of losing. Both sometimes achieve the power of American ritual.

By a practically infinite margin of advantage in numbers, the public audience for the Big Game watches television. Not only are they not at the game but, alien from the communal experience of the stands and bedeviled by frantically intrusive "personalities," television watchers never see it. The cameras and directors fragment, skew, and impoverish the potential esthetic experience. The almost entire loss of depth perception on the flat screen, the loss of the whole field or floor and thus of the frame and ground of action and flow, become the loss of almost everything. Much of what the camera eye, the replay, and the commentators' explications insist "occurred" is subtly, sometimes blatantly, false. All the patterns of tension, relation, and rhythm, everything pictorial, balletic, and musical—and much that is simply athletic—are diminished if not lost. The television fan does not know the game; he has never seen it.

Yet he does encounter esthetic experiences, and the power of the television game as entertainment cannot be denied—by many millions of dollars' worth. As popular culture, of course, entertainment is people's culture and absolutely OK as long as you keep it clean, and "clean" in this case has to mean "nontoxic to the consumer." It should not screw up his life. Its effects should be life-enhancing, or at least not life-degrading. The consumer has a right to feel that he can trust his entertainment, the popular culture, to console and relieve him, make him laugh, make him cry, make him sing or dance and feel happy a while but not rob him of his self-respect and leave him cheated, disillusioned, sorry he came and hating himself for a cheap sucker.

To pick up that word again, the problem defines itself as Dionysian—the OK and true versus the phony and toxic. For the constituents at the Big Game the esthetics are as Dionysian as for a Kurelu warrior, a Kwakiutl potlatcher, a Balinese cockfighter. And there is nothing wrong with that in the stands so long as it is true. The problem is hokum, or commercial perversion. Careful observers at least since Melville and Clemens, Howells and Crane, have registered the poisonous vices of American culture as springing from faked romanticism. It makes fools of folks. Dying to wallow in Dionysian dreams of the ideal, the herioc, we degrade the common "ordinary," which we are, to "ornery."

The constituencies want their Big Game esthetics, comic or tragic, outsized and romantic. We yearn from the realities, which are common, toward the metaphors, exaggerating, overintensifying them because they are not real. Just to list those metaphors, as many as I can think of at the moment, stirs my capacity for romance. What is a Big Game? Why chivalry, a knightly tournament; it's communal, a family, tribal reunion; it's drama, but a folk festival, too; it's a gladiatorial combat or Thermopylae, Greek; it's youthful initiation into manhood, an ordeal; it's the heart of the law, adversary conflict; or of democratic politics, the contest; it's religion and ritual, sacred fest; it's war by surrogate. Romantic? Oh, wow!

But for the players and their coaches, and for the institutional servants of the whole grand process, the Big Game and all it involves are realistic. And, absurdly but typically, it is that ordinariness which the constituencies and, oddly, the media cannot seem to abide. They insist on being disillusioned about realities because they want it all Disneyland—Disneyland out front, that is. And among the most dangerous perverters are those who, carried away by its esthetic power but dazzled by their illusions, lose the power to see that it is art and insist on trying to transpose it into the familiar "reality," which they themselves think intrinsically dirty, of American business.

Northrop Frye put the right, opposite point exactly in discussing "the principle that the transmutation of act into mime, the advance from acting out a rite to playing at the rite, is one of the central features of the development from savagery into culture." He continued:

> It is easy to see a mimesis of conflict in tennis and football, but, precisely for that very reason, tennis and football players represent a culture superior to the culture of student duellists and gladiators. The turning of literal act into play is a fundamental form of the liberalizing of life which appears in more intellectual levels as liberal education, the release of fact into imagination.

Perhaps to perform just such acts of the imagination was the triumph of student *virtu* in creating the games and the Big Game as arts and ornaments of college life and popular culture.

On field or floor the teams enact American culture, in play releasing fact into imagination. The people in the stands, responding, play their various games, all different from those of the teams. And in their ways they enact American culture too. The several symbolic dramas speak to the condition of a culture in which, much liberalized, the presences, in vibrant performance, of *homo agonistes* and *ludens* and *aleator* often dominate. The lives of imaginative business and political careers, of divinity, law, medicine, public service, and teaching as professions, of the creation of arts or of knowledge, have become long, patient fights and games and gambles in that culture. The games symbolize and support and provide release from the pains and discontents consequent on lives and careers like ours. And, shape-shifting toward *homo fraternalis*, they not only enact but create community. It would be expensive to pervert or abolish them. They would prove vexingly difficult to replace. If they present us difficulties, and they do, in controlling and channeling them, the one way to respond which will not do is the way Milton condemned: the way of a "fugitive and cloistered virtue" seeking the deathliness of nothing in preference to the challenge of a moral life.

THE ESTHETICS OF WINNING

As the Big Game may be said to be healing, "egosyntonic" to the individual psyche, it stimulates and gratifies a community. Culturally it concentrates human potential into synergistic bursts. It possesses these powers because, perhaps, it is "presentational." And what it presents on one side of the message is Winning, the esthetics of joy. On even brief examination, however, the victorious joy which makes a community of scholars want to dance and sing *etai* like Kurelu, appears to have complex parts. I count not less than seven: release; vindication; identity; *la gloire;* exultation; the sense of excellence; and, oddly, decorum.

The emotions of release—relief, liberation—come first after your perception of winning. They are survivors' emotions. They are the point, often fumbled by critics, of certain final reflections by Stephen Crane's young soldier at the end of *The Red Badge of Courage:* "He felt a quiet manhood. . . . He had been to touch the great death, and found that, after all, it was but the great death. . . . He had been an animal blistered and sweating in the heat and pain of war. He turned now with a lover's thirst to images of tranquil skies." Here is the point where the combat metaphor best illuminates the Big Game. There is no joy more poignant and immediate than being missed by the bullet or the shell meant for you. Winning the biggest mere game brings sensations of release tame by contrast.

Even before release and vindication in victory, furthermore, there come from the fear of death in combat a heightening of the senses and of perception and so a sharpening of the sense of your own, exact identity nowhere else available in human experience. I mean available nowhere but in the presence, rather long continued, of real fear stimulated by genuine physical danger. In the best of art experience or in the real observation of another's danger it can be approximated at far less cost. This same experience, the reason why war and disaster are the greatest shows on earth, is art in the Big Game.

Nevertheless, the release of winning games, precisely because it is in play, is a lot more fun than the real thing. Real release, like real fear, can shred a psyche. Game catharsis (that endlessly useful word of old Aristotle) tears no one: it was "just a game," anyhow. By the same token the release, the catharsis, can be no more than temporary—like Frost's poem, "a momentary stay against confusion." If it brings, in Martin Capell's fine phrase, "the illusion of power," that illusion wields powers of liberation, catharsis, even exorcism which account for much of the store we set by the game, for much of our yen to repeat it over and over.

The dread of powerlessness inevitable to childhood haunts grown men and women of every age. In the midst of a raging hot basketball game, as he told me, one friend, an old jock, felt a shock of recognition: "My wife," he said, "was reared in the patterns of perfect ladyhood. I mean, it really took. In fourteen years of marriage I never knew her to do or say anything not perfectly ladylike. But Saturday I realized suddenly that she was standing up on her seat with her face white with shock and her eyes blazing. And she was saying, 'Kill him! Kill him! Kill him!' "

Fear—of powerlessness, inadequacy, above all of failure—vanishes in the wake of winning. And with it go "pressure." The stress of concentration, courage, endurance "gets off," as the jocks say. And with it, for the spectators too, go the stresses of self-doubt, competitive hostility, aggression, and your guilts about all three. For the moment, and despite the momentarily hidden knowledge that you will come soon again to the test, death is swallowed up in victory.

The component equal and opposite to release in the joy of winning is vindication. In the test survived and beaten, contestant and "side," constituents and culture, may feel what it is to be right and be proved so by events, however symbolic. At the end of the symbols, emotionally the "mortal stakes" are your rights to believe in the propriety of your existence. Prior vindications overlie that deepest one of all, however. Playing the Big Game demands commitments, many and deep: of faith to risk and try; of work, pain, discipline, sacrifice, the acceptance of stress, hostility, aggression. But (and is it especially among males?) one of the dearest of human treasures goes on the gambler's line: bonding, the brotherhoods of loyalty and devotion, of that *philia*, that love without which nothing gets done and all is lost.

Vindicated, too, is the gambler who will risk the ultimates: having a baby (*mulier aleator*) or risking it all on success (*homo aleator*). Again the metaphor presents itself of war, that ultimate seriousness. For in "deep play," as in all the big games, the beginning of wisdom lies in the perception that terror, the defeat of the soul, happens only to the rigid. No matter when they die, they who "hang loose" cannot lose because they play at life and death. Yes, your skill or strength, but your luck, your claim on either Fortune or God's grace was vindicated, this time, when you won.

On its primal identity level, the use of winning to the fan, while egosyntonic, is not handsome. Winning can provide the sensation of sheer ego-ratification. I gambled, I asserted myself, I laid it on the line, and I won! I'm Me, and winning proved it. I deserve to be Me, I win! However essential, life-assertive, antientropic, self-affirming—once again, in brief, egosyntonic and psychiatrically valuable—that's primitive but not very nice. Its ugliness suggests the use and virtue of decorum in winning.

Only a shade or two less dismal (but equally necessary?), winning momentarily strengthens that endangered identity which battles daily for personal success. Few things would strike a detached observer of contemporary, postindustrial man more sharply than the triumph in all nations of the old, foolish bourgeois myth of Dick Whittington and his cat. It has taken captive Rome and Tokyo, Belgrade, Warsaw, and Moscow, to name no more obvious places. Not even the revolutionary genius of Mao could keep it down. It subverts every ideology. Little boys, and now little girls, dream of it. Long years of discipline and postponement prepare for it. Life itself is given to years, decades, generations of incessant campaigning to achieve its goal and hear the bells of the capital fling your name to the winds of celebrity. And in what comes afterward we take "no kind of interest."

But of course that is a game which ends only when they blow the last whistle and make you turn in your suit. One advantage of the Big Game, and especially winning, is its momentary stay against doubt. As art it provides form to experience, with a conclusion, with resolution, with a win. As early as the autumn of 1967, James Reston was explaining the national frenzy over sports in contrast to its apathy about politics by noticing just that point: "It could be the natural reaction of the people to an incomprehensible age where games are about the only things in the news that come to a clear and definite end." Furthermore, unlike the news, they provide experience, including the sense of a victorious ending, in which persons can participate directly and find their feelings for themselves reinforced.

On that side of the matter identity remains personal. To a great complex republic with democratic ideals and institutions, the communal, indeed the political side may be a great deal more important. It can be no less so to the institutions of higher education and the lives of their communities and constituencies. Among the many felicities of Dr. Arnold Beisser's book, one of the best is the essay to which he gives the chapter title, "Membership in the Tribe." Of course "the tribe" always supplied human beings with communal identities. And many an acute tribesman has noticed that in cultural circumstances like ours multiple tribes live interpenetratingly, thriving each in its ecological niche, in a culture at large more complex in its life than even a coral reef.

People go to games, Gahringer argued, "as a way of participating in a common mind. The Greeks knew how a spirit is born when men cheer together, or march together, or suffer together; and they named those spirits as gods. . . . And it is worth noting how often the game appears a central interest where no truly personal or intellectual community can be firmly established otherwise." So many college presidents have said the same thing so many times that we can let A. Lawrence Lowell of Harvard, delivering his inaugural address, stand for myriads. Despite their "exaggerated prominence," Lowell said, he believed "strongly" in college sports properly conducted because "such contests offer to the students the one common interest, the only striking occasion for a display of college solidarity."

Dr. Beisser sees how many and various indeed are the tribes. For the utterly rootless, even the Dodgers supply "the individual's need for something with which to identify." With other fans, he can achieve emotional reality in a community "which has developed many of the characteristics of the extended family and the tribal society. . . .In victory this is a boundless sharing of the joy which the fan experiences personally and collectively." Still further,

> As in representative government, the interests of the masses are centered on the field of action, but with the distinct advantage that the crowd can see the proceedings as they occur and make its favor or disfavor directly felt. The team influences the crowd, and the crowd influences the team, in symbiotic fashion. They belong to each other and rely on one another for their vitality.

In short, as Reston keeps saying so well, one of the American metaphors of the Big Game is politics. And so, of course, one of the essential metaphors for political reality in the republic is the Big Game. Neither could long support itself, which is in no small part what the metaphors "mean" to each other, without the winning built into both by cultural design. Writing on "English Liberty in America," Santayana opined that the best heritage from Britain to the Americans was the mix of fierce individuality with "the spirit of free co-operation," a paradox wholly English. "The omnipresence in America of this spirit of co-operation, responsibility, and growth," he said in *Character and Opinion in the United States*, "is very remarkable. . . . Every political body, every public meeting, every club, or college, or athletic team, is full of it." Without the English reference, the same point informed Margaret Mead's revision of *And Keep Your Powder Dry* in 1965. The country, she said, was built upon what I have been calling the tension between agonism and fraternity. "What we devised," she said, "in fact, was a pact of brothers, none of whom succeeded to the power of a strong father. . . . From the beginning, the country was held together by the pitting of group against group in competition." And of course the theory demanded not only that somebody win but, in net effect from all the games, that everybody win.

And so Reston again, in the more troubled fall of 1969:

> Sport in America plays a part in our national life that is probably more important than even the social scientists believe. . . . For sports and games, in a funny way, are not only America's diversion and illusion but its hope. The world of sports has everything the world of politics lacks and longs for. . . .In short, baseball and football are conflict under control. . . . Unlike the worlds of politics, business, or universities, the conflicts of sports can be seen, and have a beginning and an end.

But, as Reston notes, it is idle to suppose that politically the national devotion to games is "escapist." You do not escape, you create realizable form, you discover presentational drama, you forge symbolic pattern for life by recourse to art. And sport is art. So the metaphors of political identity and democratic faith available in the Big Game are as real as human reality gets and, so far as they go, as important as the group life or death of cultural viability. As Jaeger and Selznick say, study of "mass society" directs "attention to the quality of man's relatedness to other men and to symbols. Atomization, standardization, superficiality, alienation, apathy, compulsive conformity—this is the grim language of mass-society theory." The issues look to concern for "the quality of social and cultural participation" and "the capacity of values to retain their strength and subtlety in the face of widespread dehumanization of work and communication." The problem, in short, is how to keep the culture and its instruments working. Not to see it that way has been, I think, the trouble with the self-styled "New Left" with all its romanticisms.

The esthetics of triumph and exultation, in their institutionalization as what De Gaulle called *la gloire*, are not easily understandable, at least to the American mind, either. The exultant burst, individual or communal, is not so puzzling. Neither is that all too human, if perhaps foolish, thirst to "be Somebody" to "get some respect." But *la gloire?* Is it more than common ego-expansion or the love of domineering? Some people think so, nobody more definitely than Johan Huizinga, for all his being so often mistaken to be the apostle of "innocence" in sports. It helps the better to locate Huizinga's ideas and stance to watch him cite Ruskin at length—Ruskin of *The Crown of Wild Olives* endeavoring with stratospheric rhetoric to persuade Woolwich cadets that the pursuit of Victorian Empire was a quest for the Holy Grail. No wonder Father Rahner rather supposes that the will to win is Original Sin.

Like Santayana's philosopher on the bleachers who equated sports with whatever things in our lives "lift the whole of it from vulgarity," Huizinga and Ruskin define one term of a basic American war of values which applies intimately to sport and intercollegiate competition. Are we trying in American life to mirror the manners and values of European aristocracies? If so, should we? Or is that not to continue colonial and provincial? Is it not to whore after false gods, betraying the American Revolution and the true core of the American Dream? Ring Lardner, writing on "Sports and Play" for Harold Stearns's *Civilization in the United States* struck, whether he knew it or not, a stinging blow at the genteel tradition: "hero-worship is the national disease that does most to keep the grandstands full and the playgrounds empty."

The counter traditions were, of course, both negative and positive: "We have listened too long to the courtly muses of Europe," said Emerson. It was his theme, as it became Walt Whitman's, that America must produce her own "great persons." But would they be "heroes," or "natural gentlemen"—American aristocrats? Or would they be common and of the people? In the next generation, like Mark Twain in *Huckleberry Finn* and *A Connecticut Yankee*, Howells would fight for what he called "the superiority of the vulgar." Like Henry James he would fight the idea that "distinction" is a moral good. "So far from feeling cast down by Mr. Arnold's failure to detect distinction" in America, wrote Howells of Matthew Arnold's *Civilization in the United States*, "we are disposed to a serene complacency by it. . . .Somehow, the idea that we call America has realized itself so far that we already have identification rather than distinction as the fact which strikes the foreign critic in our greatness. Our notable men, it seems, are notable for their likeness to their fellowmen and not for their unlikeness; democracy has subtly but surely done its work . . . we have in the involuntary recognition of their common humanity by our great men something that appears to be peculiarly American, and . . . more valuable than . . . the distinction possible to greatness, among peoples accustomed to cringe before greatness."

The consequent debates and conflicts of values and assumptions have raged through the development of the national culture during this century. Nowhere is it more prominent than in the national sporting life, collegiate and otherwise. Which side is winning? It is still, as they say, a horse race.

When you think about excellence either intrinsic or of achievement, however, it begins to appear that there are certain attitudes which ought to be as common to an antique and aristocratic as to a modern and democratic belief. In triumph, in winning, a self-respect which is also respect for the opponent might well produce a governing decorum in the winner. It is the democratic decorum and compassion of Lincoln's Second Inaugural Address. It is the mask of modesty over the bronze but boyish countenance of the victorious charioteer of Delphi, a Greek aristocratic hero of an age two and a half millenia gone.

What beseems the winner? Decorum or nemesis, the Greeks thought. Does modern experience suggest anything different? Not much, say the novelists, for instance, from Fitzgerald and Hemingway through Harris and Malamud and Updike. The first, least placable nemesis of the winner who loses decorum is that he loses possession of the game itself, the art, the illusion, the experience, the best of it. The Big Game can be a "high-synergy" event, to use John P. Sisk's language, organizing and combining cultural energies to restorative vitalities greater than the sum of the observable inputs. But it can be made entropic, degrading energies and dissolving culture, too. As Daniel Boorstin puts it, "There is an obvious cure for Failure—and that is Success. But what is the cure for Success? This is a characteristically American problem." The problem, he adds, is that success, wrongly handled, breeds disillusion and disillusion breeds anomie—and so success turns into failure and winning breeds losing.

Is there no escape? Well, no easy one. It is true that people can stand anything but success and that Faustus the insatiable is the Everyman of our age. "Yen" was the Chinese for the opium fiend's insatiable thirst for his habit. It is no news that the yen of our culture for the bitch-goddess success lusts insatiably for power, for infantile omnipotence, the illusion of irresistible, manipulative autonomy. The ethics of the ages unite to condemn the dream of mastery, of exploitative power over humanity regarded as the ego's meat. But, taken wrong, the Big Game becomes the perfect trope of the yen of the ego to slash, crush, grind, smash, powder, and "wax 'em." To dominate with joyous contempt, to overrun, possess and dispossess, in effect to enslave the world becomes, on its wicked side, the "name of the game."

Do these truths mean that all goodness is lost, that we are doomed and damned forever as our modern Jeremiahs—Calvinists without God—insist? They have been very fashionable, the culture "degraders," Sisk calls them. Prophets of hopeless crisis without end, they are the people William Faulkner rejected and Saul Bellow brilliantly attacked, each in his Nobel Prize lecture. But they have been on top too long, this variety of losers. Bellow calls them "mummies." It is past time to look beyond them in our view of college sports as well as the other arts.

Much is made by degrader sensibilities of alleged violence and dehumanization in the Big Game and other sports. Is that justified? Not intrinsically. I think Dr. Beisser on his side and the acuter ethnologists on theirs are more to the point in stressing the humanizing—even, as Beisser says, rehumanizing—power of these arts of the popular culture. They can be degraded and perverted, but it takes an ill will and hard work to make them so. The issue of "violence" I think much misunderstood if not, too often for public relations and media reasons, casually misrepresented.

The game itself, and intrinsically, creates community and promotes liminality, the sense of boundaries. It is a substitute for contagious mass violence—gang riot, rape, lynchings, and arson—transferring its emotions onto symbolic dramas and discharging them harmlessly into fiesta and fantasy. To the players personally the "violence" is ritualized, symbolic, governed, and fun. We may well, however, live in the presence of mistaken efforts to persuade crowds and athletes that they ought to do away with liminality, symbolism, and illusion, and to compel the violence to become real. Should that happen, the sports will disappear until, out of psychic and cultural necessity, they are reinvented.

That the fantasies of publicist and degradist are not likely to be enacted in fact suggests itself, however, from the experience of the quite recent past. During that period, 1965-1971, of riot and confrontation on campuses which faculties seem increasingly inclined to call "The Troubles," persons responsible for the conduct of big games developed a collective nightmare about mass violence. The nightmare scenario ran this way: it is the third weekend in November, climax day in conference races, with the biggest of Big Games to play. Let us say that Minnesota is playing Wisconsin, with the Big Ten championship, the number one national rating, and the Rose Bowl at stake alongside the honor (and bets) of two great, proud, neighboring states in a game rich in tradition. With 4:06 on the clock in the fourth quarter the score is Minnesota 21-Wisconsin 19 and Wisconsin has the ball, fourth and two, on the Minnesota eighteen. Will they go for it? Will they try a field goal? Wisconsin is in its huddle, a player racing from the bench, and the crowd in an uproar.

Just as the player from the bench is reaching the huddle, a motley mass of self-proclaimed "freaks" bursts onto the field, capering wildly, carrying a smoking God-knows-what, and mixes with the teams, downing the officials, grabbing the ball, engaged in a "demonstration." What would happen? The nightmare was that in about ninety seconds the mob would arrive from the stands, murder of demonstrators on its mass mind. A bloody disaster.

Almost infinite planning and preparation went into measures to forestall realization of that nightmare of mob violence, that contagion of mass action of which all history tells such tales of uttermost horror. Fields were walled around with state troopers and police put everywhere imaginable. Stopwatches were used to time people jumping from the stands and running to points on fields. Calculations were made and vehicles timed to see how fast police could be got to such a scene on the field and how many seconds they might have before the mob arrived. Players were carefully instructed not to touch or even notice demonstrators but to get off the field as fast as possible if the nightmare came true. It was a dramatic time for anyone possessed of what Henry James called "the imagination of disaster."

Sure enough, the event, though never at the most dangerous imaginable juncture, did come true—once before my eyes. Demonstrators, leaking through the precautions while the bands were getting back into the stands after halftime, ran out, preventing the second half kickoff of a close-fought Big Game and depositing a carefully absurd rig at midfield. What happened? Nothing. Hardly anyone bothered to boo. You could hear a sigh of collective frustration as the crowd exhaled its expectation of fresh athletic drama. Then they sat still while the police strolled out to pick up the rig and escort rather sheepish and deflated demonstrators away. Then the game went on.

I have since seen analogous events. The "violence" of the Big Game crowd is ritualized, observing rules and models of a decorum not of course genteel but still "sporting" as necessary to the game.

"Winning isn't everything—it's the *only* thing," said Vince Lombardi. He was talking not about games, sports, intercollegiate athletics, the Big Game, or the realities of human life in culture. He was not even, at last, talking about the realities of coaching. He had merely found a ploy. Much more to the point is Vic Bubas, who left coaching at the top of his profession, with all the kudos and rewards of being at the top, to seek another, more serviceable profession. "I found that I had climbed that mountain," he said of his success. Much the same point provides the pivot for a fine essay written by William F. Russell, looking back from 1970 upon his careers to that date as Bill Russell. He quotes a friend: "Success is a journey with me, not a destination." That is no bad ground for a proper American decorum in winning.

THE ESTHETICS OF LOSING

Win or lose, to play the game you must "choose sides." And the primary opposition, the absolute unity in diversity, diversity in unity, breed broad paradox and fine irony, and breed them richly. Nowhere does that paradox come broader or irony finer than in the always observable fact that, while winning and losing are totally opposite, the winners lose and losers win almost every time. Though there are at least four kinds, they seldom come out pure in experience. *Winner-winners* triumph with decorum, with class. *Winner-losers* top the score but act bush. *Loser-winners* may lose the game, but they win the experience, lose while gaining the rewards of the tragic sense of life, with class. At poor last come the *Loser-losers:* they lose and act bush to boot. In the stands the esthetics of losing are experienced as keenly, satisfactorily, and meaningfully as the esthetics of winning. The losers may go home mad; but they enjoy it, may get their money's worth better than some winners. And in the long run you can't tell them apart.

It would look, offhand, and the faces, bodies, and language of losers seem to confirm it, that the winners get the esthetics while the losers get the blahs. "The winners tell jokes. The losers cry 'Deal!'" Just so. That really is much of the point. They are united and defined, even created, by the same esthetics of the Big Game. No game, no winners, no losers, no experience. The same enclosing frames of cultural expression and popular art form, the same events, unite them. The same expectations brought them to the game. If the outcomes were opposite, the same alternate and simultaneous esthetics of winning and losing gripped them in suspense until the resolution and sent them home: eager to return, held in thrall to the game, united in the end as in the beginning. Winning and losing are one and the same, only winning is the one and losing is the same. They are Yin and Yang.

These facts hold as true for the course of empire or personal careers as for sports. Daniel Boorstin's question was asked and answered long ago by Ecclesiastes, or the Preacher. Let a politician—an Ed Muskie, a Jimmy Carter—be tagged "the front-runner" by media desperate to turn politics into sports and what will happen? He will be declared a no-limit species, everybody's meat. There is an interesting seasonal relationship of our Big Game—football or basketball—to Kathleen Blake's notion of play as a way of "eating life up." With their balls, they are achieving, celebrating, harvest home games. The rhythms of ancient culture pulse there: summer and work, autumn and fruiting and gathering in. Harvest home means abundance, security from winter, safety to another springtime, defiance of entropy and death, joy!

"When the wind whistles through the oat stubble," says the Yankee farmer in July, "it's time to get ready for winter." When nature has done its work and made us safe as can be, the sun will go away. After the prime come age and death. If winning is harvest home and eating it up, losing is a little death. Nevertheless the wheel will turn. After winter comes spring, after the death of the year comes its resurrection. The winners tell jokes. The losers cry "Deal!" As the earth turns the winners lose, losers win. The cure for failure is success. What is the cure for success? Failure.

The esthetics of losing vary not much in pattern from the esthetics of winning. Losing emotions, primally human, run an amazing gamut from the lowest—"bush," as the ball-players say—to the highest—"the tragic sense of life," as Ortega y Gasset said. Among the emotions of losing are those of humiliation, distrust, fear, envy, grief, guilt, denial, defeat, frustration, melancholy, self-pity, resentment, depression, despair, desperation, rebellion, revenge, alienation, anomie, and asthenia. Though they are more numerous and complex than the emotions of winning, it may be that we hunger to know them, vicariously, and to feel them exposed and realized—but safely. So it becomes important that they be "relieved" by symbolic expression—venting, transformation, the symbolic dramas of catharsis and resurrection.

To forget the drag toward dissolution and death, the entropic plunge of things, is to forget the reality of life's joyous, defiant assertion. As we must go with that in nature which defies death, we must also know, in order to cope with its drag upon the psyche and our cultural instruments, that it is always there. Thus Adrian Stokes wrote: "No less than children, adults at play harp on the vagaries of life and death. In ball games, the context is always one of potency, often the cover for anxiety concerning the good inner object."

That the emotions of losing which set us half in love with easeful death lie at the depths of intrapsychic reality has become a commonplace. Larry Merchant says, penetratingly, that, however financially imprudent, "betting emotionally" can be egosyntonic for the gambler: "Losing such bets fills the bettor's need for self-abuse and the fan's need for suffering." But main currents of human history can flow the same ways. In his great *Five Stages of Greek Religion*, Gilbert Murray names one of the most important epochs "The Failure of Nerve." Perhaps the wiser, deeper, truer course, perhaps not, he suggests, at any rate the long stage of Greek religion lying between the glory of Athens and the achievement of Christianity seemed asthenic to Murray, characterized by "forms of heart-sinking, of feeling unstrung."

The range of loser's emotion impresses. It may be as imperial as Murray, as tragic as *King Lear*. But it may be as cheap as *You Know Me, Al: A Busher's Letters* or as ornery as "I'm a Fool" or "My Old Man." We are all losers, or mainly so; nothing is more democratic. But the diseases of persons or of history may become those of cultures too. Applying Durkheim's theory of anomie to the present condition of life in the United States, Ephraim Harold Mizruchi invented a pregnant phrase. The situation "requires awareness of two types of anomie," he wrote, "one general type of social structural strain with *bondlessness* and *boundlessness* as sub-types." Though it is a striking fact that the Big Game functions as a cultural device for providing momentary stays against both bondlessness and boundlessness equally for winners and losers, there appears to be a great deal more to say about the esthetics of losing—or what is going on over on the other side of the stands.

People can stand anything but prosperity. You can obliterate a city, but you cannot "bomb it into submission." The more bombs the greater the citizen solidarity. A town smashed by tornadoes finds itself suddenly filled with men and women tireless, eager, forgetful of self to succor and rebuild. In a nation at war the mental sanitaria empty out: people think they know what they are doing. Old soldiers in combat use friendship, sympathy, mutual support as a way of life; and a man will casually risk his being to do you a small favor. The same people ten days out of the line surrender to all the old demons of bullying, backbiting, talebearing, and stealing from one another. It is, of course, the familiar problem of William James's "The Moral Equivalent of War."

Every team, every college athletic program, has friends who are marvelous so long as you are losing and tend to disappear when you win. But they are of two marvelously distinct species. One sort are winners: they will rally with every imaginable variety of support to help you out of trouble but tend to let you happily alone when you are doing well and don't need help. The other kind however can hardly tolerate success. They grow restless, demanding, nit-picking, and miserable as soon as you win. Though the esthetics of winning somehow grate on their nerves, they live happily with the esthetics of losing. Typically "winners" as agonists in business or a profession, they crave to lose at the Big Game. And of course the game, indeed the culture, are arranged to satisfy that appetite. It can hardly be said too strongly—it cannot be overstressed as a wisdom essential to the right conduct of intercollegiate athletics—that the constituencies and fans get what they want from losing as well as winning. The terrible problems arise from the fact that the public face on competition, the proclaimed values and myths, countenance victory only. Still worse, they demand and license ugly attitudes and behavior consequent to the esthetics of losing.

Not nearly enough has been written on this subject, particularly as it applies to the fans and the culture, though some distinctly helpful insights have come from studies of the athlete as person. Here again, perhaps the best of commentators is Arnold Beisser in a chapter from *The Madness in Sports* entitled "The Problem of Winning." The problem—which will lead some fine athletes to prefer losing—is that to win you have to accept responsibility for unleashing your aggression, for "destroying" or at least humiliating your opponent, for growing up and sacrificing the claim of the immature to be loved for their weakness. The specters of guilt and alienation stand between the agonist and victory. He must defeat unconscious dread before he dare succeed: for "the athlete, although he basks in the glory of victory, also unconsciously stands convicted of murder."

And, continues Beisser, collective and cultural ghosts haunt winners. "An 'also ran' in the game is like one of the fans." As a loser he has not murdered his father; he keeps his title to "comfort and pity, the rewards of the child"; he maintains solidarity with the world of losers—everybody:

> It is the winner, the champion, who risks emerging from the crowd and who tangibly acts out their mutual desires. He bears responsibility for the collective aggression focused in sport. . . .
> The athlete on the threshold of victory faces a dilemma in his renunciation of the child for the responsibility of the adult, in his choice of the isolation of being outstanding over the mass solidarity of remaining mediocre. The

champion is the man emerging from out of the crowd of all others into uniqueness. Winning is one aspect of the enigma of maturity.

Fans and other constituents, participating as consumers of Big Game art, may and do, perhaps even must, have it both ways. Hunting with the hounds, running with the hare, they seek and find still a third way—winning/losing, whirling like colors on a disk revolving until they blend into something new and strange. Why should they care? No ground exists for a "pure" esthetic in reality. The fabled ground of Lombardi's Law represents no reality principle answerable to experience either intrapsychic or cultural. Life is not like that. There are real grounds, however, for answerable manners and judgments of value.

Winning and losing and winning/losing may each fulfill some egosyntonic function of games. Everybody loses sometimes. "Paying the price" has made a loser out of the champion even before he won; and he will never cease to pay. That is why winners wish to know of one another, "Does he have some class?" As all men die, every life game ends in loss. The esthetics of losing are everyone's experiential ground. And so, for precisely the reasons why the Big Game functions well as symbolic drama and as an occasion for public art experience, the esthetics of losing there may well become most important to those constituents whose nonathletic, or "real," achievement and experience leave them vulnerable to the same ghosts. Every fear and penalty which stands between the agonist and winning stands between the citizen and success. Why should he not, successful, enjoy the immunities, releases, and comforts of a momentary stay, in the esthetics of losing, of the penalties for success?

And it may well be true that certain parallels in the condition of American culture account for the mass and intensity within that culture of the Big Game. Winning and losing speak equally to our condition. Once more, Daniel Boorstin asks a question essential to the question of our culture: "What are the consequences for everybody every day of the effort to democratize life in America?" And he finds four disquieting answers: (1) "attenuation, which means the thinning or flattening out of experience"; (2) "the *decline of congregation*" and the rise of personal isolation; (3) "*the rising sense of momentum*"—Henry Adams's notion of a twentieth century characterized by change proceeding at rates of constant acceleration; (4) "*the belief in solutions*," which, unrealistic and forever frustrated, breeds deepening disillusion.

Obviously it is not hard to argue that a culture disconcerted by such consequences from efforts to realize its best ideals finds the Big Game serviceable. Symbolically, dramatically, esthetically, if temporarily, it ministers to the culture's symptoms of discontent. For attenuation it supplies intensity; for the decline of congregation, community; for the rising sense of momentum, clarity and a momentary stay against confusion; for the itch of disillusion about the failure of the belief in solutions it offers the balm of resolution, the sense of an ending. The point too seldom observed is that it does these things equally well with the esthetics of winning or the esthetics of losing. Which suggests that, to understand our culture better, we may need to consider more deeply than usual what are the values and uses in it of failure.

Though too much losing at anything important will destroy the agonist of any race or species in nature, within limits losing some may be valuable, more useful than winning them all. For one thing, losing is a great teacher. There Ben Franklin's saying drives its point: "Experience keeps a dear school; but fools will learn in no other." And everybody but you, dear reader, is some kind of a fool. The strength of that universal human cement of shared silliness blinds folks to the community of athletic daffiness perhaps as potently as any other communal factor. The Big Game can become a great social barrier-crosser and ice-breaker in conversation, the only topic better than the weather. And the way we talk is full of sweetly innocent idiocy, worthy of the Don from La Mancha. Nothing could put it down but the brutalest of truisms: "Why can't our quarterback complete a pass?" "Did Coach ever *hear* of a draw play?" "Why don't we shoot over the zone?" "How come *we* never have a laugher?" Well, because the other guys and gals really compete. The competitions are real, not figments of the imagination. They hold the game to find out who can win, and the only way never to lose is not to compete. These conversations really occur. Are the answers idiocies? It is a world rich in irony.

Yet losing is also the world's best school of irony because it teaches the tragic sense of life. The vision of life as tragic is worth knowing about whether at last you believe in it or not. It enters into all the great religions and all the art characterized by what Matthew Arnold called "high seriousness." But of course it undergirds and forms the background for all the world's great humor and comedy too. Shelley spoke not only for the English, famous for taking their pleasures sadly, but for the esthetics of losing in all times and places:

> We look before and after
> And pine for what is not:
> Our sincerest laughter

> With some pain is fraught;
> Our sweetest songs are those that tell of saddest thought.

Many a metaphysician somewhat to the contrary notwithstanding, I suppose there may be three lines of sight to the tragic vision. The tragic sense of life may arise, in the viewer, from any one or combination of the three: the vision of evil, the vision of failure, the vision of loss. The terms on either side of the equation must seem real—evil or failure or loss on the one side, real good truly corrupted or routed or lost on the other. The tragic sense of life consists in a proper understanding of the fact that living, however successful, is losing. It could be defined as grace under the pressure of actually losing and knowing it. It teaches a hero how to lose nobly and a loser how to go out with class.

Whether the tragic sense arises from the vision of real evil's power to inflict loss on real good, or from the recognition of natural human corruption ("original sin"), or from liminality (the knowledge of limits to power and prowess and life span), when truly registered it brings compassion to the seer. That compassion stems from the sharpening of ironic perception: there go I. Ironic perception will bring you to an honest realism, to comic vision, and at last to that humanity the Greeks saw beyond the inhuman dimensions of Apollo, Dionysus, or any god, and called "sophron"—the wisdom of live and let live. It is the wisdom of the Spanish proverb: "The best vengeance is to live well." The best esthetic of losing knows and expresses a grace like that.

Almost everything said in this swift summary of the idea of the tragic sense of life rests upon commonplaces of this century's theology and cultural criticism. Since most of both stand at sword's points with bourgeois and popular culture, it perhaps ought not to startle us to see how much more complex and closer to the heart of ethical matters come the esthetics of losing than those of winning. As tragic, sporting, ironic, and gracious, it renders the esthetics of losing noble, handsome, wise, even holy. The more shocking, then, becomes the fact that the other esthetics of losing may be, too often are, "bush" and ugly, lynch-minded and scapegoating, vicious.

Without shrinking from the appalling facts, you have to be a little careful at this point. There are pleasures in melancholy and in the arts of darkest mood. Not simply catharsis or venting but something like the old notions of homeopathic medicine, help from "the hair of the dog that bit you," may contribute largely to the values of the esthetics of losing. In their fascinating speculations about "The Quest for Excitement in Unexciting Societies," Elias and Dunning seem to be groping down the same path. Why, they interpret Aristotle to ask, "should it be that we regard as entertainment performances which arouse . . . feelings which, if we could, we would avoid like the plague"? Because, they propose, what people need and seek is "not release from tension" but the arousal of tensions "often connected" with emotions we avoid in ordinary life.

You could say that the authors might be a shade naive about general esthetics: we don't want those emotions exactly but their symbolic treatment; and we want to get our emotions vicariously, so that we shall be in fact safe and enjoy them in comfort. But Elias and Dunning do have a point which relates to losing, the little death. It is a point rather like that of Clifford Geertz about the cockfight as a cultural text for the Apollonian Balinese, a text which speaks tragically to the Balinese, giving them "life as they most do not want it."

Of all the games that people play one of the most interesting is "Loser": just so long as it is really a game; or even if the first cause is real but we can find some way to shift the shape of reality toward the sweet illusions of play. There are the pleasures of melancholy, the deep consolations of heartbreaking Lenten music or the great masses for the dead. It is no secret that people enjoy the hell out of a "Dies Irae" of any kind or, best of all, somebody else's funeral. Essential to the esthetics of sorrow is the crazy leap of creaturely exultation. "Missed me! It isn't my number up this time!" And so the New Orleans jazz band or the Scottish bagpipers wail and sob their slow marches to the grave. But they come back swinging along to "Didn't He Ramble!" or "The Girl I Left Behind Me."

The theory of homeopathic medicine was that cures could be effected by administering to a patient tiny doses of a medication which would temporarily intensify the symptoms from which he suffered. Is there perhaps a homeopathic effect, individual and cultural, in the esthetics of losing? Do they relate to those of "modernist" art, the esthetics of denial, negation, destruction, even antiart? Were Dada or Tinguely's motorized and self-devouring sculptures or abstract expressionism or concrete poetry variants of the esthetics of losing? If so, the homeopathy of losing stands close to the heart of modern, if not postmodern avant-garde civilization in the West. Perhaps it could be true.

That is all intriguing enough, the more because it could deepen our insights into certain relations between creative personalities and the Big Game. Whatever truth there may be in it further unites the winner with the loser. And it provides us one more reason to wonder whether, adapting the term from Geertz, the Big Game is not one great American, democratic, agonistic-fraternal cultural text.

But if that last statement should be true, the negative side of the esthetics of losing, the side upon which it becomes symbolically sadistic and represents what Mark Twain once angrily called "The United States of Lyncherdom," must give us the crueller concern.

On this point, I'm afraid, the urge for simple solutions muddies thought. Why isn't "sportsmanship" the good, simple answer? Probably because it's not a simple idea and simple applications of it don't work. Though indispensable, the idea of "the sporting," rooted complexly in the past, connects complexly to many relationships in sport and the rest of the culture. The people who wish to apply it simply get the same results as the Kennesaw Mountain Landis simplicitarians in every aspect of morality. They achieve repeated practical disaster, emotional and intellectual confusion, disgrace and repudiation of their "ideal."

An illuminating example offers itself in M. René Maheu, quondam director general of UNESCO. In the spring of 1970, M. Maheu awarded the " 'Pierre de Coubertin' International Fair Play Trophy" for 1969, advertising his action worldwide under the heading: "Sportsmanship and Self-Respect." The prizes went to a professional and an amateur soccer player, both Spaniards, because "both of them, during important matches, when the results were still uncertain, had declined to take advantage of the sudden incapacity of an opposing player, and had put the ball into touch instead of scoring." The case of the professional looks interesting. About to shoot for a tie-breaking goal, he saw the opposition goalkeeper collide with a back and both fall to the ground injured and declined to shoot for the goal. His team lost. He was quoted as advising "young people" going into sport "to always play fair and keep their self-respect." *UNESCO Features*, reporting the award, featured M. Maheu as saying that "actions of this kind 'strengthen our faith in man and in his capacity to overcome his passions and sacrifice his advantage and even victory to his ideal of dignity and self-respect.' "

That's beautiful, in a way, but is it cricket? Is it really sporting? Or might it be said to be self-regarding, rather egocentric, even theatrical, a form of what the jocks call "showboating"? Without regard, much less respect, for the other players of both teams, without respect for the integrity of the game, the intensity of the agon, does it not destroy the sporting moment, the fabric of illusion upon which the esthetic power of the game depends, and in the end destroy the idea of sport? A certain doubt whether M. Maheu knew what he was talking about may be thinkable.

Romance and simplicism, if they are not the same thing, muddle thought about sportsmanship. But an answerable reality principle can base itself on respect for integrity and authenticity—in the player, in the game, in the subculture of the sport with its institutional apparatus, in the fans, in the media and their public. Perhaps it becomes a matter of true love: sportsmanship is to love your game and treat it that way. Loving it forbids you to treat it like soap opera or to play it like *Hamlet*. Loving it will lend you "class."

And what is that? "Class," for instance, is what was demonstrated by Gary Player at the Greensboro Open golf tournament in 1972. One stroke off the lead for a first prize of forty thousand dollars at the end of the third round, Player forgot to sign his scorecard before turning it in, came back and signed it but reported himself to the authorities, was disqualified, and refused to complain, repine, blame anybody else, or succumb to invitations to dramatize himself as a victim. "There are rules in life and we must abide by them," he said. "I didn't want to tee off in the last round, with a chance to win the tournament, without letting officials know what I'd done." Loving the game, respecting it and the other golfers first, Player sacrificed himself for it.

Like many another moral matter, sportsmanship and "class" are almost easier to handle well as matters of taste and esthetics than as intellectual questions. As Huizinga says of play: "it creates order, *is* order. Into an imperfect world and into the confusion of life it brings a temporary, a limited perfection." Perhaps, as Dennis Brailsford thought, the very idea of firm rules, much less fair play, took its rise from the need of gambling nobles to preserve the possibility of their "play," from their need for gamblers' honor. It is the spirit of order and structure for the sake of good play and respect for the other agonist, his courage, his skill, his grace under pressure, the spirit of his love for the whole game which the athlete internalizes as values. The spirit of those values becomes that good taste to do and never to do which is "class." And "class" is esthetic.

It is finally a matter of taste, which no doubt rests on ascertainable moral values and choices in belief, whether you choose to "have class" or to "be bush" in your esthetics of losing. To watch the eagerly publicized versions of "bushmanship" theatricalized by Ilie Nastase is to wonder idly whether the whole performance is not an exercise in Marxian "critical realism"—an effort to destroy by conspiring with the Americans to degrade their own manners. As gestures of total rejection, whether politically revolutionary or not, the uglification of taste, style, manners, message has become a standard variation upon the patterns of our times. Is it an ethics of repudiation or is it just "being bush" that leads constituencies in the stands to act like "fans"?

At his worst, a fan becomes a body of petrified ignorance entirely surrounded by prejudice. He thinks in totems. At the Big Game to him the players, the coaches, the auxiliaries never seem real people. They serve for illusions and abstractions, counters in a game he plays with himself against the principalities and powers of the Spirit of Fierceness. Whether they sound the same or, ideally, have become nicknamed and totemized, not even the names of players and coaches on his lips denote real persons. To the fan no college exists, only Awful Animals, Inexorable Forces, Saturated Colors, Mythic Warriors, or Fightin' Provincials or Ethnics or Saints. Sometimes fans do turn back into people again, and only when that happens can a fan permit the realities of a world of other persons to prevail. But he may exclude that reconversion from his world of athletics. Professional sports commentators of every medium are paid to entertain fans.

Nothing you can say against the sports fan, however, does not apply to the devotee of another art or culture pattern. Uglier deeds have been done in theaters and opera houses than have yet occurred at any American sports arena. I suppose it could be argued that it may not matter so much what rock fans or professional hockey fans do. But it matters in a particular way how fans and other constituents behave at the Big Game precisely because colleges and universities are involved. However the character of Charles O. Finley matters or does not, altogether different issues are involved in the characters of Coach Joseph Paterno or Coach Robert Knight. Whatever, therefore, goes on in the world of fans, winning and losing a college or university can never permit its ruling attitudes to be bush.

Defining "bush" is not easy. The opposite of "class," it is the mean, small other. No tragic "motiveless malignity," it owns the spirit of a cheap malice, a smart-ass consumed by envy mixed with fright. There is a bush personality featuring surface arrogance undergirded by cold funk. I can think of conspicuous personal examples but would rather not work in such terms. Not Lucifer the star of the morning plummeting in grand revolt from heaven to hell, the busher's is the spirit that denies and muddles and bitches and stabs you in the back: only so it can realize itself. It would prefer to have nothing in place of something—so as to confirm its hope that although it can never be anything neither can anybody else. Wins bad, loses bad, the bush needs things ugly. Above all it yearns to bring down class and stamp it into the mud—where it supposes itself to be. It plans, sacrifices, and waits, smilingly, flatteringly bitter, for the chance to betray, to sell out or subvert, to ambush or scuttle the reputed good or great—only so can it feel its power.

To be bush is to deny every mission and possibility for which a university exists. A college, to pick up the phrase from Mark Twain's *Connecticut Yankee*, is a woman factory, a man factory. It turns out persons with enhanced and liberated powers to grow up and realize upon themselves. The bushers' reality corresponds to the absolute reduction, even the transvaluation, of values. Though it may be life as they most do not want it, their esthetic of losing is *l'esthétique du mal*, like that depicted in the art of "underground" sensibility. It prefers corruption and despair. As Frederick J. Hoffman said of that sensibility in *Samuel Beckett: The Language of Self*, "The underground man is aware of himself as a 'louse' or a 'fly,' a mean creature; but his awareness is always countered in one way or another by a form of assertion." The university needs urgently to explore that sensibility; but to strive to *be* everything opposite is its fight for life.

It is the same as the need of the entities "class" and "bush" each to protect itself from the other. Psychically they are matter and antimatter. Esthetically, class can stand to win or lose and confess it. Bush, dying to lose and gain the chance to burn somebody, must never admit it. Why do the bush at heart exult, all shamefully, in failure, negation, bad luck, collapse? Because they are secretly self-destructive, guilt and self-contempt raging within, thirsting to counter meanness by the assertion of self-aggrandizing corruption and destruction of others— not other people, of course, but those symbols and illusions out there at the Game everybody pretends is so Big. Since they cannot grow up, bushers need scapegoats.

It is, I am convinced, this evil side of the esthetics of losing against which the whole enterprise of intercollegiate athletics must steel itself and war. There stands the enemy, not in the joy of winning, however ominous the threat of an esthetics of power might seem. Though Beisser does not talk in just these terms, they are consonant with some of his best insights. Though Kathleen Blake sees that in Lewis Carroll's eyes the development from play to agonic sport turned innocence to sadism, I think the evil is bush. The busher, really, it is who in Reuel Denney's *The Astonished Muse* becomes a "reality purist" demanding the literal in place of the symbolic. Denney is right when he sees that "the sports public often responds with an eagerness to the promotion of sports sadism and masochism . . . a brutishness that reminds us of lynch law." But the sucker in the case is the bit of busher in us all. Just what part and place in this are occupied by the sports media is perhaps a question of judgment best left to the media—who are rather good at judging themselves if left alone to do it.

The busher in the self and his influence in the college must be restrained and counteracted. So you have to fight him within the walls sometimes. Beyond that, his pain deserves our pity. The ugliness of that born loser, the "action player," and the demonic side of *homo aleator* (nay-saying, agitating, exploiting, wrecking) belong to the topic: failing the gambler's honor they are bush. Figures of myth, tricksters and picaros, loom in the background: Thersites, Loki, Reynard the Fox, Lazarillo, Falstaff, Brer Rabbit, Old Scratch, Leo the Lip, Cosell. Each occupies his niche in the universe of fun, fantasy, and psychic compensation. But what the colleges have to fear and hate is its force within the communities otherwise happily formed around the Big Game, the force of the bush. It is almost incredibly potent to corrupt. And corruption, by an apparent law of its nature, begets escalation: escalation begets scandal; and scandal begets collapse. The only recourse is a control which cannot be too resolute or begin too early. It was never the business of a university to become a school for crime, an arena for lynchings. It is the business of a university to teach the good life, the defiance of entropy, the joy of winning in beauty, the power and solace of the tragic vision. As it would fight pleurisy or plagiarism, it must fight the bush.

CHAPTER FIVE
"Coach"

In the sports-crazy modern world the expert teacher, trainer, developer, motivator of super athletes has become a common phenomenon. But nobody elsewhere stands beside the legendary wizard of the American Big Game. He expresses and symbolizes cultural impulses swirling and conjoined to something like tornadic power: the student *virtu* which invented and evolved the games and took them into the mainstream of college life; the almost hysterical response of the constituencies; the intrusion of the public and exploitation by the media; the expertise of generations of professional sophistication; the sometimes desperate efforts of the institutions to exercise some degree of control. He stands in the eye of the storm: when it blows with him, he is exalted, bestriding the festival, godlike; when it turns and blows the other way, he is strong indeed if it does not tear him to shreds. He becomes, all dimly, the American Vegetation God, watcher of the golden bough, king today, burned tomorrow. We call him "Coach."

He must be a man of parts, indeed. If you were out to recruit a coach, you would look at factors like the equation between his age and his record, like his regions of origin and experience, his personal reputation, the traditions out of which he comes. As with any candidate for a major and sensitive post, you would wish to make sure of his integrity and, if he were young, his potential for growth. But the checklist of professional qualifications for a good coach is staggering. He must be a technical expert, knowing the game in all its variations. On the field he must be a gifted teacher; and coaches are: some of the best teaching in America is done, most especially in scholastic athletics, by coaches. Yet college coaches have to be better teachers still, and they are so good it is a professional pleasure for a professor to watch a good coach at work, teaching.

But off the field a coach has to work effectively as an executive, handling a massive flow of correspondence and other paper work as well as telephonic communication. He has to be able to organize, expedite, and schedule people, units, and equipment. He must be able to deal effectively with staff colleagues, subordinates, and the allied auxiliary people with whom good relations are essential: academic, medical, administrative, even arty people—all notoriously difficult. Further, in dealing well with players the coach must exercise the talents of a good clinical psychologist. He treats with intense, competitive, tough-minded youngsters who know they are gifted, who have been warmly entreated, even enticed, to join him. They have many sorts of problems, often real, and the coach has not only to keep them in balance (and in school) through the griefs and troubles of youth, of boys from deprived backgrounds, of students exposed for the first time to actual intellectual training—all the problems well-staffed offices of "Student Personnel" treat in the student body at large. The coach must keep them struggling against personal and competitive failure and help them grow and learn and mature in order at last, perhaps, to succeed, to win. It takes large resources of perception, sensitivity, humor, love— and integrity.

The foregoing may be called intramural qualifications, but the job demands extramural talents too. It is a coach otherwise rarely gifted indeed who can stay, much less advance, in his profession unless he can wield the powers of a first-rate salesman and recruiter. It is demonstrable from experience that the saying is not true that "eighty percent of coaching is getting the studs." But it is true that no matter what his other qualifications, a coach who cannot recruit an adequate share of athletic talent cannot win.

Extramurally, he had better be a good colleague, for coaches share knowledge fraternally, incessantly. They spend hours on long distance phones, especially during the season, gossiping, relaying new ideas. The network of scouts and friends and the system of exchanging films before a game spread the word of an invention, a perception, the revival of an old idea, a "wrinkle," all over the country in a matter of days. All the forewarned coaches will experiment and put it in their pattern of play, if only on the assumption that the other fellow will do the same and may use it in the game and that therefore *his* defense or offense had better be familiar with it and prepared even if he does not put it into his game plan. God help the coach who does not enjoy the respect and affection of his colleagues enough to be plugged into the network. Not until the clinics come between seasons will he find out what the going ideas were last year.

Finally, extramurally, the more a coach commands the powers of a public relations expert, the better. At clinics, conventions, banquets, luncheons, alumni meetings, corporation or professional gatherings, motivational seminars, he must speak well. Talent as an actor or entertainer will serve him wonderfully. Some of the most successful coaches have created public masks, *personae*, of theatrical quality. And of course he must be a politician, especially with the sports media.

All the foregoing qualifications require that half-definable thing, class, too. And yet a man might possess them all and remain an assistant all his professional life without a sufficient abundance and balance of certain personal gifts and qualities which no society ever has in oversupply. Any coach will tell you that the first and least dispensable is intelligence: quickness of perception and response. Second comes leadership, the power to command the loyalties and the obedience even to sacrifice which are perhaps essentials of male bonding. With that goes an aura, the projection of what is sometimes called star quality: it makes everybody look up when one figure enters a crowded or preoccupied room. But perhaps it is more than that. If you have the eye and have seen enough of them, many people believe, you can tell a real Coach just by looking at him.

It might go without saying that Coach is a fighter, determined, relentless, resourceful, wily—a winner. No fool, however, he matures in judgment to become a great fighter by other means—a diplomat. He is supremely *homo aleator*, craving action, and a winner born to gambler's honor. Finally, returning to the largely indefinable, Coach has something of those personal qualities often observed in primitive medicine men or shamans: charisma, the power to channel mana. Secretly, or privately, many of them are believers in extrasensory perception, or prevision, or extrasensory communication, even psychokinesis—or perhaps all of these. So, of course, some generals, many artists, some doctors, some executives, many gamblers and politicians also think. Or at least they act as if they thought that way, and subordinates, supporters, and foot soldiers agree.

I do not say, or suggest, that it is to be known that any such powers exist or ought to be credited. They were, however, anciently credited and are currently believed in by many and subject to certain kinds of serious investigation. Should they in fact be nugatory, their shadowy presence in the pattern of coaching relationships would still consort with the folkloristic, if not primitive, associations of the Big Game with certain roots of culture.

The historic British Eighth Army, with more varied experience, perhaps, than any that ever fought, had a saying which, though it applies to much in life, lights up the world of coaches: "The only reason any army ever wins a war is that it fights another army." You will hear it said of the Big Game in either sport, "It is a game of mistakes." With all the coachly qualities given in one man's personal mix, he must survive in competition with his peers. Winners survive, though most do not last long enough to become truly established. The average tenure, for example, of Big Ten football coaches since 1901 is less than five years (considering current member schools only). Of the roughly 154 conference head football coaches during that period, however, about twenty-two have served ten years or more. Not considering that some of them served more than one institution but subtracting their numbers and years of service, the average tenure for the rest drops to three years. One in seven, it may be said, survived to become Coach.

My guess would be that the national figures are rather more discouraging to the beginner. Are prospective coaches thereby discouraged? Very seldom. Why not? Because they are the sort of people they are, they have those qualities. Because they are in love with the game, the art, and the life. Because the rewards of winning and the satisfactions of being Coach are great. Because there have always been men, and they of the best in their way, who would rather be dead lions than live dogs. And because being part of a great university or college is one of the vital adventures of the spirit in our times. "It's like being in the Church in the Middle Ages," you hear people say.

Both because winning is not everything and because it is a factor in winning too little considered and yet of the first importance, there is one other quality and qualification which calls for special discussion. It could even be one of the keys to the future. If you talk to a retired coach, even one elevated to a high administrative post, he is almost sure to tell you, "The one thing I miss most is the contact with the kids." Where he values his part in the lives of the students, the good coach becomes one with the good professor. That is where the action is in the true college. Perhaps it becomes a matter of where you draw the boundary of your parochialism. Some professors do not wish to or can not look beyond the bounds of their research, or their seminars, or their special students, or fields, or departments. Some look primarily to extramural service. Some, however, try hard to work well with research and teaching and in the closest possible harmony with the character, traditions, mission, present needs, and future potential of the particular institution. I have long identified and admired such as "university men," a special breed.

"Coach" may either become a free-standing power and monument in his own right, like Warner or Bryant, like Parseghian or McKay. Or he may find the match of his qualities with those of the character and traditions of the college and build his life into it as a university man, like Stagg or Zuppke, like Wooden or Schwartzwalder or Neely. As with professors, the outcomes may depend on fate. But it seems obvious that long, stable, well-matched careers by student-oriented university men are not only highly advantageous to coaches. They are of the utmost importance to the good names and prosperity both internal and external of the institutions. Though presidents and trustees, and members, servants and friends, of the colleges ought to assign first priority to recruiting and holding such coaches in such situations, there is all too little evidence that they think about it. And that lack of thought and forethought have become fruitful sources of chaos in intercollegiate athletics.

On the other hand, "horses for courses," the radically different sorts of tradition at different places call for coaches matched to each. At some places the elaborate, luxurious athletic dormitory, known to students as the "ape house," houses every man, willy-nilly. He is set apart and kept inside the athletic establishment as totally as coachly ingenuity and discipline can secure him. His every other connection to the rest of the academic community is filtered through and subordinated to his life as athlete. In thorough contrast, at other places careful efforts are made to see that athletes have nonathlete roommates, that athletes are distributed as evenly as possible through the living centers, that they share as fully as possible in the rest of student life and are made conscious of being athletes only when actively engaged in the sport. The middling permutations and combinations fill out most of the possible variables. The coach and his staff try to take maximum advantage of the virtues for them of each way.

However he does it, the modern coach must strive for and get some sense of "family" about his staff, squad, and team. It is easier for the basketball coach because he deals with so relatively few players. But the attitudes and characteristics of the family will be of lifelong importance to the student athlete. Experience shows that Coach, the father, will communicate, for instance, his academic values to the squad. They will achieve, as a group, just about what he expects or demands. They will become serious about solid majors and preprofessional motivation in proportion to coachly concern and counseling. Quite commonly, graduated "old" players will turn to Coach for advice and encouragement at the cruxes of their adult business lives. They keep contact. "Not a week goes by," says Schwartzwalder, "but the doorbell rings, and they come back. They bring me their wives and children to see."

Though I wish I were better satisfied with what little writing I have seen on male bonding as an instinctive phenomenon, it is imaginable that it plays a part in the relations of athletes to Coach as it does in those of military types to the "Old Man," and so forth. Perhaps we do better to stay with the metaphor of family, which works for the institution as a whole (alma mater) and for the relation of professor or director or conductor to students in many of the partial expressions of academe, from the most scholarly to the least. Reality as well as metaphor seems to lie in the image of academic enterprise as a very complex "family in passage" for everybody in the community. Dr. Salvador Minuchin, one of the pioneers in the psychiatry of family therapy, provides a key to the situation in observing that, setting aside "the medical-biological model," we need to use a model of adolescent experience like that of "ecological fields" in order to see that part of the essence of adolescence is to be moving from family unity and simplicity outward to complexity and plurality. To go to college is for the adolescent "a definite break with his previous systems of support."

Academe must provide effective and exciting new systems of support; and it does, athletics among them. But no "new family" need be so immediately effective as that maintained by the coach. It may range in character and type along a continuum of variants which ranges from the severely patriarchal/military at one pole to the loosely comic/egalitarian at the opposite extreme. Again, the match of coach and pattern to collegiate tradition and character is essential. But family success must be quick and thorough in the coach's house. The Big Game will test it in a refiner's fire.

Nevertheless family counts more than winning. It simply must. That way points the direction of the only honorable future for intercollegiate athletics. As I see it, integrity and authenticity are the possible tests: integrity of intention, authenticity in result. The Big Game can be supposed viable if it meets four tests of integrity and authenticity, all of which look to the idea of family: (1) What happens at and in the game must keep faith with its tradition of expressing the nature of American student life and community. (2) The people on the field or floor, allowing for the fact that the specialists are specialized by the culture, must genuinely represent the character and qualities of the actual undergraduate student body. (3) The coach and his "family" and his program must match the traditions and character of and belong to the larger family, Alma Mater. (4) Structurally the athletic enterprise must be integrated into, be organically a part of the academic institution, not a separate but related or "service" enterprise.

The criterion at the bottom line is organic, familial. Amid all the pressures and confusions endemic to the Big Game, self-evidently terrible, every other imaginable criterion looks easier in the short run. Supposing, as I do, that closing it down, doing away with the Big Game, is not a viable alternative, or even desirable, however, the truth is that nothing else will work. The first of those tests I trust has become evident from previous discussion of the evolution and esthetics of the Big Game. The second belongs most properly to the discussion of recruiting in the chapter to follow this, and the last to discussion of institutional relations below. For the present we must stick to Coach and his family problems.

The problems I mean, of course, are not domestic, not those private ones of Everyman as husband and father, though that is a tempting subject. Mary Stuhldreher's wonderful *Many a Saturday Afternoon* shows what could be done with the great topic of "Coaches' Wives." The wife with fortitude and patience and loyalty, with good sense and humor, can make a coach or, failing them, break him. In some of the best instances, she contributes richly to the life of that other, extended family, the squad.

Individual differences aside, the coach's need is to unite his people into a family without segregating and alienating them from student life and the academic community. A tough proposition, although it is not impossible; but it demands a nice and sensitive discrimination of the times to apply and to relax centripetal force. Academically and culturally more diverse, but more competitive, better motivated to overachieve than the run of the student body, athletes need to be pushed, to be actively integrated with academic experience. The coach needs to see to it that college experience does not pass them by. Insofar as football and basketball are subcultures, for instance, they are hardly more so than the musical, dramatic, journalistic, political, or social organized activities of the campus and, except that the pressures rise higher, not more divisive. They can be overcome.

Within his squad family, the coach must deal with a variety of subcultural types. John Pont lists them as: "the players," sportsmen of the most traditionary sort; the "win is everything" Lombardi kind; the artists, lovers of the game; the self-disciplined; the undisciplined; the evaders of self, the game, the coach. Out of all this complexity the coach must, each year, forge a family, and yet, if he be a university man, keep its members in right relations to the household of the campus.

Though such a coach truly deserves the support of the whole community and its constituencies, people seldom think to give it. All too often, if not most of the time, the realities he must face look like those ancient, monstrous and bloody myths which glared from the primitive tribe upon its candidate for worship and death as the king of the seasons, the symbolic vegetation god. It is a curious fact in the world of the postmodern American universities.

It is not that Coach *is* Attis-Osiris-Adonis-Dionysus, the corn god, the scapegoat. But you do get some fascinating new light cast upon him and into American culture when you flip the switch of that metaphor. Nobody can exactly pin down the facts about the old religion, but fortunately it makes little difference to us here. From the eldest evidence of the most primitive ages to the *avant garde* art of our present, an immense variety of material has suggested to eminent judges that the human psyche indulges readily and gratefully in scapegoating human sacrifice to propitiate the unseen powers of survival, fertility, and luck. Parallel impulses appear in the rhythms of democratic politics. Cognate emotions exercise themselves in certain long-lived American religious patterns. The connections of all this to the grand old traditions of mobbing and lynching people seem as obvious as its connections to the way we treat the coach.

That we are dealing not with genuine religion but with secular religion, the worship of the golden calf, with certain outcomes from a festival which is only sort of sacred, suggests parodic cult. But that the religion is phony probably makes its consequences in action more dangerous because less responsible. Not to entangle ourselves with Frazer or Freud or Jung or Gilbert Murray or "the myth and ritual approach" to explanation of life and art in general, perhaps the point can be put this way. There appears to have been in relatively primitive, even barbaric, religious and agricultural practice, a dramatized myth of the flourishing, victory, defeat, death, and rebirth of gods who symbolized the seasonal rhythms of nature. Averaging out the myths, you see them, one divinity set against another, politicized, as the beneficent gods war with the malign. Now we have dramatic plot. The grain god arrives, flushed with youthful potency, and fertilizes the world in triumph; opposed, he is betrayed, slaughtered and dismembered, leaving the earth to mourn in barren want. What if he should not arise? Death for all. But of course in due season he springs to life, resurrected as himself or his successor.

All very nice in Bulfinch's *Mythology*, those pretty fables turn to gore and terror in Frazer's *The Golden Bough* and its successors. Not the myth but the cult, not the plot but our present suspicions about how it was enacted have altered our feelings about antiquity, the primitive, and the roots of human thought. Let Gilbert Murray say how it seemed to him with the Greeks:

> The renovation ceremonies were accompanied by a casting off of the old year, the old garments, and everything that is polluted by the infection of death . . . of guilt or sin. . . . Each Year arrives, waxes great, commits the sin of Hubris, and then is slain. The death is deserved; but the slaying is a sin. . . . We must cast away the old year; we must put our sins on to a *pharmakos* or scapegoat and drive it out.

The tradition suggests in many times and places, moreover, that the victim, sacrifice or scapegoat, had to be godly or royal and pass from all that's noblest and most desirable to death and bloody dismemberment. Thus the human actor, king for a season, monarch of joys, condemned to worship and immolation.

Though there are parallels in the careers of politicians and media fad personalities, nobody in American life traces a curve of fate nearly so close to that of the vegetation god of pagan myth as good old Coach. Silly as it would sound to say that Woody Hayes is Osiris, certain resemblances between the corn god surrogate and Coach become almost uncanny. Big Game times coincide with the American harvest home and winter festivals. If anything survives deep in the national preconsciousness of ancient impulse, can it be accidental that autumn-harvest-hybris-death-retribution, in pattern, always demanded enaction? The esthetics of winning and losing both count for such symbolic drama, and the roots of tragedy and comedy feed there alike. Tragedy springs from the death and sacrifice of the corn spirit in reaping, from the resultant sin, guilt, repentance, cleansing, and atonement. Comedy springs from the exultances of harvest home, survival in store, abundance at hand, fear set aside; but of course it always had its roots in orgiastic springtime, too. The obvious ambivalences might be supposed to account for the festive, devouring mood of winning and at the same time for the fact that the loser is as interesting as the winner—if only because he is due to get his psychic if not professional blood spilled.

This would sound like nonsense but for the fact that emotionally, culturally, professionally Coach gets treated as if it were true. When a Big Game coach is hired and introduced, the lengths to which flattery, protestations of devotion, and all the kudos of personality cults are carried can be shocking. He is showered with gifts and benefits. When he wins, these are multiplied. When he loses, or even sometimes when he does not really lose but some accident triggers the emotions of mass violence, they kick his scapegoating butt out into the boondocks. They cut his professional throat and water the astroturf with the blood of his job and his reputation.

Sports Illustrated for 9 December 1974 quotes Coach Pepper Rogers as having remarked on a television show: "A good season for the alumni is when the team goes 11-0 and the coach gets fired at the end of the year." Is that a silly crack? By no means. I have before me a Western Union telegram from the years when such were physically delivered. The recipient was a college president just installed and the subject was near the midpoint of a season in which his team won better than 70 percent of its games. With the name changed, of course, the telegram reads in its entirety: COACH PHILBURT MUST GO TOO. THE ALUMNI. The 3:00 A.M. obscene telephone calls, the poison pen letters, the scandalous tips to the press become routine to Coach. He knows they also happen to people who get media exposure for tragedy or misfortune. But some of the calculated harrassment is harder to take. The banners and signs at games, the leaflets showered from the air, the din in the media, the attacks on children and wives, the subornation of players, the garbage dumped on the lawn, the movers' trucks mysteriously dispatched to the house with orders to pick up the family furniture—these are things which seem not to happen to criminals.

Every coach has his favorite illustration. They remember the day when, for the first time in many years at Ohio Stadium, the home team was substantially behind after the first half and things looked hopeless for the second: at halftime an airplane flew over dragging a banner reading "Goodbye Woody." Coach Tom Mont wrote an almost Swiftian piece, circulated in mimeograph under the title "Patent Pending?" It proposes for sale, "A ready-made effigy kit. . . . The burning model" treated to let off "a sour smell that is in keeping with the occasion. . . . A braided rope in the school colors adds tremendously to the hanging models." And a "super-deluxe coaching model" contains "a built in tape recorder which plays the school fight song and then 'Hail Alma Mater.' "

Not fun, however, only the tears of things are in the two stories, quite true, of coaches burned in their homes. One was wakened at 2:00 A.M. by a phone call which purported to come from the Associated Press. Did he have any comment, it enquired, about the news that his son had been shot down by enemy action over North Korea? It was, of course, fortunate that the war department could affirm in the morning that no such casualty had occurred. Another coach had to go to the state patrol to bring home his teen-aged daughter. Her car forced to the roadside, she had been beaten up by two men who left, saying, "Tell 'Coach' that was for him."

But, as Northrop Frye says so eloquently, "the element of *play* is the barrier that separates art from savagery. . . . At play, mob emotions are boiled in an open pot, so to speak; in the lynching mob they are in a sealed furnace of what Blake would call moral virtue." Where are they at that strange phase of American intercollegiate athletics when the community of scholars, its constituencies and friends, are wittily engaged in the game of burning Coach? In a democratic culture, and doubly so in a university partaking of a people's culture, it can be true that *The King Must Die* only in true play. There must be a mock monarch and a make-believe death: above all, none of the blood can be real. But we get run away with by Professor Denney's "reality purists." In all too sober fact, burning Coach does become a lynching. How else explain the extraordinary history of mass hysteria which Mary Stuhldreher can tell so movingly about one of the most civilized cities in the country? Or perhaps, once again, they are at church—St. Parody's; or, since the patterns are rather more Protestant, Travesty Methodist.

I said to an old, long head, a cradle Catholic and long burned-over coach, because I was not able to grasp the point of one all too obviously gathering mood of lyncherdom,

> "Chris, what's eating these people?"
> "Oh, you know. Every few years they get tired of the old coach. They want to have all the fun and fuss of getting rid of somebody and running him

out. Then they can have the thrill of hiring a new one and all rededicating themselves and having a big time."

It would not be fair to guess whether Chris knows about "hitting the sawdust trail" and "sitting on the mourner's bench" and "getting saved" and "backsliding" and "having a revival" and "being redeemed" once more—all the vocabulary and rhythms of the old-time religion. Or whether he would see how applicable were his observations. In parody, the secular religion has transferred the old rhythms from revival to athletic politics. Nothing could be more twistedly American.

But what is an institution of the higher learning, its officers, trustees, faculty, and students doing mixed up in any such complex of horrors as that? Whatever immunities may reign in the spectators' seats at game time, surely there is no other time or place for a university to succumb to fanhood. You cannot grasp the enormity of the coach-burning, the lynching mood in an academic community and its constituencies, unless you have lived through it a few times, preferably either with your sympathies on the coach's side or with a duty to be fair to the persons and responsible toward the real interests of the institution. In their conduct of the institution's affairs, its officers and faculty may never be permitted to be Dionysian, far less bush. To act, think, or feel so about any other aspect of mission or personnel, to be anything but as controlled, as sensitive to main values, as possible, would bring disaster, even constitute malfeasance in office. The truth cannot be different for intercollegiate athletics and coaches. Yet Big Game coaches are regularly subject to treatment as employees, as members of the academic community, which can accurately be characterized only as fanlike and bush. They and their staffs are the only persons in that community of whom it is even imaginable that they should be so treated. In any analysis the least fair, responsible, ethical, the facts admit of no excuse or defense.

Big Game coaches, however they individually conclude to act in the face of the facts, learn from brutal experience, personal and professional, to contemplate the starkest of reality principles. It is that of an unmitigated Social Darwinism: "Win or die." No matter what mealymouthed self-righteousness preaches "ideals" to him, general experience seems to tell Coach about intercollegiate athletics that (1) it is business, and, ethically worse, "show biz"; (2) "winning is the only thing"; (3) everybody thirsts to meddle; and (4) they are always looking for a chance to burn a coach.

Needless to say, the hard Darwinian ethic, complicated by the rewards and punishments of the modern celebrity system which is meat for the media, flourishes in our times. If you start to list the public or professional services, to say nothing of business, where the ethics of "win or else" do not reign, you will stare at a blank page. Institutionally, functionally, emotionally, psychically, if we have ceased to say "Win or starve," we have perhaps that much the more come to say "Win or be abject"; and "Win relatively or be relatively nobody"; and, more subtly, "Win absolutely or be relatively somebody." It is perfectly true that the games symbolize and their esthetics present those essences of the American experience and of the cultural matrices in which it is formed.

Though it is not really so, the situation seems less complicated in the world of professional sport, where they know they are in show biz and are prepared to act on that knowledge. Professional baseball managers, an odd guild, migrate calmly enough. "I was hired to be fired," they say. But these celebrities, like the "baseball statistics" for which nobody else cares, are, compared to the great coaches, media products, cultivated as grist for the insatiable hoppers of the media mills. Part of the intercollegiate mystique is the intense affective involvement of the public with Bryant or Parseghian, Paterno or Pont, Hayes or Royal or Broyles or Majors or—one could go on and on with the mighty and begin again with their parallels from basketball. And yet, if "the name of the game is Win," and beyond that you hope only for a little class, all you need are the heroic virtues well understood long before they were written down in the great pagan epics: "*suaviter in modo, fortiter in re.*" *Fortitudo:* strength and courage, yes, but it will win better if it is arrogance and fatalism, too. *Prudentia:* a hero with "smarts," with diplomacy, with a captain's power to finger the stops of that simple instrument, man. *Temperantia:* "Be bold, be bold!—be not too very goddam bold!" Think before and after; know when to save and when to spend: keep your cool. *Justitia:* if you can be fair, if you can mete to every man in the measure of his desert and his need, if you can take the long view: honesty is the best policy. Given the talent and the luck, these are the rules for winners, known of old, long and long.

It would be as silly to suggest that these heroic virtues are out of place in the university as it would be hypocritical to suggest that they are not in use there every day. But what happens if they are allowed to run free, unchecked in the life of the academic community—for any of its aspects, much less anything so hot as intercollegiate athletics? The trailer runs away with the truck. The Big Game subcultures, already technical and esthetic, already manned by athletes selected out and specialized by the larger culture and by professionals forged in a hard guild, become alienated from the campus, from the academic mission, from that student life from which they took their rise. Culturally alienated, their institutional servants, the administrators who of course used to be coaches, become alienated as economic entities and as political factors of formidable power and influence among the athletic constituencies, with the media, and therefore with the public. In Alabama they tell the joke that one day Coach John McKay was coming to visit and Coach Bryant had a sudden emergency with his quarterback and couldn't meet the plane at the airport. So he sent the governor.

A case can no doubt be made for saying that the ways of the real world and the practical ethics appropriate to them support the "business" and "win" notions of intercollegiate athletics. It is said that such ethics and concepts are right for the sports, making them appropriate to the educational mission of an institution charged to prepare its students for life. It is said that such sports become one of the most effective teaching devices known, and a marvelous instrument for uniting everybody except the kooks around the realities and simultaneously giving them a great, good time. Therefore, *QED*, the bigger, the intenser, the more victorious, the better. Hire the artists in residence and get the best! Viva Lombardi! Entropy follows anomie. The academy begins to exist for the sake of the game.

To me the *artists in residence* theory of intercollegiate athletics, which is at least as old as the dawn-success of Fielding H. Yost, seems as simplistic, unworkable, disastrous as the equally ancient and opposite *let the grass grow tall in the stadium* theory. Everybody knows that there are many and weighty reasons religious, philosophic, ethical, cultural—even Darwinian—for believing that the heroic, pagan, Social Darwinist ideals achieve melancholy results. The Scriptures of all the world, to say nothing of the treasures of Western literature, unite to undercut Coach Lombardi. In business or games or life, are the perceptual bases of "winning . . . is the only thing" not simply immature? Can it be the business of the academy to retard the maturation of its people?

As I know him, Coach does not believe, as Vince Lombardi himself did not simply believe, in "Win." But Coach cannot help feeling massive pressure to behave as if he believed so, the alternative being immolation. He would like to see the situation controlled. It is imperative to the academy to get it under institutional and community control.

Their interests coincide. But then why have the coaches, powerful men, and the institutions, massively organized and well officered, signally and scandalously failed in their efforts to control? Because the situations are complex, not simple, and much more dynamic than the academy has been willing to believe. Because there have been massive failures of nerve and vision. Because fragmentation, ambivalence, expediency, and dishonor have too typically afflicted all the parties—institutional, federated, professional, and public—to the problem.

No college or university can do its job unless its processes can be so arranged that in it the consequences of competition are mitigated, or retrievable, or temporary, or postponed. The very nature of human knowledge, with its necessary principles of limitation—the uncertainty principle, the indeterminacy principle—require that. We stand on the shoulders of the past so that others may mount over us. To err is human. Art is long, life short. We are in the people growing business. We are a family and a community which exist to nurture learning and scholars. The scoreboard, the box office, the bottom line are different, mainly symbolic, with us. We march to the beat of a different drummer. We hear what the years and ages say, not the days and hours. You could of course go on and on.

Certain principles of parsimony therefore apply to expenditures of all kinds, from individual life to academic integrity and thence to institutional well-being, for the Big Game. Yes, it has to be that hard: as hard as high art, the play principle, true competitiveness and unremitting development are bound to make it. But no, it does not have to be *that* hard: it must not surpass certain limits or pierce certain ceilings. How do you tell where the ceiling has to be? Answerable measure resides in reality and authenticity principles which look to wholeness. You have to find a good ecological niche in the academic coral reef, great or small, for Coach and his family. You have to be sure that, for love and limitations, they belong to the family and have their place at the family table and fireside. They must belong to the community, follow the categorical imperatives for communal success, and enjoy the benefits thereof. Above all, they must not be permitted to become mere neighbors or allies or auxiliary enterprises. Their relationship to the body academic must be organic. All the metaphors lead to the same end. Nothing will do but to take them, and keep them, in.

The failures of three-quarters of a century, scandalous, spectacular, consistent, seem to show that no other means of controlling intercollegiate athletics will maintain their authenticity. So far as I know, all other methods fail. The worst method is control by rhetoric. No other of all his tribulations will more deeply, justly embitter the heart of a coach than to be told, cavalierly, that the academy has ideals of integrity, sportsmanship, gentlemanliness, amateurism, high-minded disinterestedness, fastidious honor. He hears that its faculty and officers have made rules to govern his rather suspect conduct and attitudes. He is informed that the powers—the president and trustees, the faculty, the athletics committee and faculty representative—have entered into treaties within regional or national associations to govern him. He is told, very likely he receives an official letter of admonition, that if he violates any of those ideals in spirit or those rules in fact he will be separated from the family, excommunicated, cast into outer darkness, fired. But the same community, the same career and life situation, very likely the same persons, tell him, "Win or else!" It would make a cynic of Sir Galahad.

Let the same community and persons act bush in victory and defeat. Let them vent their emotions on the academic and athletic constituency cocktail party circuits, through the incredible gestures of fandom, in the media—and Coach can arrive at only one perception. Let them meddle in his recruiting and tinker with his staff and players. Let him find that his coaching colleagues and opponents are having the same experiences and that he is in danger of being destroyed by their inability to match rhetoric to realities; then he will feel compelled to one conclusion: they are kidding about the rhetoric, and the rules are empty verbiage. Let Coach A be disciplined for infractions of a sort he knows B, C, and D have committed with impunity, and all will feel forced to conclude that the academy is morally as crooked as a stick and hypocritical as a Pharisee.

In practice it gets worse than that, as complicated as Watergate. Hundreds of cases show what happens. Indeed, the wonder is not that some coaches succumb to cynical conclusions and behavior but that others fight and suffer for integrity. The easy road for Coach as cynic is to decide that a little illegality is no bad thing, especially since they are really only kidding about the rules and all that. Then he can set himself, superb gamesman that he is, to beat the rules. Having done so, he will establish a kind of underworld control by thieves' honor—there are certain things nobody should do; and by the ancient *lex talionis*—an eye for an eye; and by an intricate system of "getting something on" everybody else so one can control "blowing the whistle," or "turning people in." The method of relative control by mutual blackmail does not work, either. Sooner or later somebody explodes or something breaks.

Now, aside from the fact that nobody should be permitted, far less enticed by circumstances, to live or operate that way within a college or university, all experience shows that the cynical way leads to disaster. At its worst, the coach's cynicism, which can otherwise be overcome by personal integrity, drifts into moral disorientation, which cannot, as much contemporary evidence suggests, be overcome by anything. Communicated to the players and the constituencies, winked at if not connived in by officers, faculty, and students, moral disorientation infects the academic community, the constituencies, the media. It plagues the institution with scandal but, much worse, with loss of self-respect, which turns into self-hatred, which leads, of course, to anomie. The academy is thereby delivered into the hands of entropy, its permanent, mortal enemy.

Thus, by failing to control the Big Game you can render it of no effect or value. But so for the academy and so for the nation and its culture. What is the case for answerable control of intercollegiate athletics? Certainly one of the salient points is that, not controlled, it ceases to be an asset to academe and the culture and becomes a danger. The moral disorientation which springs from lack of control is supremely the cultural disorder of our times. It menaces the national meaning. Could it be stamped out by eliminating coaches and games, the sacrifice would be well worth while. But who will seriously stand and say that any such thing could be so? To say nothing of the culture, who will say that nowhere in academe but in athletics does the plague of moral disorientation rage? We cannot control the culture, and I am not sure we can control the faculty. But I think we can control intercollegiate athletics.

I would begin by laying down the firm principle that, as is already largely true for the other sports, nobody among Big Game coaches can get fired for losing. The national rules for faculty tenure, subscribed to by all respectable universities, say that a professor may be fired, under the rubrics of due process, for proved incompetency, moral turpitude, insubordination, or failure to perform his regular and stated duties. In practice, very few get fired for anything. Incompetency or a developed incapacity, when they become intolerable, are customarily handled by a compassionate early retirement or transfer of duties, and tolerability is notoriously elastic. The practical truth is that, once established, staff employees have a large measure of security and continuance in university employment too. Almost without fail, the coaches of the other sports teach, hold faculty appointments, and attain academic tenure. Under present NCAA rules, there can be nine football coaches in all and three basketball coaches. Why should those twelve apostles of the Big Game, and they only, be without job security, without reasonable expectation of continuance, vulnerable to immolation, the Cinderellas of the academic family and community? The situation is absurd and, because it negates control, disastrous.

Once you know that Coach is not for burning any more, the first thing to do is, electrostatically speaking, ground him. Or, theologically speaking, demythologize him. If you are not going to sacrifice, don't deify him. That's more than half the battle won. Many of the sensible and humanely academic moves to make in hiring a good head coach differ not at all from those usual in hiring a dean. You want a man of abilities and character so high and personality so suitable there is every reason to believe he can hardly fail. But in case he or the college should find it best to rotate him out, you give him academic tenure in a post you know he can fill. With a coach it is a good idea to see to it that he can, as musicians say, "double": he could do an excellent job coaching another sport. Failing the possibility of academic tenure, you provide him a guarantee that some among his high and versatile qualifications will be put to work, his employment continued, on the staff side of the institutional payroll. The demands for executive and personnel and public relations talents in a modern university, with its complex missions and facilities, are insatiable. Almost any coach is, in truth, better fitted by talent and capacity for hard work to fill the majority of those jobs than the person now working there.

The advantages of such approaches to establishing Coach in the academic community are in part obvious. They regularize and humanize his relationships. They have a lightning-rod effect on fan emotions and bush impulses and set the lynchers' yen at nought, returning the game to its proper site and esthetics. The vegetation god is dead. Long live the game and the coach at home on campus!

In part, however, they may not be quite obvious. I suppose that the odds are long that few, perhaps not 5 percent, of Big Game coaches can effectively serve out the academic longevity—through ages sixty-five to seventy, depending on the institution—of the tenured professor. How many still active Big Game coaches much older than fifty can you name? After middle age sets in, many of them can no longer bear the stresses, perhaps physically, perhaps psychically. Or they "lose the kids," as they say, no longer able to communicate, lead, inspire, make it fun—or, therefore, to teach or to win. The result becomes misery for everybody, and there has to be another coach. How much the effective longevity of coaches might be lengthened by a decent, regular relation to the academic community is hard to guess. Though I hope it would be substantial, the odds remain long that if you don't hire a coach to fire him you must plan to place him in teaching, in staff service, or in other coaching sometime before the age of retirement normal to the institution.

Of all the persons professionally employed by the contemporary American college or university the ones who have it worst are assistant coaches in the Big Game sports. With few of the rewards and perquisites which can come to Coach, they are utterly and annually dependent on him for employment and even, in general, for continuance in the profession. If he is burned, they burn too. If he is threatened, they may have to walk the plank. It will not do. The coaching profession itself, it ought to be added, must bear some of the blame for the failure of certain experiments in responsibility. Established culture patterns are by nature hard to deflect, harder to break. Coaches tend to internalize even the worst values of fandom. *Homo aleator* says, "OK, so I'll burn! Make me King while I last!" The American celebrity system, with its cults of personality and kudos and cruelty may be a disease of the modern world, but it is deadly seductive.

Many people know the true story of a spectacularly successful coach at a place we will call Magnolia University. He had a salary and fringe benefits so good they were hard to believe. In addition, the university had built him a beautiful house on its choicest site, and for every year he stayed he was given another substantial fraction of equity in the house. But he presented himself as an eager candidate for every major opening. Finally he got one, a "hardship job" where no coach had been able to win consistently. As one old timer chuckled: "Billy got bored with success. He's not so bored now."

Everybody knows true stories of assistants who were elevated to the head job because they were known to be great teachers and had been thought for years the nicest guys and finest men on campus. Elevated, they turned into tyrants and finks. Others, for instance small college coaches with impeccable records for idealism and fastidious integrity, have turned into crooks and traitors. Great pressures, not alone in coaches of course, can induce fatal personality changes in people. And perhaps the most difficult of all for the person himself to handle or for the outsider to judge or anticipate, are the internal pressures, the demands of self upon self, endemic to coaches.

One final true story, from a place we will call Saguaro Tech, features a young coach who took my fancy indeed. I saw that there were others arising around the country like him, and I began to talk about the "new breed." I began to say, "We need one like him." He was handsome and clean-favored and well-spoken. His backgrounds were impeccable, and he fitted as well at the faculty club as at the country club. Intelligent, gentlemanly, knowledgeable, he was a great catch for Saguaro. With him they should have been set for thirty years with a stable program, respectable in victory or defeat.

What was more, the Saguaro administration understood what it was doing. The then dean of faculties was and remains one of the most respected educational statesmen in the nation, and he took pains to be unmistakable about the university's position in talking to its brilliant young coach in the midst of the process of hiring him. This is close to what the dean said, verbatim:

> "Coach, we want you to understand something as we offer and you consider the head coaching post at Saguaro. In order to be Coach here you do not have to win.
> Let me expand on that. Though we think you are by far the best choice we can make, you have never really been a winner as a head coach. You have never had a big winning season and your overall record shows more losses than victories. We want you to understand that we have regarded that fact as an asset. We intend to do something positive at Saguaro for major intercollegiate athletics in this country. And we want you to understand beyond any shadow of a doubt that one of the reasons we wish to hire you is that you are not a winner and we are out to emphasize the fact that you don't have to win to coach at Saguaro.

Nevertheless, that coach, in one of the most painful episodes I know, was to leave Saguaro in disgrace after a cheating scandal in which he was profoundly involved. The program at Saguaro has been a shambles ever since.

What made him do it? Internal pressure, the psychic factors that make a man Coach. Does it have to be that way? No. Engaged once in recruiting a coach, I sat with a committee and interviewed the possessors of a dozen great names. Some said, "Just give me what it takes, I'll get the two greatest scholastic superstars in your state for you." Some volunteered, "Hire me and I'll get those superstars for you." Some said no such thing but listened and nodded when told that we required solid compliance with the rules on recruiting and aid. When we told Bobby

Knight that we required compliance, he said, "I have been waiting to hear what your position is. Let me put it this way: if you had said to me, 'Come with us and we'll get those superstars for you,' I would have had to say, 'Thank you, gentlemen, very much for your time' and leave the room."

The moral is not that Coach and intercollegiate athletics cannot be controlled. The moral is that no simple answers will do. No easy, stark decisions will work. The phenomena are complex and difficult. Answerable control is hard, and it does have to be that hard. But it is not and does not have to be so hard it is impossible. Hard work, intelligent and informed and consistent and unrelenting work, has to be invested in the control of intercollegiate athletics. To do the job you are going to have to work as hard as Coach works to win—if only to gain his respect. It is hard but not impossible; and it seems to me that it is indispensable.

Book 2.

*"What To Tell the
New President About . . ."*

So much of a book like this has to depend on metaphor that it seems natural to use another. The virtually universal structural pattern of the American college or university provides a board—sometimes of overseers, regents, or governors, but usually trustees—of officers ultimately responsible for its total conduct. In turn, the board employs a chief executive officer, usually the president to whom all other employees answer and who answers to the board. The president who does not steadily face the realities of his intercollegiate athletics situation puts himself in jeopardy where they play the Big Game. If he does not keep it under control, if he tries to ignore its realities, it will come and get him.

So for purposes of metaphor let us imagine a president who does not quite understand his new situation—an act which requires strength of imagination. As a metaphor he will not resent remarks aimed over his head at the reader. And yet, the new president is an ideal reader: intelligent enough to understand more than I know how to say to him; eager for the good of his institution; fired with zeal for the welfare of higher education in our time. So let us fancy him seeking light and leading, demanding education, even advice. What should he reflect upon? What needs to be said? What should every young president know about college sports and American life? Even to begin to think of answers is to see that you would have to break it down into topics: "What To Tell the President About . . ."

STUDENT ATHLETES AND WHERE THEY COME FROM

First and last they are the people who count in college sports. They play, they do and are the thing; without them nothing happens. If they are all right so is everything else that matters; but if they are not, it's all wrong. As with everything else, it is the responsibility of a president to see that things are all right with his student athletes. And, as with everything else for which a president is responsible, some presidents are gifted with a particular tact for and insight into athletics and some are not. In either case the only practical option open to the president is to find and keep first-rate people to perform the duties he must delegate. Student athletes are among the sheep for whom the shepherd of the university must have a special solicitude: more wolves are after them. First-rate coaches led by a first-rate director, like sound, effective structures for academic control, will provide Siwash traditions with a present environment which is right for the student athlete. All he will know about it, of course, is all he needs to know: that Siwash is "great," that he relates to it with love and joy. Essential to that good program are sound relations to the academic community on both its faculty and student sides. Steps must be taken to see that the athlete experiences the lives of the scholar and the collegian. Those steps must be made to succeed even if everybody has to fight for it.

Though some academic folk would prefer not to trouble themselves with thinking about it, the student athlete has become a specialized product of contemporary culture, and the facts make a difference which has to be taken into consideration. He, and now increasingly she, starts as a special sort of American person. Or at least he started as an athlete, like all the other guys, during adolescence and jumped ahead of them physically or temperamentally. Early in adolescence most boys want to be athletes for reasons about which psychologists talk solemnly. My scoutmaster, a gruffly compassionate steam fitter, knew all about it. Empirically, in other words, the early child-study and social child-concern movements predicted the structures of meaning for which Freud, Piaget, Erikson, and their followers have supplied theoretical and clinical explanations which continue to move forward excitingly in the work of Minuchin and the other family therapists.

Historically, it looks as if modern child study, including the taxonomic discovery of adolescence, ran hand in hand with the rise of sports. At any rate, we seem agreed that youngsters go crazy for sports as they become adolescents and that it is a good thing. There appears to be agreement about a number of benefits to be derived from the adolescent sports mania. They are helped to achieve goals they need desperately to reach: socially acceptable and safety valve control of raging new aggressive and sexual drives; the conquest of fear; establishment of the fact that one possesses powers and can realize upon them—and the consequent self-respect. Sports initiate youngsters to what will be certain realities of adult life, bridging the gap between unfounded childhood fantasy and actual adult possibility. Players discover the capacity to deal with groups of peers, making contact, learning teamwork, finding that the others are really like oneself; learning to work, sacrifice, succeed; learning to handle success and failure and endure beyond both; learning the value of accepting, internalizing, exploiting rules and codes, and learning the facts of both leadership and followership.

Quite evidently the adolescent addiction to sport, especially agonic sport, functions well to teach these essentials, and by experience. Many forms of gang and deviant, even criminal activity by adolescents do the same, and just as well. The trouble is that they invite retaliation and criminalization. They deliver the adolescent to adulthood almost surely bound to disaster. The difference leaves much to be said for the sporting, playing, symbolic way with its modes of catharsis and liminality.

Though of course not all adolescents follow the sports road, perhaps as many nowadays as two million out of every year's children do. By what processes of selection are the relatively few thousands chosen who become serious athletes, varsity competitors in intercollegiate athletics, for instance? We do not seem to know. The processes, obviously many, remain mysterious to me. In trying to think the problem through I have rejected several hypotheses as insufficient. And I am not much helped by such literature as I have found. Its failures appear in large part to rise from difficulties in research design: how to differentiate the serious, or, as the literature often prefers to say, the superior, athlete from nonserious or nonathletic persons.

Perhaps the same things that make people successful at anything make them so as athletes. What makes them athletes? Apparently all kinds of influences, motives, preferences, opportunities, and talents. Is it a question of body type? The answer can perhaps stand for variables in psychic, familial, and class factors, too. Extreme endomorphs and ectomorphs seem not to make good athletes, and though you see them in student populations, of course, you do not see them on teams. But there are mesomorphs who cannot, as they say in the country, "play a lick"—or prefer not to, which comes to the same effect. And on the teams you see tall and short, skinny and fat, blocky and lean, rawboned and sleek, bodies statuesque in sharply profiled musculature and bodies all whalebone and sinew, big boys, little boys, people with every variety of skull formation: athletes, superior athletes, come in almost every human sort and figure. So, in fact, do professors.

Stereotypes are dear to our ignorance, as in the comic pages, or to our prejudices, as in political cartooning; but college athletes come in every psychological, temperamental, and intellectual figure, too. As the beginnings of undergraduate intellectual sophistication take their rise in love of type, in its end that sophistication becomes the power to recognize the deficiencies of stereotype. Long dominant in the sophomore mind, therefore, has been the image of a stereotype now called the "jock." He was tintyped by James Thurber as "Bolenciecwcz," an outstanding star on the Ohio State football team. In class Bolenciecwcz was a problem for everybody, "for while he was not dumber than an ox he was not any smarter." *QED*. If we have become more sensitive about ethnic stereotyping than Thurber, the "jock" stereotype will be surrendered, if it ever is, more reluctantly.

Like artists and achievers of every kind, successful athletes must be, at a minimum, four things: gifted, hungry, intelligent, and toughminded. Intelligence, though it may be other than verbal or mathematical, is so major an asset that no achievement exists without it. Not all the gifted, most natural athletes emerge from the ruck of sportsobsessed adolescents to compete successfully even in secondary school. Desire and toughness carry some of the relatively little gifted to amazing success, leaving better talents behind. But no other factor can compensate for entire lack of giftedness. The folklore of sporting comment devastates certain realms of myth and fantasy with laconic finality: "Good hit, no field," or, "He may be small, but he is slow."

What creates tough-mindedness in one and leaves it out of another? What makes good character? It is the mystery of temperament, of the heart, perhaps the soul. Does the culture shape athletes? No doubt, but questions remain about a certain circularity in the process. Do some strong, rather balanced, success-oriented persons lean to sport? Or are they like that because sport made them so? Do the affinities of our sort of culture for athletic and agonic expression draw such people to sport who might have looked elsewhere in a different culture? Or does the process of enculturation produce such people and teach them to use sports (among other means) to achieve success both for themselves and for the culture?

For a number of years I fancied the explanation that desire, hunger, eagerness to pay the price, might best be explained as products of deprivation. Boys deprived of privilege, status, opportunity, or self-respect may collapse or be frozen in place by the pressures of deprivation; or they may, at least some of them, fight their way out and up and through. They would be hungry indeed, and the price might seem small to pay to them. They would have to be tough-minded from the start to rebel and fight their fated handicaps. They would make the most of talent. That would explain the authority with which the Irish moved in on the collegiate WASPs in athletics, to be followed by the Slavs, by the Italians, by the blacks. It would explain the snatching away from East Coast Megalopolis of the Big Game by the rest of the insulted nation. It would explain many facts, including the willingness of the jock to swallow—accept and internalize—the campus stereotype.

If you look at major football and basketball rosters and learn the histories of the individual student athletes, you will see reason to favor the deprivation explanation. Not 1 percent of all the little boys who begin in any year to play their first football on lawns or vacant lots or playgrounds or in the street will survive to become members of a major varsity football team. Of those who do, an impressive percentage will have something to prove by reason of class or economic or ethnic deprivation. That number swells when you add the orphans and the boys from homes broken by divorce or desertion, those who have something to prove by reason of psychic deprivation. But I found the people who know most about college athletes, the coaches and recruiters, not satisfied with the deprivation theory. It works perfectly, according to his recent book, to explain Bob Cousy. But there are enough contrary instances to give you pause and account for the reluctance of the coaches to accept the deprivation explanation as generally valid even though there are implications in it of major value to them and their profession. Family is hard to use as an explanation. The variables seem about as many as the natural permutations and combinations permit. Some excellent athletes were simply brought up to it in athletic families.

There is a volume of commentary on the possibilities of foolishness about this sort of speculation, however, in the story each of the famous Kuechenberg brothers told the press at various times:

> Our father was a human cannon ball, who used to go around county fairs and

rodeos being shot out of a cannon. Usually to make it more exciting they'd shoot him over something, like one of the carnival rides. He always used to say, "go to college or be a cannon ball." I remember we had an uncle who substituted for my father once. He didn't clear the ferris wheel and got cut up pretty badly. That made up my mind for me.

What does unite the shy with the extraverted, the deprived with the privileged, the very gifted with the "made" athlete, is a temperamental constant. Though these words were Ben Schwartzwalder's, you hear them regularly from coaches and athletes. They speak of "positive people." The positive believe; they want to give of themselves. They would rather suffer than be passive or bored or slighted: they want to make something happen. Never challenge one of them unless you are looking for an active response. They crave action—if they can find nothing better. They represent principles recognizable to Lorenz and Huizinga and to students of the gambling impulse. If I were recruiting an athlete, I would want to know of course about his primary endowments of giftedness, hunger, tough-mindedness, intelligence. But then I would be eager to know whether he seeks action, loves play, enjoys risk. Given a satisfactory balance of these factors in enough members of a team, the rest is coaching.

Therefore I feel no hesitation in talking about "love" and "joy" in athletic and collegiate experiences. The graduate athlete who comes away not having felt those emotions, who has no alma mater, has been sadly defrauded. He has never been to college. And college sports, known directly or vicariously, provide, not exclusively, occasions and opportunities for good college experience. I have had the luck to know teams intimately which ran, voluntarily, proudly, the half mile to get to practice. They not only won but suffered miraculously few serious injuries and no academic casualties. Why? *Per aspera ad astra.*

Coaches say, "When you have learned how to win, you will never lose." They do not mean that you can never be beaten but that you can't lose. The way to win is to play for joy and satisfaction, even the satisfaction of self-sacrifice. It is to play to fulfill your potential and to realize upon yourself as, among other things, *homo agonistes, homo ludens, homo aleator.* Giving yourself creates morale, which leads to joy: except that such experiences are circular, not linear. Thus you create the esthetic rewards, the bonding, the communities everybody needs: *homo fraternalis.* Incredibly perhaps to certain minds, "What the Thunder Said" at the climax to T.S. Eliot's *The Waste Land* fits the demands and rewards of intercollegiate athletics nicely. What the

148

thunder said was, translated: "Give. Sympathize. Control." Exercised in the Big Game, those admonitions become ways of joy and love. People who know such things by doing them are, well integrated, extraordinary assets to a student body.

But here we have come to the heart of the mystery. Winning, even winning, is not only not everything; it is not even the real thing. Coaches like to quote the great "Peahead" Walker, who said, drawling, "I've tried winning. And I've tried losing. Winning's better." It is, on the whole; but that is all there is to say for it. The player who cannot accept himself and his game unless he wins is as sick as the loser who cannot bear to win. Because the real thing, the heart of light at the inmost core of the athlete's experience, is an ecstasy. Like other ultimate experience, sexual or religious or creative, it is incommunicable. Nobody can share it. Nobody can teach it. The relation to it of the intrusive observer is like the relation to sexuality of the pornographer. It is wholly other (though of course there are relationships) from the esthetics of the spectator, no matter how pious.

It is true that the player, like any artist, may practice his art in multiple roles, at various levels of experience. At the Big Game he can be a fan, a constituent, a technical expert, a wily schemer for mastery, a servant of his father the coach, "in and out of the game." He may "turn on" to his ecstasy as easily at practice as in the midst of the Big Game. It is what he means when he says, "I love the game." It and not the money or acclaim, certainly not all he must suffer from fandom, the entertainment industry, and the celebrity system, may keep him scratching to stay in the game as professional player, as coach, as manager, anything that will keep him close all his life if he can make it. Though the ecstasy is pure by reason of its intense authenticity, it is also true that, other things being nearly equal, the people who play most richly for it are going to win, perhaps almost incidentally.

Though Huizinga wrote movingly of the magic, sacred and free and sure, of play, and though testimony from athletes, most notably Bill Bradley, abounds, not really much seems to be known about the athletic rapture beyond the facts of its existence and prevalence. Clearly it has kinesthetic, psychic, communal, and artistic dimensions with qualities especially appealing to youth. But of its actual content not much more is clear.

One of those dimensions speaks a language far too deep for words— or philosophy—and especially appeals to the young as an instrument of self-discovery. In play, even in work rightly done as in sport, the body speaks a nonlingual, nondiscursive equivalent of a tongue, whose only symbols or abstractions express themselves in gesture. The heft of muscles, rhythms of neural control, the glide of sinew, the beats of heart and breath: these are a language the body speaks to itself and exults to comprehend. Its name is kinesthesia. The earliest motive, it is the first, most perfect reward of sport; but of course it is only a beginning. You can learn to play poems in that "language."

Psychically, sport may be egosyntonic, as psychiatrists think, for roughly Freudian reasons. But it may also be intrinsically rewarding far beyond crass considerations of therapy. Young people seek, through patterns of stress in form, that hyperalertness and sensitivity, that density of felt life, that joy, those intimations of extrasensory connections characteristically found among the ingredients of ecstasy. And some continue to find them in games—caught up, rapt in trances turned deeply inward or richly out. Albert Camus is often quoted as saying that in sport he found his only existential experience of morality. And the frequent association in our time of athletic with religious emotion can hardly be supposed to be simply gratuitous. It is probably, at least in many cases, something other than simply esthetic.

All that, however, is about people for whom athletic experience fulfilled itself. What of the rest, the great majority of students, whose experience peaked in secondary school or before? It was often, though ecstatic, quixotic, making the college Big Game an occasion for dreaming. The writer of the following, who wishes to be anonymous, is a mature, successful, notably well-balanced man who obviously cherishes experience he is compelled to see as comic. "At Steamboat Springs in my time," he says, "we almost never won in football, and we were mainly used to it. . . . But our worst night came against the Rifle Cowboys one October." Rifle scored on the kickoff and twice more in the first ten minutes. Their second string rolled the score up into the twenties and left the field to give their frosh some practice.

Of course nobody liked it, but the pattern was familiar. Our coach bellowed from the sidelines and sent in futile plays. Fans were few. Mothers and girlfriends had learned to stay away from the blood and the cold. But our fathers were there. Each week that paternal clan gathered to shout lusty encouragement before the kickoff. After the first two minutes of play they would begin to berate the referees; and midway through the first quarter they would loudly accuse the opponents' freshmen of foul conduct. During the second quarter and halftime, mutterings directed against the coach would seethe through the crowd. But during the last half, they would relax and swap jokes and cattle prices. The team tried not to notice much during those Friday night debacles, and we were pretty good at it.

That was why we failed to notice toward the end of the half what happened when, against fiery roars of protest from the clan, the coach sent in a sneak instead of a punt on fourth down and lost five yards and set up another Rifle touchdown. Just when the fury of the mob was whipped to a froth, a father threw a thick red apple and scored a direct hit on the back of the head coach's head.

Between the halves, he remembered in retrospect, there was "no Knute Rockne oration." The coach spoke only, quietly to his assistants, and he made no effort to intervene during the action of the second half until, "The final gun signaled the end of the slaughter; and, helmets in hand, we raced to the bus." Last man aboard was the quarterback with gasped out news. Full battle was raging on the field between our coaches and our fathers:

> We rushed to the scene; and there they stood, slugging it out—coach against father, father attacking coach. Several stiff paternal forms graced the turf, and the red badge decorated coachly foreheads, noses, chins. Fists flew and curses rained through the air.
>
> Donning our helmets we plunged into the fray. The quarterback blocked a left from his father; the center a right from his. Two ends caught the flailing arms of the line coach; the fullback pinioned our chief. In and out of the scramble dashed the safety, pushing grown men at random.
>
> At last they separated; there was silence. What then? At first nothing but amazed stares filled the awful vacuum; but then one sheepish grin, then another spread from father to coach. And then they were turning away chuckling and smiling wryly.
>
> What were we—the sons, the players—to think? I didn't know then; I don't know now. That a fistfight between our fathers and our coaches should be the highlight of our football careers (as it turned out to be) seems an irony too cruel to bear.

Every romance, every ecstasy demands and finds its mirror opposite in the comic, the quixotic, in bathos. But the foregoing tells the loser's story *con amore*—to the losers of the world, to the human race, with love. These are among the experiences out of which student athletes come. It is obvious enough, however mysterious his essential experiences, that the athlete does it for himself, for itself (the game), for those others inside the magic ring (friends or foes). What is not so obvious is how or why it should be that he also does it for others—the spectators, the constituencies and communities, the town.

"Talking" his kinesthetic poem to and for himself, the athlete says it to and for us also, like a poet speaking better for us than we can for ourselves. He is an artist. And so we delight in the way he wakens the mute ecstatic within us of our dreams: and so he is we. At the Big Game it is obvious that the stands will be crowded with quondam boys for whom adolescent sports experience formed one of the most rewarding, best-remembered developments of their lives. Nostalgia and the chance for safe, brief regression charm them to the stadium and waft them into the game. As Coleridge said, the success of art depends on a "momentary suspension of disbelief" in the beholder while the practitioner weaves his spell. No art ever had an audience more eagerly participant than an arena full of graduate adolescents.

Often during the century since the artists of the "boy book" began to probe into the world of the boy, observers have wondered if his developing life did not somehow repeat the evolution of civilization. If "ontogeny recapitulates phylogeny" is true about the biological life of the embryo, might biography not somehow recapitulate cultural history? For all its penalties, might the achievement of manhood represent a victory and the spectator, for all his nostalgia, be renewing the affirmations of his own triumph through sport over the pains and disabilities of adolescence? But if the athlete as performer is our artist, our vicarious selves, as a person he is also our child. We are his people, his family, his town, and wield the shaping powers of the culture, our life. In the end, it all comes back home.

Like the American boy, the American school is a product of the community—which in turn stands in more or less reciprocal relations with the family. As a general proposition the family, the community, the school—and therefore the advertising and entertainment media—function unanimously to help pick out, support, and exploit the athlete. Ignoring moralists and other carpers, the people involved seldom answer and almost never ask questions about it, proceeding with that firmness and continuity which suggest that you are looking at live culture. Certainly it is at the point of the school where the community exerts its leverage. School expenditures for athletics and for Big Game auxiliaries (bands, twirlers, etc.) are often massive, cheerfully budgeted, and justified as educational per se.

The argument that such investment represents a diversion of resources better spent on actual academic facilities cuts no ice with the school board or supervisor. Nowhere in the world, far less the United States, is there a constituency which could be tuned up to a fistfighting pitch over the school library or laboratories or teaching talent. A school administrator is a sensitive politician: there are no others.

The argument that athletic endeavor damages the secondary school academic achievement of the athlete appears to be as prejudicial as the notion that jocks are stupid. Real academic achievement in the American secondary school system is hard to judge anyhow. In general, we do not expect it to be an issue. We leave intellectual education to the colleges and the serious life of the mind to the graduate and professional schools in the United States. Though much in the run of "educational research" articles devoted to scholastic athletics leaves a reader bemused, no study shows that the athlete is mentally or academically inferior to his nonathletic peers. On the contrary, he tends statistically to do rather better in grade point average. The better and the more dedicated the athlete, the better the student, say Schafer and Armer.

The truth is that the athlete's special situation skews his academic experience from his emergence in junior high school throughout his secondary and undergraduate years and perhaps afterward. From his contemporaries and the community he may feel sharp pressure to conform to the jock stereotype; many an athlete has felt forced to keep the emergent life of his mind a secret. Unless he is lucky in his family, he may find the same pressures at home. At school his relations to what intellectual life exists may be complicated. Some teachers will scornfully put him down for a qualified idiot and penalize him. Others, equally unfair, may pet and patronize him, awarding automatically inflated, meaningless grades, making it clear that nothing is expected of him in class.

Perhaps three laudatory things can be said educationally of secondary school athletics in America, granting the difficulties of making definitive sense of the grade point average. Scholastic athletics help meet some of the Jeffersonian desiderata for public, democratic education. They select some of the competitors and achievers and bearers of pressure, some of the positive people—as Jefferson thought public education should find in the general populace the *aristoi*, the naturally best—and train them to the service of the republic. And they train those they find in disciplines essential to attainment. As William Pearson Tolley kept insisting, the athletes learn and they demonstrate, at least most publicly if not best, in the university the force of the Greek wisdom: "The good is hard."

Of all American boys who can become athletes, those find the scholastic and college athletic enterprises most significant who were handicapped by low status, whether it was economic, racial, educational, residential, ethnic, or immigrant. No panacea, athletics present a ladder of social mobility which, though it narrows sharply toward the top like most ladders, reaches surprisingly high. Throughout the current century, more and more boys have used it effectively. Though defenseless before the radical sensibility which would burn anything unless it promised to solve all problems at once, that ladder deserves the sympathy and reforming protection of every liberal or compassionate American sensibility. What began as an exclusive possession of the rich can now help to teach democracy to the poor.

It is a common observation that athletic opportunity provides something enticing to do at school for the not quite socialized boy. It keeps him there and keeps him at it, instead of his dropping out, sometimes until he begins to catch hold. The lower his family status the more he is apt to need such help and, according to Schafer and Armer, the more likely he is to get it. In particular where family income and status are low, athletes are much more likely to plan to go to college than other, comparable boys; and where rank in graduating class is low, athletes are more than twice as likely to plan for college. When, in short, he is recruited for intercollegiate athletics, and especially for the Big Game sports, the college student stands a significant chance of having already benefited substantially from his experience. If he started handicapped, he has already risen up the ladder; and opportunity undreamed of by his father may lie ahead. If he started privileged, he knows and has learned how to adjust to the other half like few if any of his compeers.

Battling the Bolenciecwcz canard on behalf of the student athlete too much resembles the hopeless job of battling the stereotypes of ethnic prejudice. Some intellectually gifted athletes are prepared to exploit their talents in college and graduate or professional schools; some, incredulously at first, discover gifts of which they were not aware; others never bother. Many successful athletes have ordinary academic skills, some struggle. There are no "dumb" ones, not among the survivors, though there are many who can camouflage intelligence and sensitivities from eyes they think hostile. In George Plimpton's hilarious *Mad Ducks and Bears* a number of good stories illustrate the growth of his perceptiveness in catching that point.

Of course proportionally more of them survive academically and achieve degrees than their undifferentiated classmates (as virtually all studies record). They could hardly help it. Their motivations to stay and play, to win at any competition, to please the coaches, all help them. Tutoring and study tables help. At one point I found myself meeting with an academic vice president to find out for a faculty committee what his overview of student experience had brought him to think of the tutoring program for athletes.

He was crisp. "Education," he said, "is this university's business. Anything that educates students is good in itself."

Later, it transpired, a quite different committee—one appointed to investigate special programs for students economically and culturally deprived—found itself unexpectedly interested in the tutoring program for student athletes. Seeing that the athletics people were by conditioned reflex on the defensive, they hastened to say, "No. Please don't misunderstand. All our figures show that yours is the only tutoring program on campus that achieves demonstrably positive results. We want to know why it works."

It has been my good luck over several decades to know quite a few student athletes pretty well. Perhaps it would say something worth while to glance at a gallery of vignettes. Not among them are the Rhodes or Marshall Scholars, the Phi Beta Kappas, the 4.0 blazers. I suppose I think these people are interesting as human beings, "simple, separate persons."

Stan's lives, before he came to college, had been those of a Polish orphan asylum and then the Army, first as a football player, then as a G.I. deep in the assault across the Rhine: Remagen and all that. Then had come drifting through a couple of colleges, one year at a time as a tramp athlete before a sudden, incredible dawn. He discovered that he too had a mind and that it was the source of pleasures and gifts never dreamt of before. He used to study the habits of professors until he knew when you were almost always in the office and free. Then he tacitly scheduled you and called weekly at that hour with carefully prepared questions, topics of conversation, and unconfessed vocabulary lists. If you used a word new to him, he wrote it down as soon as he had left the office; and next week he made a point of using it in return—partly to make sure he had it right, partly out of curiosity to see what else it might unlock. He has since achieved an Ed.D., success as a teacher and administrator, significance as a state official.

Joey came from a tiny, worked-out Ohio coal mining town so tough a boy had to fight his way out of the neighborhood to go and play ball and fight his way back in again coming home. When he came to college in the heat of September he hung his suit jacket in the closet of the Delta Tau house. His roomie said, "You get half the closet for your clothes." And Joey said, "That's it."

When the frat boys told him, "Go down and take your nut test," he went, yawned through it, and scored a moron's I.Q. rating. In the spring of his junior year, having decided he wanted to coach and been told he would have to qualify for a teaching certificate, he reported to the Department of Education. When they saw his transcript and that I.Q. figure jumped off the page, they said, "You'll *never* get a job with that. Try it again."

He raised his raw score more than thirty points—a theoretical impossibility. He became a successful coach, picked up advanced academic degrees, and is now a tenured professor.

Hopkins was his first name. He was the sort of young black stud they would be happy to see on his state university team nowadays but who had to go North to play then. I remember his coming with solemn eyes to complain of his English instructor: "He's be*hind!*" Investigation revealed that Hopkins and his instructor were numerically even. The instructor owed him three themes he had not graded and returned, and he owed three he was late turning in. Nevertheless, justice lay on Hopkins's side. How could he progress without feedback from his work?

The other Hopkins I remember from the great Constellation plane, before jets, when you flew low enough over the Rockies to see them glittering apparently near at hand. If Hopkins had heard about them, he had not believed and had felt no preparation for seeing the continent on his first flight to the Coast. He gazed searchingly into other faces to see if they shared the same astonishment. He was on his feet for hours, darting from window to window, watching. Other players reported that Hopkins loved the motels on away trips: they were the nicest places he had lived in.

He did not survive academically to become a junior. Were the years wasted on him? I cannot believe so.

Jimmy stood perhaps 5'3" and, perfectly formed for an athlete, weighed perhaps 150 pounds. Recruiters reported that he had one thing to say: "We're poor and I have to have a tender. Just give me one chance. Just let me show you." He had sparkling high school statistics, could punt and pass, was a darting, quicksilver running back in a time when triple-threat tailbacks were nearing extinction.

"We gambled," said Coach. "We never regretted it."

In the big time Jimmy wasn't tall enough to pass well from the pocket and he wasn't fast enough to burn anybody outside. You could send him off-tackle only so many times. But while he lasted in any game he was the best they had. "He understands the offense better than I do," said the coordinator.

Looking back, Coach said, "It dawned on us that he used the tutors more and better than anybody. He used them to make A's in those tough premed courses. When the medical school accepted him at the end of his junior year, we had to say, 'God bless you!' He doesn't owe us a thing."

Jimmy has published one if not two books. He is a distinguished but rising young surgeon.

Fred comes from one of the meanest black ghettos in the nation. Most of his rooftop boyhood buddies are dead or in jail. "It occurred to me," he said, "that I was going the same way as soon as I stopped being lucky if I didn't pull out. I set myself to be good enough to get to college. If I do well, I'd like to train myself to be able to go back and help." He played a full and distinguished football career, becoming a key team leader. He took a degree in four years, has done successful graduate work and performed well in both government and private industry jobs. He keeps moving up. He's not back, but he is helping. A reporter asked him one day, "Is football exploiting you?" "No," was the answer. "I am exploiting football. I love it, and it is giving me an education."

In point of cultural origin the student athlete comes to college from a figure of culture in many ways dangerous to his mature success in life. It is in effect neither a farmer's nor a hard hat's way of making a living nor the failed dream of suburbia but what may amorphously be called "the town." Even in the great cities, neighborhoods and sections constitute congeries of towns. Almost never does the town, full of competition if not confrontation, qualify as a community. In fact, what joint and communal life the town has tends to revolve around its schools, where it invests, heavily if dimly, in the futures of children. There it cherishes the promise of achievement in the young and rewards it. But its best shared life centers upon scholastic athletics and unites passionately in the esthetics of winning.

The student athlete coming to college arrives specialized by experience substantially different from that of his peers. Statistically speaking, every college student is the product of the town, its culture; but the athlete, specialized, is a revealing expression of his family, school, town—of the culture. College may change him as it enriches his experience and helps him mature; but he comes there ready-made. Like other college students, the athlete represents the cream of the scholastic crop. But he has been carefully and knowledgeably selected off the top of the pool of supply. No national resource is so exactly and exhaustively utilized as the supply of potential collegiate football and basketball players. And the whole process of town culture with regard to athletics operates to inform—and misinform—the athlete about these facts. It may become a solemn responsibility of his college to see tò it that no further harm befalls him at it and to repair the damages of his precollege experience. Though it surely is morally responsible to avoid so behaving as to intensify hometown disabilities, it can hope only to mitigate, not control, the culture.

A thoroughly American paradox reveals itself at this crossing of concerns. If democratic and popular culture is to work, it must work to console and heal and enhance the life of the people. That has always been the Jeffersonian, Lincolnian, Emersonian, Howellsian, Rooseveltian point, opposing the Hamiltonian, Whig, Bourbon, Ivy League, and elitist view. Mark Twain, with his divided mind, put the case against popular culture in his portrait of Bricksville, Arkansas, in *Huckleberry Finn* and the case against the genteel tradition in his tale of "The Man That Corrupted Hadleyburg." In both cases his perception was that the people in both towns were perishing for action: anything—a dogfight, a circus, a shooting, a lynching, a con game, a scandal—to lend them an emotion, to lift the pall of cheap, useless, meaningless boredom beneath which their hearts, minds, and souls wilted.

The entertainment industry purveys billions of dollars of product now to Bricksville, Hadleyburg, and to John Updike's Brewer, Pa. But is it popular or only a product? Is it democratic? Does it work as culture must? Or is it still just any circus? The same questions apply, of course, to the shaping processes of athletics in the American town. American culture is a living branch of European or Western culture. And the most cursory perspective of that culture reveals a striking evolution. From earliest historic times, sport in Western culture was reserved for "persons"—elite persons, aristocrats, that is—and in large part denied to sub-elite, and especially to peasant, nonpersons. Sport was therefore a badge and a shaping determinant of values, of value in persons, and indeed of individuality. There was a longish middle period where, especially in Britain and therefore here, sport and personhood broadened down. Now, in the democratized, industrialized, and (at least theoretically) personalized modern world, sport is everywhere.

I who think the Whiggish "true sport is for us rich and happy few" sort of notion will not do also think that the question is open whether the present situation will at last turn out for good or ill. John Kieran, an acute observer, noted forty years ago that in the wake of World War I "most of the great changes on the sports field are due to great changes in the economic or political condition of the contestants. The spread of democracy brought a sweeping revision along the whole sports front" and "the progressive breakdown of class barriers." I would, to be plain, see the whole enterprise in Hell before it were returned to the palmy days of the condemnation of Jim Thorpe. But though I would not revert to Frank Merriwell if I could, it seems to me that there is not the least danger of that. The currents in the culture are far too strong. What remains to be seen is whether scholastic and college athletics can successfully navigate those currents on a culturally valuable voyage—remembering that success is a journey, not a destination.

The student athlete who comes up out of the circumstances of ghetto basketball may focus the college problem more challengingly than any other. "Street-wise," he is often a performer and competitor of dazzling individual skills. But in proportion as he is street-wise he may be academically defiant and innocent of team play, especially on defense. In many ways he represents the modern equivalent of the old poolroom subculture, whose athletes went into the "fight game" and shunned college like virtue. The old club fighters were often one narrow step, if that, from criminal careers; and they possessed no illusions about the integrity of their art or the authenticity of their relations to it. Like "rasslers" nowadays, they worked as entertainers engaged in supplying occasions for wildly emotional fan behavior of the most sentimental sort. Sentimentality may be defined as emotion detached from human connection or compassion, from the sense of responsibility to think or respond or care, from, above all, responsibility to act morally. True sentiment is the business of an artist, sentimentality that of a showman.

Though it is not the heart of the problem, it is true that, like the fighter or the rassler, the ghetto basketball player is used to performing "one on one" and for "show time." He is so accustomed to the attitudes of a vulgate fandom that it may be difficult for him to accept the fact that team play as taught in the colleges by Dean Smith or Bobby Knight—or even, now, in the professionals by Al Attles—will beat "alley ball." College experience beats street education, too. And from the time forward since Thomas Jefferson's design for the state universities, the primary mission of American higher education has been to serve the persons in it most promising to the future of the nation. Intercollegiate athletics, particularly when they can pick up such Americans as ghetto ballplayers, still do that better than any other instrumentality.

The problem is to see that they do it as positively as possible for all their people. And, though of course individuals vary broadly, the problems of the more nearly average athlete moving from scholastic to college status are only on the whole less profound than those of ghetto youth. Some towns carelessly, absentmindedly risk placing the athletes in real developmental danger psychically and socially. Everybody sees casualties of the sort John Updike registered brilliantly in *Rabbit, Run;* and other sorts occur. All the American and Big Game factors, miniaturized but often thereby concentrated, and all the human factors which stimulate athletic participation rage through the culture of towns. And there they are sometimes mitigated by too few such countervailing influences as those at work in college and university communities. Intensified by parochialism, by definition short on class, the athletic enterprise of a town, like much else in its life, can become almost pure bush. That life, indeed, at its worst originally stood as the model of what the ballplayers meant when they coined the word.

The far-famed "teen culture" hurts. Its worship of athletes reinforces the adolescent need to be somebody in defiance of the adult world; but too often the adult town culture doubles and redoubles that reinforcement—confounding and confusing the adolescent need for defiance and rebellion. Confusion about adult overacceptance of teen culture drives some adolescents to bizarre if not delinquent behavior. It may drive the athlete deeper into "his thing"; and his competitive thing, with its new principles of weight and interval training, of isometrics, and especially of overload may draw him very deeply indeed into training activity as escape from all else. If you are gifted and you play 72 holes of golf and hit a few hundred practice balls every day, you can become a young lion. If you play four or five hours of basketball and then practice every shot in your repertoire, insisting on hitting twenty of each in a row or beginning all over whenever you miss, you can become competitive. How does a lad bear that sort of thing? He works in a dream, intoning for himself the imagined words of an announcer: "Here is Billy Jock. He shoots! It's up and traveling, folks. What will happen? It's in! He did it! He wins the national championship! Wow!" In certain areas—music, mathematics, poetry, scholarship—such concentration is not only common enough but may be essential to adult success. The reading child and adolescent draw away to levels of skill and command which no intensity of late-blooming graduate school application can overtake. The trouble for the athlete comes from the fact that there is almost no adult future for his skills; and it comes from the intrusion of the public.

Single-mindedness and egosyntonic fantasy befit an adolescent thirsting for identity, the chance to be somebody and get a little respect. But what follows development arrested by becoming a big shot? Or false identity drawn from essentially inapposite attention and the celebrity treatment? Rabbit Angstrom in all his tortured, destructive, pathetic varieties follows. Too many a high school athletic big shot has gone over the hill forever at commencement day just before or after his eighteenth birthday. He will never have it so good again, and he may never be able to recover from a fall which need never have occurred. Where there is social or psychic deprivation, of course, his youthful vulnerability may be that much the worse.

The one source of most of the trouble lies in the fact that a bush town is a sort of collective adolescent itself, starving, thirsting, perishing to believe in itself, to feel important, to get some respect, some recognition, to win the bragging rights, to achieve identity. A town so small it has only four main entrances will erect a banner over each, a yoke beneath which every visitor must pass, saying, "Johnson. Home of Billy Jock." Or the chamber of commerce will rent a billboard, bragging: "Jerusalem. Home of the Saints. State Champions, 1980," and listing all the scores, all the players, the coach and all his assistants, all the honors won by players. Or the same may adorn milk company or brewery trucks. For years later, weathering softly in the rain and wind of the seasons, the brag will stand, the fading bumper stickers sit in the used car lots. The very worst thing which can happen to an athlete—or, for that matter, a coach—is to believe what they say at those testimonial banquets. They say, "Our hearts overflow with gratitude. We will always remember. We love you forever." What they mean is: "Just wait, Big Shot." After a certain amount or intensity of winning, the town coach, if he is wise and has a good chance, moves. The athlete, unless he is unlucky or unwise, moves also—to college.

Perhaps, in the final analysis, one of the safer generalizations you could make about the situation of American student athletes might be that, all things democratic considered, it is all right to treat them no worse than the world agrees to treat Olympic competitors so long as they are *bona fide* students. The point the Big Ten Special Advisory Commission makes strikes to the heart of the matter for student athletes female or male, black or white. To remain eligible to compete from one year to another they must demonstrate regular progress toward valid degree programs in solid majors. If they fail to do that, their grants-in-aid should be continued as long as they continue to try with promise. *Bona fide* students who complete degrees at about the same rates as the student body in general can honorably perform as student athletes.

For most student athletes the worst fate that can befall them is to be captured by the delusion of becoming Joe Namath: if you go far enough, you can do commercials. The American star and celebrity systems stand among the worst diseases of the national imagination anyhow. Nathanael West painted them in their true colors. But the entertainment and advertising industries, dominating hometown values and illusions, conspire to mislead the kids shamefully—or is it shamelessly? Woe to the academic community which does not know how to light them their way back to answerable human and citizen reality. What *does* it have to offer?

I enjoy and admire what is meant by a "real pro" and an "old pro." They have and exhibit true class after their fashions. By definition, however, student athletes, even as I, ought to take them as metaphors for mature success in the grownup, the adult life which lies above and beyond intercollegiate athletics. Most of them ought to discard the "pro" dream as a vocational model. "That myth," says Bob James, Commissioner of the Atlantic Coast Conference, "is one of the peskiest things we have to deal with." Academe must help its athletes get their heads straight about it. Because they are students, student athletes are persons in the making. Personal growth toward mature fulfillment is their occupation as promoting it is the business of the college. The coaches are professionals, like the administrators and the faculty. Doctors and lawyers and artists and teachers, civil servants and bankers and preachers and politicians and manufacturers—all are professionals. So are media and entertainment industry people. In those and hundreds of other skilled callings you can be a real pro for the entirety of your life. Even in such chronically underemployed and desperate fields as acting or musicianship or poetry you can be a professional all your life.

But the games are boys' games (is there yet a sport invented by and for girls?). They belong to youth. As such, they climax with the capacity to perform them, essentially in the college years. Athletically, there is no answer to A.E. Housman's perfect poem, "To an Athlete Dying Young." We all do. Play, recreation, exercise—these last lifelong. A middle-aged athlete has a fool in his shoes. They are not games for grown-ups. Bill Russell has been piercingly right in his description of how essentially silly it is for grown men to be running up and down a floor in short pants, playing a boy's game. He's definitive.

As it has been my privilege to say to student athletes, especially seniors, who wished to hear, there are four reasons why a student athlete might wish to turn professional: (1) You can't bear to leave the game yet. (2) Your status and probable opportunities are such that you continue to need the social ladder. (3) You can endow yourself financially for life. (4) You probably can't succeed at anything else. Unless one or more of these reasons really compels him (so far it is never "her"), any student athlete ought to hang up his boots and embark upon building his adult life at once. For the odds are at least hundreds to one that if he does so he will be better off in fifteen years than anybody who tries the pro's. Those are facts.

One of the signs that the pro's are in show biz is that they regard people with the same attitudes—attitudes varying from callous indifference to casual malice or rapacious exploitation. They treat college and university athletic programs the same predatory way. Even when there is a little—for there is never much—money in it for an athletics program, therefore, it seems highly doubtful that academe ought to have much to do with them. When it has done its duty to explain the probabilities, the academic community ought to act, except for the help it can give him, as if it were a happy accident when one of its own achieves professional sports success. The exception should be all the help coaches and administrators and faculty can give their athlete in negotiating contracts with professionals and in advising him on investing and safeguarding his returns. In its policy and legislation to the contrary, it seems to me, the NCAA has been dead wrong. As we would keep our prospective student athletes out of the hands of the flesh-peddling sharpies and corrupters, so we must keep out students out of the hands of the flesh-peddling agents and other leeches. It is part of what we owe them, and we have the expertise to give.

RECRUITING AND AID

From the earliest times, American colleges have recruited students—if only to have enough warm bodies in attendance to justify their existence. Otherwise their motives have been legion: recruiting and training a ministry, making gentry, conserving the values of Western civilization on this continent, providing opportunity for the gifted poor, civilizing Indians, raising up talented servants for the republic, creating a life of the mind in America—or an American mind; encouraging talent in the arts or sciences, improving agriculture or engineering or manufacturing or business. Students have always been and now are actively recruited for matriculation at particular institutions for these or any one of a myriad other motives, some arbitrary or eccentric.

The methods of collegiate recruitment, in use from the beginning, include propaganda; personal proselytizing; the use of personal and institutional influence in the home community; and financial subvention of the student's attendance through loans, arrangements for employment on and off campus, and outright gifts of cash in the forms of scholarships, fellowships, and other grants-in-aid. Adding endowment income and gifts (largely derived from the constituencies) to grants from federal, state, and local governments and from foundations gives a figure of more millions of dollars than I know how to compute available for help in recruiting students to higher education. But it must be some hundreds of millions; and we take it for granted that the institutions will compete for the size of their shares: it is the American way.

The point of summarizing what everybody knows is to confront the not infrequent comment, made in the tone humorists call deadpan, that colleges recruit students to play games. If they did not it might be the only aspect of campus life for which nobody were recruited. It would be a reason for wonder, given the whole American tradition, if no athletic recruitment took place. During the years when the NCAA pretended that its members in good standing did not proselytize, the discrepancy between fact and fiction became so virulent a source of moral disorientation that the association's first effort to close the gap they called the "Sanity Code." If by "sanity" they meant an answerable principle of reality, the defect of the experiment proved to be imbalance—too much code, too little sanity.

There is, of course, a sort of sanity in the answer every coach will give you in moments of quiet disillusion, when the pressures seem too much and, like Stephen Crane's young soldier marching away from Chancellorsville, he turns "with a lover's thirst to images of tranquil skies," to "prospects of clover tranquility."

If you ask him, "What can be done to stop this rat race?"

He will answer, "Just play the students, the kids that come to school on their own."

But the trouble, and he knows it as well as any veteran coming out of combat while the war goes on, is that his vision is, in the most romantic sense, Utopian—an escapist dream. There are several ways to put the point. Student recruitment was woven into the fabric of American higher education with the foundation of Harvard College. There is a ruling practical sense in which nobody comes to school on his own. It's "unAmerican." Furthermore, recruitment for athletic competition is a practice older than college athletics, older even than the distinction between amateur and professional. It antedated organized collegiate competition, was rife in the sporting world about which students knew everything long before they ever associated to compete among themselves, and was carried forward from the early days, certainly the "lyric period," in its worst forms.

The control of intercollegiate athletics really began in order to control the recruitment not of the student athlete but of the "ringer." To say nothing of war and chivalric combat, the use of the ringer is at least as old as competitive sport; and some of the classical Greek Olympians of the palmiest day were tramp athletes. Of the time-honored ways to win by actually cheating at horse or dog racing, one of the most prevalent has always been to "ring in" suckers by switching a look-alike fast runner, a "dead ringer" (or a dyed animal, a "dark horse"), for his slower counterpart. You run Slowpoke until the right odds are 40-1 against him, then run the ringer, under Slowpoke's name, and clean up on the bets. No antique or mere country phenomenon, the ringer may be encountered within the moral bastions even of suburbia and academe. He pops up in Little League Baseball, I am told; and I have met him myself, both as a "sandbagger" (possessed of an artificially nurtured and mendacious handicap) and as a true "dark horse" in faculty golf league tournament play.

The idea was bound to strike college athletics early. The folklore resounds with tales of the gypsy coach whose team never played at home but who traveled with half a dozen skilled players and made up the rest of the team by judicious recruitment Friday night and Saturday morning among the saloons frequented by riveters, caulkers, hod-carriers and other muscular types who would enjoy an afternoon spent making a day's wages for bashing college boys. One church-going gentleman of the old school assured me that, until marriage stopped it, he played ten years of football at a total of three colleges and used a different name at each. It seems to be a matter of record that no less than seven members of the University of Michigan varsity of 1893 had never bothered with the formality of matriculation. The official historian of Ohio Wesleyan wrote: " 'In 1897,' says C. Sumner ("Doc") Welsh (ex 1898), 'the few of us got a little money together and sent down to Morgantown for Yost to coach and play a tackle in the game with Michigan.' " Asked about it, Fielding H. Yost, with the perspective of that incredible career, said something significant: "As to rules, we didn't violate any; in those days there weren't any rules."

The evolution of the fact of rules (to say nothing of their character and qualities) for the conduct of intercollegiate athletics illustrates Thomas Paine's aphorism: "Government is given to us for our sins." Not the fact of recruitment but the sins of corrupt recruitment gave us the rules governing it. In athletic recruiting there are three cardinal sins: (1) gathering in and playing the ringer, or nonstudent; (2) using excessive inducements to attend and compete for Siwash and not Red Raider U., or vice versa; (3) the use and promise of (or mere reputation for having available) excessive aid for the student athlete once he is in residence and entered upon the swing of college life.

You can quickly name the reason why practices like the above are sins: they have evil consequences. Other things between Big Game coaches and teams begin so nearly equal as they are, a small advantage in recruiting one year will empower the Red Raiders to beat Siwash three years later; and a consistent edge in recruiting will make Magnolia so devastatingly superior to Athabasca State as to drive the latter off the schedule. How many coaches would burn at Athabasca in the process one shudders to guess. Much depends on fair degrees of opportunity for equal competition. And even when things are fair, success or failure in recruiting makes or breaks not only Coach and his family but the health of the program in all its relations to the academic and other communities and the esthetics of the game. Here is where Coach with his charm and charisma, his name and the good name of his program, to say nothing of the talents of the staff, count for much. The qualities of relationship of the college or university to all its constituencies count too. If recruiting is life or death to the won-lost record, it is the same to representativeness in the squad. Much depends on whether Siwash is recruiting Siwash people, notably the continued authenticity of the game.

Though you could not tell it from the jeremiad rhetoric of artificial self-righteousness that runs through the literature about athletic recruiting, a great deal of intelligence and sensitivity, moral issues aside for the moment, enter into good recruiting. If, for instance, John

Wooden got his sort and UCLA's sort of people, he could win over teams with theoretically better material. You could multiply examples. Recruiting has more factors than chess and can perhaps in the last analysis be done best by people with superior intuitions. You recruit "futures," guessing whose play will mesh best with that of others; how a youth will perform when he has become a man; how personalities and backgrounds will fit into the family, match the student body, produce happy, effective seniors; who may become leaders; whether a youth can survive academically, socially, psychically. You figure the odds on everybody, knowing that you will at best get only part of your ideal list, knowing you will make mistakes.

As an English professor I have acquired just enough of that smattering of ignorance about accounting which makes a man profoundly suspicious that, no matter whether figures lie, liars figure. And as a faculty representative to intercollegiate enterprises I have seen quite enough balance sheets to make the English professor suppose that accounting as applied to athletics bears certain marked resemblances to surrealist poetry. In short, I don't suppose anybody has better than the vaguest idea what the national expenditure is for the recruitment of athletes annually. To say nothing of the various camp followers and Baker Street Irregulars of the Big Game, coaches spend a great deal of their salaried time in travel and on the long distance telephone, recruiting. Athletes and their communities spend a lot of life and a good deal of money on it also. Big Game athletic talent is the best exploited of national resources, and we foot the bill for it handsomely.

What Coach seeks first, of course, is the *sine qua non:* demonstrable promise of Big Game competence. The stars light in his eyes when he says of a boy, "He can *play!*" Back on campus he knows he has squad members who have, at least for the present, fallen on the wrong side of the distinction the late Casey Stengel used to make between "ballplayers" and "ribbon clerks." For Coach the equivalent of the latter perform on his JV or his "scout" squad. Maybe next year or the year after they will play, but until they do they are his recruiting mistakes. Everybody would like genuine college superstars, but they are in fact almost impossible to recruit. At best you want scholastic superstars and hope they will turn out blue chips—people who could play for any team. The rest, to tell the truth, is luck and lottery: sometimes to recruit a superstar who rises to an equivalent college level, or sometimes to have a blue chip blaze forth as a star; hopefully, never to be stuck with too few blue chips, too many ribbon clerks. How many are enough "blue chips who come through"? Perhaps a dozen a year in football and three a year in basketball, on the average.

And yet, even without rules to break and all the evils attendant on a consequent life of treachery and deceit, historically it proved to be impossible not to sin so desperately in recruiting as to require the establishment of rules and standards of conduct. If you rule, and the institution earnestly enforces the rule, that nobody shall be eligible to compete who is not a regularly admitted and matriculated student, who is not in a representative course of studies, who is not progressing satisfactorily, by the standards applied to other students in general, toward a regular degree, you have eliminated the ringer. A good faculty committee can administer such rules justly and humanely. If Coach will then see to it that the desirable match exists between his family personnel and the college, you have met the rule against ringers in the spirit as well as the letter.

Be it remembered that where student athletes come from in their communities and secondary schools tends to enrich, from a democratic point of view, the athletic pool with a higher proportion of people from deprived or relatively low economic and social backgrounds. The proportion of ethnics in the Big Game families often far outshines their proportion among a student body at large. Among the jocks you might meet people you never see at home, as Walter Camp suggested. It seems harsh to say, "Woe to that critic who therefore finds the athletes not representative!" But what else is there to say? Only this, the coach who recruits—and the faculty and administrators who let him do it—athletes with slim or no chances of surviving academically in a college are foolish in the short run and corrupt in the long.

You can list the reasons why Coach ought not to try even that form of ringer: (1) Intellectually underqualified student athletes don't survive. I once studied an entering class of more than forty football players on athletic scholarship which happened to be characterized by a recruiting resolve to ignore academic promise. Almost half failed to survive the freshman year, and two-thirds were gone by the end of the sophomore year. Perhaps a quarter of them ever played at all. After one injury early in their senior year, none of the surviving 11 percent played. (2) Such losses wreck recruiting continuity and structure, which results in (3) ill-planned squads, out of personnel balance, without experience, and short on leadership. (4) Since athletes who survive for four years grow physically, learn much from coaching and competitive experience, you lose consistently to well-built, coherent, experienced teams with senior leadership. (5) On campus you alienate the players and your program from the academic communities and nourish the jock stereotype. (6) Off-campus you lose recruiting credibility in the field to the point where, eventually, you destroy the confidence of the college in all its elements, leaving yourself prey to the coach-burners. (7) Finally, you diminish the reputation of yourself, your profession, your game, and the institution.

Why, then, do the wicked flourish like the green bay tree? They don't flourish so well as you hear it claimed. When they do, perhaps it is the will of God, but perhaps it is because there is a way out. If the institution will let you, you can, I hear, at some places conduct a fake college within the college for athletes only. What that constitutes morally seems obvious; structurally it constitutes alienation of athletics and their operation as an intrinsically noncollegiate associated enterprise—like a shopping center, let us say, owned and operated for endowment income.

What makes this sort of thing really worse than ordinary forms of white-collar crime is that it defrauds the athletes of life and opportunity, which are both more precious than cash, and that it turns the college into a school of crime, perverting it and corrupting its students. Why, then, allow recruiting? Why not just make them cut it out? Because there is no way to stop for college athletics what is so deeply grown in the American grain. Throughout our higher education, and for Jeffersonian reasons, in science, in art, for scholarly and professional and leadership promise, talent and high motive are recruited for the social good and institutional prestige. Every sign indicates that, though jobs for the mediocre fall off, in business, industry, research, education, and government recruiting for talent will intensify. The most critical shortage everywhere is the shortage in true talent. The feasible solution for intercollegiate athletics is to control it, limiting hypocrisy and abuse, promoting the good of the student athlete, the games, and the colleges.

With no theoretical intention, the rules of conferences and the NCAA which govern intercollegiate athletics evolved on the same principles as English Common Law—from precedents established to meet specific cases. It is a realistic method but not tidy; and it worked pretty well for the Intercollegiate Conference of Faculty Representatives, the oldest of organized conferences, with its regional homogeneity and relative natural equality of universities. Like the common law, however, it tended to produce flexible but tangled procedures. At the NCAA level, of which more later, it tends to produce jungle. Nevertheless, the problem is democratic in nature. No doubt an ideology both true and sufficient to the scope and variety of the problems would give better results in athletic as in national governance. But where is that counsel of perfection? Without it, better muddle along with good, mere, messy old human problems.

After recruiting ringers, which is the first, the second of the great cardinal sins in the recruitment of college athletes is improper or, in the wake of the rules, illegal inducement to choose one place in preference to others. In the trade they call that "buying them" and say of the athlete, "He was bought." A famous early case, often cited, can perhaps not be better put than it was by Robert H. Boyle in *Sport–Mirror of American Life:* "Yale lured James Hogan, a superb tackle, to New Haven at the turn of the century by giving him a suite in Vanderbilt Hall, free meals, a trip to Cuba, free tuition, a monopoly on the sale of scorecards, and the job as cigarette agent for the American Tobacco Company." As Yost said, nobody was then breaking rules; but the bizarre package of benefits wrapped together for Mr. Hogan suggests that Yale, as usual in those days, went all out and won. Won what? Why, the bidding war for the pleasure of Mr. Hogan's company for the span of a college generation. Bidding against what? Well, quite clearly offers which only a most ingenious parceling together of inducements could top. Offers by whom? Ah, who knows? But it wasn't Notre Dame or Texas or Southern Cal. Not then.

Did Walter Camp know about the Hogan deal? Officially, probably not; but it is humanly impossible to suppose that in actual fact he did not: in short, double standards had come into practice. That their multiplicity reproduced the plurality of standards customary in business and politics perhaps explains much. Was Hogan the only Bulldog with a deal? Not bloody likely. And, in the light of the bidding war implicit in Hogan's deal, was Yale's the only Ivy League team manned by stars recruited through improper inducement? Sure it was!

I do think that Yost and Camp and men like them undertook to comply with the rules once they had been formulated and honor pledged to them, though in saying that it is not necessary to suppose that nobody from Yale or Michigan ever fractured a rule. The Hogan case is so fascinating, so exactly illustrative of so much of the heart of the problem, that if it were not true you'd have to invent it. Hogan's package, so brilliantly, zanily constructed, ascends toward the stature of myth: it can stand for ten thousand others from Hogan to the as yet unknown scandal of 1980.

Hogan's story really was told by that Princetonian who would have traded an arm to be Hogan but had to settle for literary genius. Its name is *The Great Gatsby*. In the first place Hogan's package justifies Stephen Crane's generalization, "Every sin is the result of a collaboration." Not just Coach, and especially not just some poor, expendable fall guy of an assistant coach is ever responsible for a recruiting infraction. Athletes, parents, scholastic coaches and guidance counselors and superintendents, media people, fans, and community leaders collaborate. So do students and faculty and administrators, trustees and alumni. How many people must have helped put the ingredients into Hogan's deal? How much cash passed through how many hands? How many strings were pulled or debts of influence incurred or called in? Who came to owe what to whom and what was expected in return?

When you begin to ask questions like that, you approach one side of the very heart of the matter. For all he was deeply appealing in ways which have misled a few critics, F. Scott Fitzgerald's character "Gatsby" was both ersatz and a bum. But he was a bum with a genius for playing roles of achievement and self-deliverance and heroism and romance which must be older than fairy tales. Such dreams have deep roots, both beautiful and terrible, in American experience. They are in one sense of the essence of democracy, in another of the essence of snobbery. What is the story of "American aristocracy"?—"Three generations from shirt-sleeves to shirt-sleeves." But what comes in the middle?—high life.

It seems self-evident from the goodies on his Christmas tree that Mr. Hogan was no gentleman: think only of that trip to Havana. But what were Yale and its gentlemen teaching him? That, as the masses suppose and the media assure them, the life of "class" in America is that famous Fitzgerald party of unlimited affluence which never really ends, that green light to the orgiastic future which never goes out. To play a little variation on the famous theme by Fitzgerald and Hemingway, what is the difference between a poor boy with no character and a rich boy with no character? The rich bum has money. Was that the lesson Yale taught Hogan? If not, how in the premises did William Lyon Phelps teach him to be a Christian gentleman or Walter Camp teach him to be a democratic gentleman? Who taught him reality principles upon which, generalized as ingredients in a moral imperative, American culture could hope to survive? Or did they arrange with him to sell his talents for a college generation in the sunshine of the high life before he returned to the twilight natural to low, common life?

I really do not mean to harp on Yale. Show me a college or university where they have played the Big Game and I will show you a program where they have made deals of which Hogan's is only a classic, not even the primal example. The real issue is moral and looks to the problem of the use of affluence and the high life by Baker Street Irregulars, whether of the underground or fifth column, to recruit Big Game prospects. When it happens it is much too often an issue of class, the rich preying upon the poor. It becomes much too often the crime in actuality for which, falsely, Socrates was condemned to drink hemlock: the corruption of youth, in this case by introducing them to actual vice, or at least to conspicuous consumption, and encouraging them to believe that these are real and desirable values. There arises in the practice an element of the devil's bargain: young people are encouraged to rely upon the validity of attested principles of reality which are in fact false, which lead to moral disorientation and the death of the possibility of that which the great religions and philosophies unite in agreeing to be the good life.

Perhaps it is important to stipulate that "evidence which would stand up in court" is naturally hard to get in the world, far less the underworld, of intercollegiate athletics. Honest coaches tend, in self-protection, to log every contact made, every act of any sort, in recruiting every prospect. Yet it is patent that such things could be faked.

You cannot subpoena documents or witnesses, put witnesses under oath or cross-examine them or prosecute for perjury. Real due process is almost impossible. Further, no topic on earth is more a subject of whiskey-talk—brags, complaints and other lies—than recruiting; and whole books appear to have been founded upon consultations in bars.

As a faculty representative I passed through a period in which I was regularly the butt of charges that the rules and the faculty always punished Siwash and let the Red Raiders get away with murder. The typical conversation went:

> "Do you know what those bastards down in Springfield have done now?"
> "No. What?"
> "They've bought Joe Star's daddy a twenty-thousand-dollar cruiser to get him to go to Raider, and they've signed him. I know it for a fact. What are you going to do about it?"
> "Well, you know I could do a lot if I really had the evidence on paper. Would you write me a letter setting down the facts?"
> "You could, eh? Well, by God, it'll be on your desk Monday morning!"

No letter of just that sort ever came to my desk: vituperation and general complaint, yes; facts asserted and attested by a name signed at the bottom of a document of allegations, not once. There must have been fifty such conversations before the storm blew over.

And yet there can be no doubt about the factuality, sometimes voluntarily documented, even stipulated, by a repentant institution, of improper and illegal recruiting practices. Categorized in their thousands of cases, these would fall under a relatively few headings: explicit proffers of cash, gifts, or advantage—as opposed to tacit understandings; deals made with parents or guardians—as distinct to those made with boys; the shading off of "inducements" before matriculation by degrees of introduction, initiation, promise, continuation, and, for successes, escalation of excessive aid, luxuriant reward: "You get it if you make good at Lacustrine Tech."

What, specifically, are we talking about? The shopping list is impressive: (1) Family deals: new and better jobs for Dad or Mom or Bud or Sis; perhaps a new roof or the mortgage paid off; perhaps just cold cash. (2) Summer jobs for Joe Star, if not other people too, at prime wages: Blessed be Siwash, for theirs is the inside lane to the State Highway Department. (3) The advent into the life of the boy and his family of a cordial, infinitely helpful new friend, the "sponsor," to whose hospitalities and good offices there may seem to be no bottom, who becomes a pleasant Santa Claus for four years, and may take you into the firm thereafter. (4) The promise, or if it is not a promise the powerful implication that the path to professional or business success lies through the halls of Hedera College or the corridors of the University of Grosse Pointe. They may promise to get you into the great Magnolia Med. School, or you may only meet the cordial dean and a number of doctors who played ball for Magnolia. Perhaps they will tell you who will hire you after graduation, or perhaps they don't need to. When you have met all those presidents of banks or brokerage firms, all those vice presidents of mighty corporations who shake your hand and tell you they have a lot of other Athabascans in the firm and they're sure you'd love the old college too and you don't get the point, maybe you're too dumb to play anyhow.

At what points does an illegal inducement become an impropriety and shade off into a practice against which good morals could make no rule, in which common sense and respect for individual rights can find no impropriety? We do need to keep asking, as the late Commissioner William R. Reed kept pointing out, "What are the permissible practices?"

Certainly not gifts of great value or sweetheart deals on clothing or automobiles. Certainly not jobs for which there is pay but no work or in which there is lucrative pay for a jobholder unqualified to perform it. Not loans which everybody knows will never be repaid; and most especially not semantic juggles in which high rates of scholarship aid come to the athlete defined as not athletic aid because, so they say, "We grant no athletic aid."

Without pretending to psychoanalytic expertise, I suspect it might be fair to say that the most trying of the Irregulars must be somehow trapped at an "anal" level of development. Inquiry of almost any coach will bring the comment, "Yeah, we have one or two like that, too." His pattern is to invade a locker room when, perhaps forty-five minutes after a game, it has been opened to the usual flood of relatives, friends, old players, prospective recruits, and hangers on. His coming seems particularly likely after a loss, and what he does is circulate among players "laying on" each of ten or a dozen of them a twenty-dollar bill. His "sympathies" are irregular, unpredictable, as he deposits his little load now on one man, now another.

The act naturally embarrasses a player, who feels like a fool or a prig, an apostate from the cash nexus value and reward system if he refuses. But he feels humiliated and moved to cynicism when he accepts. In general, so identifying it in the language and perceptions of the culture of poverty, the player "takes his shit." The Yahoo who dropped it proves hard to control, his persistence apparently compulsive, and effective defenses against him difficult to devise. What in American culture with relation to college sports does he represent?

He infuriates coaches, who know, as the Yahoo knows, that he corrodes team and family relationships. His act is not at all the same as "getting into" the game or even "getting a piece of the action": it is too nearly autonomous for that. Does he represent something toward the far end, a bit of the psychopathology of the esthetics of losing? Or is his act a perversion of the Irregular's will to power? But no, not Yahoos, either.

Finally, not "high life" as by whomever defined or financed. No eager girls laid on whether for pecuniary or patriotic motives; no night-clubbing; no Lear Jet trips to hunting lodges or voyages on yachts or Kentucky Derby weekends—on the house.

Then, what is permissible? Does amateurism not demand that, just exactly that, nobody get anything at all? Well, if it does, there is now—and I believe never much was—any reason to take amateurism seriously. Permissible practices do not break rules—though rules writers had better take care that in the natural course of things it shall be possible to comply. Permissible practices let the life of the student athlete be collegiate and natural. Control must invade as few individual rights and privacies, it must wreak as little real injustice, as possible. Common hospitality, parties, favors, social life within the student body, the college town, the natural communities, constitute permissible practices. So do normal hometown relationships.

I am at variance with what gradually has become the thrust of NCAA regulations against the use of alumni in recruiting. I know you have to educate and organize your alumni to understand and be ready to comply with rules and to help police the wild Irregulars who menace all control. But I know from experience and observation that it is possible to do those things. And I feel that to sacrifice or outlaw alumni recruiting of student athletes is to destroy the most natural and valid, the most organic and trustworthy relations the prospective student athlete at home in his town can possibly have with any college. The effect at length is further to segregate and alienate the athlete from the processes of normal academic life.

From whom does any prospective student learn about a college, about the sort of people who go there, the sort of people it turns out, the whole complex and atmosphere of character, values, concerns, and traditions associated with it? In his town and most naturally, from the people who inevitably represent those things: they *are* Siwash. A college is a people factory, and alumni are its products. If a student goes to Siwash and in a normal course of life comes home to live, she or he will continue in special associations with Siwash alums for life. Trained, educated, sensitized, organized, local—they are almost the only valid recruiters.

I should not, of course, for that reason—nor because the rules compel certain invasions of personal rights and perpetrate certain sad injustices—refuse to obey them. I should seek to have them changed. For the letter and the spirit of compliance and of proper recruitment and aid of student athletes are important just as far as they control certain immoralities which produce great evils. Improper recruiting, excessive aid, and rules infractions miseducate the young, perverting the college into an academy for false values and crime. They corrupt coaches. And nowadays, however it was in the past, when the student athletes know the rules and have become sensitized to corruption and perversion, they tend to be cumulatively counterproductive for the corrupt coach.

I have heard John Pont, told by an Irregular that he would "buy Somebody for him," decline, saying: "If I let you give him that, what am I going to say to the rest of the squad?" Asked for illegal cash inducements, Pont has told young athletes in the presence of their importunate fathers, "Look, if I give you anything illegal, I own you— and you own me." The danger is that such will become a bargain between the right to coercion on one side and the threat of blackmail on the other. Rumor says that a series of just such incidents coming to a head destroyed a famous coach. He bought and bought and won and won his way right out of the game.

This coach attracted national attention by asserting to the media that, as soon as he jumped from his college coaching job to a professional team, he had no further responsibility for the couple of hundred rules infractions in his recruiting and aid of players the university and the NCAA were engaged in tracking down. He didn't work there anymore, he said. The situation strikes me as an exact example of the worst result in players, coaches, and academic communities of persistent irresponsibility, deceit, living by multiple standards and fragmentary rationalizations, trying to live by the code, "Winning cures everything." That result is moral disorientation, loss of the capacity to tell right from wrong, left from right, up from down in the moral world.

This coach enjoys the reputation of having "bought 'em" wherever he coached. Experienced watchers believe that he got away with a lot because, having other sources of income, he regularly invested his salary in illegal recruiting and aid. Yet perhaps it is still not so much the cool *aleator* who goes hog wild once moral disorientation strikes him. Let a man of good will and the inner assurance of good conscience, a moral man, be so routed by the pressures and terrors of Big Game coaching and so worked upon by the underground and by the fifth columnists in high places that he decides to strike the devil's bargain, and he may go off the deep end as a cheatin', lyin', wheelin' an' dealin' sonofabitch resembling nothing so much as a Viking baresarker, a man with a death wish. One such coach told me that he had faced fifty recruits, a few each Saturday after Saturday all one winter, and said: "Our deal is the full ride and fifty dollars cash a month, every month." It had to be a form of suicide.

It is well known that the same sort of thing can befall student athletes. Make a bum of a boy and he will play like one. Put enough of them together on a squad and they will use the power of blackmail to take over the family, displace the coach, ruin the program, lose, and get everybody fired in disgrace. The point-shavers of the great basketball scandals of a quarter of a century ago were only playing along with the "point-spread" mania of the media and the gamblers, not losing games. It was hard for them to see any harm in it. Wasn't everybody "shaving it" more or less? Suddenly federal judges were calling it crime, and some of the nation's most promising professional athletic careers were snuffed out. Even the survivors, who have made good other ways, carry deep scars. I wish I believed that their mentors in moral disorientation suffer with them. On the contrary, the commonest response in a mass academic community to being caught out and sanctioned for failures in athletic rules compliance and propriety is an outburst of righteous indignation, denial, vituperation, countercharges, and closing sympathetic ranks around the cheaters. Only a good coach lynching can be worse.

Neither the recruitment nor the regular administered grant-in-aid of the student athlete is intrinsically unusual or improper. There are valid justifications for both. Many an otherwise deprived youth would have been deprived of college, too, without them. Mr. James Michener has just publicly added his name to the list. Further, institutionalized through feasible and humane rules firmly enforced, recruitment and grant-in-aid procedures strengthen the control of intercollegiate athletics by the institutions and their agencies. They tend to organize the Irregulars, to force monies to come out face up on the table from underneath it, to achieve control through coach and player eligibility rather than through making examples.

The remedies for bad practices and their dreadful results may seem simple; but they demand the sacrifice of confining fan attitudes and contest esthetics to the arena and to game time. They demand good sense. They require the warm, active support of soundness. The academic community, its institutional instruments, and all its constituencies must provide active moral support for the good coach. It must provide moral and financial support for the good program and the sound tradition. Like players, the communities must behave like positive people.

WOMEN STUDENT ATHLETES

The true frontier of intercollegiate athletics in our times is sexual. There a revolution has long been churning in the deeps of American women's culture, altering emotions, images, hopes, intentions, beliefs. It has been longer operative than the radical sensibility—with its yen to believe that the revolution was imagined last night and must be perfected this morning—can permit itself to recognize. In the 1890s, with the rise of men's intercollegiate athletics, a "new woman," much commented upon, arose in the colleges. She went out of doors and got her face tanned. She rowed and sailed. She played tennis and golf and swam competitively. She joined basketball and field hockey teams and played for championships.

The Gibson Girl appeared with her clubs on the links. The Curtis Sisters and May Sutton and Eleanora Sears rose to national and international stature, blazing the trail which turned golden in the twenties for Trudy Ederle and Helen Wills and Glenna Collett. The women of the people arrived in the thirties with Babe Didrickson and, after World War II, Althea Gibson. During all that while, well-organized programs of intercollegiate competition for women rolled along throughout the country, and the secondary schools, though spottily, followed suit.

Much of that development was halted, perhaps thirty years ago, by a rise within the persons in control of women's intercollegiate athletics of a persuasion that competitiveness, though masculine, is not a feminine trait. Sheer altruism, gentleness, sweetness, and givingness, they said, represent the female psyche. Though sound exercise and fun do girls good, they argued, competition perverts the nature of womanhood. Therefore departments of physical education for women generally suppressed their competitive athletic enterprises, disbanded their teams, declined to send representatives to meets and tournaments.

Having lived most of my domestic life outnumbered by females in the house, I felt doubts about the theory that competition and aggressiveness are foreign to the feminine nature. I mourned the loss of women's teams and traditions of competitive programs, feeling that women often suffer grave adult deprivations from not having learned how to lose when young. If you are lucky when young, you survive the humiliations of failing at games and looking bad and being jeered and mocked and bullied and put down. Boys who don't survive that universal, inevitable experience sometimes live their refugee ways into serious intraphysic difficulties in consequence. If one perseveres, it may be a long time before he succeeds or wins—or even wins acceptance. If he has talent or desire or heart, he may be compelled, as a pup is magnetized toward the big dogs, to go and play with the big boys, the older ones. There, though he will develop faster, he will lose for a long time before he learns to win. Nonetheless, if he can carry the process far enough, he will find himself at the top. To get there he will have learned, in large part, how to win by losing. And he will know, above all else, that you can risk and lose and keep coming back, that the realities run deeper than the score, that, though winning is better, that's all it is. Proportionately, more men than women know these things in our population, and the men are happier and freer for knowing.

Though nowadays the philosophies have largely shifted within departments of women's physical education, it seems clear to me that issues remain: in a sports context, *are* women different from men? or are they, allowing for obvious skeletal, muscular, endocrine and secondary physical differences, psychically the same? Ought they to compete head-to-head? If real differences appear, are they by nature or nurture, innate or culturally created? Much depends in these as in other matters on faith and the will to believe, on sensibility and intuition. Even if you decide, as I do, that philosophically the best bets are that women are here to stay, that the time is past for deciding that they should have equal opportunities with men for self-realization, that we ought to try acting as if the human oneness and likeness are more important and decisive than differences, you have not solved many problems. Human reality is cultural and comes by nurture. We know much about the vulnerability and fragility of cultures, and the human catastrophe of the loss of culture. We know too much at firsthand in our time about the humane, cultural consequences of the famous observation on the behavior of a Roman army: "They created a desert and called it victory."

So what is the answer? I think it is to look from ideological combat to behavior and practice and try experimenting, try as many sensible and sensitive ways as can be imagined. In the colleges, above all, I'd encourage and support the women student athletes to work out their programs, possibly to invent their own games. The truth is that nothing else will work anyway. If you look from philosophy to behavior, it seems obvious enough that certain problems in intercollegiate athletics for women are going to be internal to the programs, others external. Let's begin by considering the internal sort first. Though the categories are more convenient than either necessary or mutually exclusive, it seems useful to consider the internal problems of the future as (1) definitional, (2) developmental, (3) professional.

By definitional I mean the problem of models, the question of just what kind of athletic program the student-athlete, the coach and her staff, the responsible administrative officer and her staff, and the several university constituencies may all conceive themselves to be engaged or concerned in. Are the men's "varsity" programs and the Big Game—implying "all-star," implying recruited and aided student-athletes governed by the rules of conferences and national associations, implying high pressure competition, greatly gifted coaches, big money, and massive public attention—the right future model for women? Many well-informed women's administrators think not. If not, is the model of the informal, low-pressure, self-organized and self-determined "club" sport (admitting the grest differences among them) the better model? Or should the women hybridize varsity with club models for a vigorous new bloom?

Otherwise, is it likely that the feminization of sport—or of any other human institution—will, can, or ought to produce a novelty, something in human life never seen before? If, as American thought generally demands, you accept the idea of a universe and a culture both open-ended so that novelty can occur, it follows that the novel be unforsee-able, unimaginable until present and perceivable. Does it also follow that males disqualify themselves from presuming to intuit feminine novelty? Again, may be, the question issues into a matter of faith. Novelty has occurred before and must again. But how many human hearts have been burned-over since the first prophet led his folk to the first hilltop in their ascension robes and the night passed and the ordinary sun rose on the common day and the millenium first failed?

What I call developmental might almost as well fall under defini-tional: yet a somewhat variant issue appears if you ask not, abstractly, what we must achieve, but, more pragmatically, what assumptions we might make about how to change, step by step, from what we are doing now to something better. Should women's sports develop from the recreational toward the competitive? or from the participatory toward the championship? Or is the answer rather both/and than either/or?

Most particularly, what about excellence? One obvious answer lies in the vein of "in comparison with what?" Was Jim Thorpe greater than Jim Brown? Was Althea Gibson greater than Evonne Goolagong? Nobody will ever know. But we do know that Mark Spitz was a lot better than Johnny Weissmuller, that times come down and weights and distances go up in sports where measures are objective. Well, how high must "up" be? Dare we try for the utmost, the best in women's intercollegiate athletics? But dare we not? From the men's point of view I should say that these remain problems both vexing and not readily resolvable. *Can* things be different for women?

From one point of view, it looks axiomatic that the future of athletics for women, perhaps especially woman student athletes, depends much, in its potential to satisfy and interest, upon creativity. We need attractive, cohesive, truly competitive sports designed, presumably by women, for women. As in certain kinds of dancing women make men look out of place (and vice versa) so in certain sports. Women have made particular gymnastic events theirs. The same for particular styles in figure skating. No doubt I overlook something. But at most of the games invented by and developed for the other sex, women produce inferior performance and look rather awkward at it. When you think of the reasons why the males do better, one obvious answer leaps out: those are by origin their games, with centuries if not millenia behind them.

Though women cannot now invest a century, why need they? Everybody knows, with a wealth of data sufficiently exact, "how it is done." Basketball "took off" within the lifetime remaining to the adult who had the idea. Women's athletics need ideas and the freedom to experiment.

Obviously enough, these, like other human problems, will be resolved variously, pluralistically, rather sloppily, sometimes not at all. But as we all work at them our efforts will involve us in what appear to me to be some rather ominous professional, that is to say, structural problems. Issues of this sort easily become personal, even petty: but that does not make them easier to smooth away. Much of the thunder and lightning of national and international conflict, sad to say, much of the imperial warfare among the federations, the NCAA, the AAU, the USOC, and the world Olympic movement boil down to questions like who gets to make the trips? or pick the coaches? or tell the athletes what to do? or swell around and sit at the high table and hobnob with the nabobs? Do you have to be a hereditary nobleman? or a commissar? or a millionaire? and if any of these, what is the date of your commission?

To start near our own level, should the women's advisor or the woman professor give way to a coach? should Coach Bryant (who does not) or Doc Counsilman (who does) both teach college classes? In either case, should there come to be female counterparts to Bryant, and should *they* teach? Since there will have to be an executive head for women's intercollegiate athletics, should that officer be female or male? If, as seems likely, she will get the job, should she be a dean in a school or a director in a department of athletics? And if the latter, what should her line relationships be to the director of athletics?

It seems probable to me that developmental forces will carry women's intercollegiate athletics a lot farther toward the model of men's varsity programs than they have gone before. Such developments will differentiate the outstanding woman athlete more than before, push her closer to the pattern of unlimited competition for total self-realization and achievement, encourage her to demand better coaching, encourage the coach to demand status equivalent to that of comparably devoted and gifted men, and tend to draw the structural program of women's intercollegiate athletics out of the academic departments and toward membership either within or beside the departments of athletics which presently exist to carry on the programs of men's varsity competition.

If, finally, the professional, structural status and conditions of the people who compete in and conduct women's athletic programs change, there will arise a serious question whether the determination of the present executive heads to keep clear of the men's conferences and associations can succeed. Are women sufficiently different from men to avoid the snares of corrupt practice in the recruitment and aid of student-athletes? I fear for the practical consequences of some of the present rules of women's organizations. Will a Big Ten or Pac-10 or NCAA championship long continue to seem un-whatever-it-is to the woman athlete, the woman coach or director? And if, at last, any considerable part of such development occurs, can the women create and keep to themselves an athletic empire not subject to the ordinary instrumentalities of academic control? I do not think so, and I suppose that no such thing ought to occur. In the long run and whatever the true and happy differences or novelties, women's intercollegiate athletics will tend toward the general control of, let us say, the university athletics committee. Might that some day bring us a female faculty representative or director of athletics? It might well, indeed.

In all these connections I think it is worth reporting on a historic meeting in which I was privileged to sit when, within the oldest and strongest conference in the country, the group of heads of women's programs sat for the first time with the Joint Group of Directors and

Faculty Representatives and then with the faculty representatives alone. All three groups were attempting to agree on recommendations to be made to the Council of Presidents for a response to the obscure demands of the "Title IX" legislation of the Congress as it might apply to intercollegiate athletics. Among the women, all mature, experienced, thoroughly responsible professionals, it transpired, unanimity existed on only one point: they thought "Title IX" an unmitigated catastrophe, counterproductive to the welfare and prosperity of programs for women's intercollegiate athletics.

In the truest tradition of the conference, they reported that the existent modes of institutional governance for women's athletics ran the gamut of possibilities. At one place they were totally integrated into one structure with the men; at another two perfectly separate and parallel structures had been built; the rest, more or less developed, lay between those poles. Discussion was passionate and sincere, the women arguing that nothing ought to be imposed upon them, that they needed help in being heard, that they had a right to be "equal but different." They asserted a real difference in philosophy from the men but did not say what it was. When they turned to behavior, they confessed that there were deep differences of opinion among them and that they felt almost desperately the need for time to work things out.

They seemed clearer about what they do not want. They wish, decidedly, not to lose their opportunity for feminine identity. They will not be coopted by the conference or the NCAA. A majority feels doubtful that at the institutional level they should risk identity in integration. Some of them pleaded eloquently for the right to be different and sought support in that. Others demurred. The net impression was that of active, well-versed intelligences dealing sensitively with difficult and obscure issues.

The group of men was not less impressive, with perhaps a hundred collective years of experience in the field and including in its membership three who have been NCAA presidents. They accepted the plea for not trying to resolve issues prematurely, despite pressure from the Council of Presidents. But their members who had served on joint committees with the women spoke their sense of difficulties. One said he doubted that circumstances or outside forces would brook much delay. The law, he said, and internal institutional impulses toward neatness and symmetry had to be reckoned with; and there are forces at work in society which many misunderstand. Women must consider whether they really can evade the athletic logic of the culture, whether they too do not need the protection of effective external controls like the structure of the conference. Further, he urged, they must consider the likelihood of their destroying the apparatus of academic control, both internal and external, for men's athletics if the women and their rules hold aloof. What court, for instance, could now uphold in equity a rule of eligibility which restricted male but not female student athletes?

Another laid out his sense of the real alternatives. They were, he said, in behavior to: (1) do nothing: cool it (but time is running out); (2) develop women's programs differently from men's (but "separate but equal" is in the worst possible constitutional odor—it is a dubious possibility, no matter how philosophically attractive); (3) homogenize the programs; (4) "create something" structural and see who joins. The presidents, he concluded, could be told that these are the options. In the last analysis, a federal bureau or the courts might have to decide what to regard as adequate.

The question, the only real one, is what the women student athletes are going to decide they honestly want to do. They are fairly entitled to equal amenities, services, protection, access to facilities, and support—if they can decide what they want it for. But they are also fairly entitled to say that they do not know yet and need the time to work it out. Why should we not create programs of possibility for women? They could be temporary, trial modes to let historical developments flesh out or fade out or evolve creatively from them. Among Old Blue women, does anybody really want to play field hockey again? or do they want ice hockey? or bandy? Do they want to play hard ball? or give a damn for soft ball? Do they really want to respond to the dream of rough sports for women? how many could make the varsity golf or tennis, swimming or diving squads? What shall we know until we find out a lot ot things like this?

The first thing you hear is that nobody can afford it, which is nonsense. A lot of coaches could add an experimental women's program to their duties and enjoy it and still not work very hard. Among the realities about money are choices. As I count them, six athletic activities ordinarily take place on our campuses. They are: (1) varsity men's intercollegiate competition; (2) women's sports, intercollegiate; (3) "club sports" (men's, women's: are there, seriously, any "mixed" sports?), intercollegiate; (4) intramurals; (5) activities courses; (6) recreation. For most purposes it is useful to say that the last two are either academic or informal and paid for out of academic or general budgets. Intramurals are generally supervised out of academic budgets. But the first three are all intercollegiate. Ultimately they ought to come under the control of the athletics committees, and they ought to be supported out of the budgets of the directors of athletics. We have them and know that we must continue to have them while they develop along lines which will tend toward the destructive unless their development can be controlled. If, in doing that, it should turn out that funds had to be found, through budgets or endowments, for men's varsity and women's varsity (should they come to that) athletics and club sports, a foresighted university would save itself a lot of pain and penalty if it quietly got up the money.

Our business, even with our most external constituencies, is the best reality, no matter how poor it may seem, we can find. But it does seem to me that one can glimpse advancing reality in the area of relations between athletics for men and athletics for women. I think of the ex-coach for whom I bore a certain responsibility who felt a rude shock. He was committed by contract to compete against a team which featured a coed. "Foul!" he cried. If his young gentlemen had to play a girl, he reasoned, they could never compete at their normal level of excellence: it would be cruel, discourteous, unthinkable. And besides, he urged, think how humiliating it would be if she won. He changed jobs not long thereafter. For, as the late Theodore Bardacke pointed out in one of the unique pieces which used to grace *San Diego Magazine*, matters do move. At San Diego City College they turned up some kind of woman athlete. But Bardacke should tell his tale:

Robin is a pert, five-foot, three-inch bomb who explodes on a tennis court. Her male opponents from other colleges don't quite know how to handle her. A four-year college who schedules State in football came into town for a match and Mr. Bacon listed Robin to play the number-one position. When he presented the seeding to the visiting coach, he looked up at Bacon and asked, What kind of a name is Robin for a boy?"
"Oh, didn't I tell you? Robin is a girl."
"She's a what?"
"She's a girl, a first-rate tennis player."
"You're kidding Bob. I don't think my first man will play her."
"That's OK, just default the match."
"Well. Well, let's ask him."
The coach called over his number one player and asked him if he'd object to playing a girl.
"Is she some kind of an Amazon?"
"No," interjected Bob, "She's 5'3" and weighs 110 pounds."
"Ah, come on coach. It would be too embarrassing."
"OK, embarrass her. But you *must* play her or default the match."

The score was 6-0, 6-0. The match lasted only 29 minutes and the number-one visiting man won only eight points.

Citrus College, a conference opponent, arranged a male motorcycling streaker. Robin didn't even look up. And so it goes.

Soon the scream will be heard. "Break up Robin and her merry men."

BLACK STUDENT ATHLETES

See "Student Athletes and Where They Come From" and "Women Student Athletes."

In one important sense there ought to be nothing more to say. The black student athlete must be treated by and relate to the academic and athletic communities exactly the same as the nonblack, certainly not disadvantageously. But in other at least equally important senses the black person has to be treated differently. Facts, the realities of circumstance, demand it. Yet at the same time careful calculations of effect have to be practiced not to set black persons apart, alienated from the family, in academic or athletic ghettos. It is a situation, unavoidable in the wake of a tragic history and, in the fact of present injustice, loaded with paradox. It requires the exercise of the finest possible discrimination in favor of the black student athlete by the whole of academe and especially by the leadership of the intramural black community.

Black athletes, like other black students, are entitled to a special portion of "the old college try"—precisely because their case is difficult. I did not appreciate fully the rueful saying that "race prejudice will get you coming and going" until, in the midst of a slowly successful fight to get full acceptance for blacks within an athletic establishment, a first-rate young man came to me with a new dilemma. His sociology professor had offered him a self-confessedly arbitrary and political choice: though he had earned a B, he could quit his championship team in public protest against "black exploitation" and get an A; he could keep his athletic loyalty and take an F as a course grade.

But what the college owes to black students are the tools of competency. They need to be equipped to move, learn, succeed in the mainstream beyond both the culture of poverty and that of the black experience. They must, if necessary, be removed from the culture of poverty yet not alienated from black culture. They are bound to suffer more or less culture shock—from which the athletic experience can

186

often, by the way, provide some shelter. They must be properly discriminated for.

About one issue regarding the black student athlete I have changed my mind during the past ten years. You can hear indignant objection to the "exploitation" of blacks by schools which take them in, play out their eligibility, and send them on their way without degrees or salable educations. Is that in fact immoral? intolerable? I used to think so. Professor David Baker, among others, gave me pause.

As everybody knows, black athletes frequently come from within or from just at the edges of American poverty. Suppose, now, you have a young man athletically gifted; you could add, because it is not infrequently true, that he has survived to make himself imaginable for college because he has the requisite personality endowment—of the sort attested by Floyd Little, for example. His family background is deprived, his schooling the product of blight, prejudice, and conflict. Does it then become a crime of exploitation to bring him to a college to play sports, travel, associate with that community for four years even if you know he cannot honestly graduate? You hear it said so, loud and often.

But what is the real alternative? Will it do to say, "Sorry, son, history has given you the short and dirty end of the stick. Go back to your ghetto or canebrake?" Dave Baker asks, "Why not give them all we can?"

I find that I cannot arrive at anything but a rule of "best judgment," knowing it is bound often to be wrong. Some of the best coaches—and not for cynical reasons, because the effects are devastating when you are wrong—agree. Setting aside, of course, the cases about which there is small doubt, you have to judge: Who can obviously not hack it? Who, in spite of formal evidences to the contrary, might very well send down strong psychic roots into his education and exploit it decisively? Who, though he probably can never catch up scholastically, might well profit personally from his years on campus so richly that his life will be changed for the better anyhow?

I should feel amply justified in an institution's accepting a certain number of solid risks. The national need is so great. The alternatives for the man not taken are so bleak. The risk and losses, though real, to the institution are so survivable: these would stand as the grounds of my justification for not "throwing the book" at the gifted but marginal black athlete. Would I do the same for nonathletes? My dear sir or madam, as the case may be, every institution of higher education, the federal government powerfully pushing, does not the same but much more for black nonathletes all the time.

But I would no more let a black athlete be an athletic tramp than I would let anybody else. Interestingly, the one unique and most encouraging black athletic commission in the country heartily agrees.

In 1972 the Intercollegiate Conference of Faculty Representatives (Big Ten) took a vote of its controlling body, the faculty representatives, to establish a Special Advisory Commission "composed of black distinguished persons with a background in athletics," following that in 1974 by the appointment of Dr. Charles D. Henry, former chairman of the Physical Education Department of Grambling College, as an assistant commissioner. The members of the Special Advisory Commission are weighty persons indeed, and Henry was well known as, among other things, a formidable debater and leader in black interests in the NCAA.

Their early recommendations, which have largely been implemented, looked in two directions. Though they did not use the term, they proposed to "blackwash" both the institutional apparatus of conference members and the conference machinery. That meant getting more black members on institutional athletics committees or councils, in departments of athletics offices and posts, as coaches, trainers, officials, cheerleaders. Perhaps more surprisingly, they proposed to upgrade the conference academic requirements for eligibility to compete in spite of the fact that they were already stiffer than general national requirements. They also wanted a regular fifth year of grants-in-aid for students short of hours but without unused eligibility. But they insisted that the student athlete earn it academically.

At that moment, Big Ten eligibility rules required progress toward a degree year by year, showing at least promise of attaining the normal goal. What the work of the Special Advisory Comission secured was a change by the faculty representatives, effective for students enrolling "on or after June 1, 1974." The change establishes requirements for eligibility to compete which make it impossible for a student athlete to survive on "Mickey Mouse" and random "snap" courses. He must be making "progress in a program of studies through which" he "can qualify for a baccalaureate degree within no more than five years." Every year he must be substantially closer in prescribed numbers of hours of credit applicable to that degree and in "cumulative grade average." Failing either in any year, he cannot compete. If he continues making prescribed progress through his first four years but has exhausted his eligibility to compete, he is still eligible for a fifth year of a full grant-in-aid in order to complete the degree. That is a major, pioneering clarification and, so far as I know, still unique to that conference which first availed itself of some of the resources of expertise from its own black alumni who combined athletic with post-athletic career distinction.

THE ATHLETIC DORMITORY

Integrate it.

CONTROL: INTERNAL

As a fascinated college president watcher of thirty years' standing, I've observed that surprisingly often the best thing to do with too tough a problem is to put it on the back of the stove and let it simmer until it steams itself tender or the needful ingredients come to hand to make it right. The method works for a lot of hard cases, but it does not work for Big Game athletics: the damn thing will blow up every time. Nothing but regular attention by creative people who care can control the situation in college athletics, and then barely. It will not wag along or go away, and it cannot be controlled by emergency action after the lid blows off.

As this book has tried to make plain, what is going on in and around and behind the Big Game is all more complex than anybody realizes. And it's nitroglycerine, because it reaches deep toward the intrapsychic and cultural roots of our people and the behavior it elicits is largely irrational. I was once more sanguine about the ease of control than I am. Perhaps you have to be a little naive to try to buck the principalities and powers of fanhood, but I hope and trust not.

It is, of course, disconcerting to be deep in commitment to academic control and then discover that your president is an "Irregular" or that some of the trustees are fifth columnists; but it has happened. I once heard of a trustee who, without seeking the permission of the other institution's president or director, without consulting with his own president or even his colleagues, put in a call to a neighboring football coach and offered him the post of combined director and coach, at more than the combined salaries of the incumbents and without regard to their contracts. Perhaps he just wanted "to make something happen" as they say.

The best resource available to a president who must control his intercollegiate athletics will always be considered resoluteness in support of his own positive people. Coaches, directors, faculty representatives, deans of students, registrars who carry the president's word for sound control can win it for him, most of the time against the gates of hell. Meeting fanaticism with humor, exploitation with humanity, chicanery with intelligence, alienation with faith in academic missions, the president can prevail through his people. He cannot do it alone because he cannot and must not afford the energy taken from more central, imperative duties. But he can win with his own team. I don't think there is any other way.

To do that requires the same attention to assembling your people and making support evident as the accomplishment of any other mission. The great difference is that success in controlling athletics is indeed a journey, not a destination. The president has to find people he can trust to do the job until they need help and then come for the help as soon as they see they will need it. The only good fires are those which never get out of hand, and he has to be available and prepared to respond like a fireman when an alarm comes in. And he had better reconcile himself to the expectation that it will come less frequently, less urgently, in proportion to his team's success at fire prevention.

Though everybody's tendency to play the fan at inappropriate times and places, to romanticize the Big Game and oscillate between romance and cynicism, tempts us to opposite impressions, there is nothing mysterious or sinister about the instruments of control. As a job of work it must be done as a novel or a symphony is written—one piece at a time like a man sawing a cord of wood, except that in this case the woodpile is never finished. Patience with unending and exasperating detail will win through if it is governed by sound design. But too many of the existing instruments "just growed." Too many represent little Sargasso Seas of the compromised and defeated wrecks of once passionate or panicky reforms. But steady, effective, applicable instruments are what we need. Stability and continuity are everything.

To prevent fires we need the right instruments. First and last, of course, these must be persons of intrinsic quality: it is no job for hacks or toadies. Next, perhaps surprisingly, we need a good, strong, well-planned, and warmly conducted organization for the Irregulars.

Finally, we need an intramural and academic commission—call it committee, council, board in control, or anything—to work at the center and act as the court of last resort.

Hard experience has taught that the best way to handle the Irregulars is the same as John Adams's design for the United States Senate. Organize them into groups where they will check and balance and police each other, where you can get at them to educate and restrain them, where they can safely ventilate. Encourage them to pool the money they want to give and pour the pools into the Siwash Foundation, where its expenditure can be checked and accounted for. Let them organize and work in support of alma mater rather than wander to and fro, up and down the earth, seeking whom they may devour; it is one more function for the great American principle of association. Under many a colorful heraldic or heroic name, such organizations raise impressive sums in support of athletic grants-in-aid and latterly toward endowments for athletics programs which go far, and promise to go much farther, toward freeing the Big Game from commercial reliance on "the gate." Adams was right. Uncontrolled, the Irregulars have a history of raising hell with intercollegiate athletics which would waken the competitive instincts of Attila the Hun. Channeled, their energies can turn many a useful academic as well as athletic wheel.

As to the ultimate and inward commission, it is easier to say what you would want it to accomplish than how best to design it. That the design must fit the traditions and needs of the given college accounts for wide differences among the instruments around the country that work fairly well. That none works so well as it should signifies the same thing as the fact that many of them are in process of change: the stresses just now are terrific.

It pays to remember that the structural aim of the commission is to integrate athletics into the academy, keep them organic and in the family like such other expressions of student life as music, theater, journalism, societies fraternal, honorary, intellectual, or student government, even academic departments. In our time, success in the design of the best possible instrument for securing that aim depends on a nice equilibrium of forces. The name of the game is balance: to mobilize, educate, lead, and protect a coalition of everybody. We are compelled to try to accommodate, balance, discount, socialize, co-opt, and institutionalize diverse, sometimes clashing interests. Worse yet, the "interests," however loud and bitter the face they may turn toward others, are plural, full of contest and indeterminacy within themselves.

Providing them the means of mutual expression and appropriate influence is a job which could not be done if it were not necessary. It can't in fact be done: we have only to try as hard as we can without sacrificing function to the complexity of means.

I have known it to be necessary to point out to the president that he must not permit the presidential interest and responsibility to be compromised. So far as possible, he and his administrative officers would be wise to have policies but sit above the battle. Nobody administrative above the level of the director and his coevals like the dean of students or the registrar ought, ideally, to be involved in the daily conduct of athletics. That permits a president and trustees the luxuries of Olympian detachment—until all the instruments fail.

Traditionally, three interests found representation in committees on athletics: those of the department, the faculty, the alumni. In the 1960s, quite properly, students demanded formal participation and won it. However diverse, these represent natural population within the academic family and have the advantages which arise from being pluralistic and accommodative themselves. But the temper and recent history of the times have thrust forward other sorts of interests: for instance, feminist, ethnic, and ideological (radical, conservative—and middling in many shades). They have to be balanced both in and out.

From a simpler time I wrote the following letter to the late William R. Reed, whom I thought a great person, because he had asked for suggestions relative to a paper to be prepared for a National Association of Collegiate Directors of Athletics convention:

Dear Bill:

In reply to your query about thoughts for NACDA concerning "Needs For an Athletics Committee," I guess I'd say that I'm sure a Committee is a big pain in the neck that no Director needs—if his program never gets into any kind of trouble. But of course I'd only be half serious about that, because I think a good Committee could make a contribution even to that ideal Department in which nothing ever goes wrong.

First and last I think the use of the Committee is to be a bridge. It keeps open communication to the faculty and its instruments of participation in University government. It's also a safety valve, letting the steam of prejudice and passion blow back and forth from the coaches and players on one end to the faculty fan *and* the faculty hostile on the other end. In this way it can give a great deal of support, even protection, to the Director in the middle.

Less dramatically, a good Committee serves as a consulting board for the Director, or the President, even the trustee, as well as the professor and the student with an athletics problem. The best troubles are the ones that never quite happen, and some tough ones can get headed off at the bridge-head if there is somebody concerned but disinterested (with nothing professional in it for him) to talk to. And of course a Committee is a great place for floating trial balloons: an idea that seemed good but won't work, a question so knotty you can't quite see how it really goes, can come before the Committee with no harm done. In a good Committee you can consult know-how, contacts, and know-what that nobody could pay for.

Any time, but especially in a crunch, of course, the collective prestige of a good Committee is also invaluable. If the right people speak up in the crucial meeting, the day is won. You have them, and they are uniquely prepared, if you have the Committee and it has done its work.

Implicit, of course, all along is the idea of "the *good* Committee." It has to have first-class people, of real weight, wisdom, and academic prestige— with the real respect of the whole academic community. They have to be intrinsically able and well experienced in academic committee work and academic politics. Most essentially, they have to be genuinely interested in intercollegiate athletics. Give people like that terms long enough so the Director can educate them in the realities, and you've got an ally and a resource worth its weight in platinum.

Good luck with your talk!

The assumption basic to that account was that the instrument ought to be mainly a faculty commission. I still believe that, but with a sense that matters have become less simple. For one thing, the events of 1967-72 largely cost the faculties everywhere their credit, even in their own eyes, as competent for institutional governance. Though they are gradually recovering both reputation and composure, I do not expect to see the situation as of, let us say, 1962 again. Nevertheless, I should still tell our metaphorical president that he can entrust his presidential interests and those of the Department of Athletics to no better hands. None exist. Properly selected and educated, women and men of the faculty must constitute and must exercise the powers, essentially diplomatic and judicial, of the central instrument and court of last resort, the means of academic control of intercollegiate athletics.

In the conduct of practical affairs professors are often rather timid folk: that is why they became professors, and the life permits them to shun conflicts. But anybody who thinks they are not competitive and aggressive simply does not know the often relentlessly Darwinian facts or the sometimes startlingly Byzantine facts about the academic struggle for promotion, preferment, celebrity, money, and power. An arrived "university man" (no few among whom are female) is the survivor of at least three hard schools. And they have tenure. It is hard to frighten people like that and a bad idea to threaten them. They can take high degrees of heat off the president or director who can say, "Well, you know I'd like to; but you know the faculty!" Or even, "Well, but those goddam professors. . . ." And no harm done.

For these and other reasons the faculty representative or chairman ought, at least in the president's office, to stand at parity with the director. And among those other reasons perhaps the most compelling is that, as all experience shows, the one true method of academic control governs *eligibility*. It governs the eligibility of players to compete, receive aid, represent the college; and the eligibility of coaches to coach, to recruit, to belong to the community, and to represent the college; and the eligibility of directors to make contracts and other commitments; and of directors and faculty representatives to represent the college. Finally, in a meaningful conference, or the NCAA, it plays the basic institutional role in determining who is eligible to belong and worthy of competition.

In proportion as the academic instrument wields these powers, not absolutely (nobody at all possesses absolute or arbitrary power, or can, in a good academic community), you have control. I repeat that decisive faculty weight in the commission must make it in the last analysis an instrument of faculty control. But we do have to balance in everybody else. Good "university women" serve at least as well as men—if you can find those not compromised by conflicting interests (on the whole, Department of Physical Education people tend to be compromised) who are willing to make a costly investment in college sports. Ethnic minorities probably have to be overrepresented in proportion to their numbers in the academic population; and that's fine insofar as the individual professor, bombarded by demands to "represent," can bear it. But how legitimately and justly to accommodate student interests and rights I have found problematical.

In the first place, the students who most need and deserve representation and its benefits but are least likely to get them are the actual athletes, men and women, but especially the Big Game competitors and auxiliaries. Students, an inherently transient population, move naturally through undergraduate careers from obscurity to a brief, exhausting blaze of glory and extinction. However loaded with prizes and honors, a senior in the spring has become an undergraduate nonperson. As the Romans spoke of the dead: "He was." Further, the discovery I made as a sophomore presents itself to everyone interested in "student government." It is hard to find anything really to govern; nobody can afford the homework necessary for even minimal participation in the realities; it tends to be a charade. So Stu Gov people incline to fill the slots in interesting commissions with themselves and each other if they can. It is hard to identify the right representatives.

I incline to think that the ideal solution for problems of this sort is the organization of a parliament of student body athletic interests which should elect student representatives to the ultimate and authoritative commission. Let the Women's Athletic Association, the Lettermen's Club, the Band, the cheerleaders, the Boosters' Club, the federation of club sports, or any other such body with solid athletics existence, send proportional representatives to a Student Athletics Commission and the student members of the commission come from that body.

Advisory to the central instrument, too, I would have in the best of all possible worlds an instrument of student athlete personnel affairs advisory to the commission in matters of athletic eligibility. Amid all the vortices of pressure and passion, with the media helplessly avid to exploit, the protection the academic community gives to all students against the consequences of misdemeanors and rebellious conduct needs to be doubly sensitive and just and skilful in dealing with athletes. Most student trouble with the authorities gets little or no public attention. Even deaths and suicides are, usually quite properly, made so little of that many good people think, erroneously, that football is statistically a significant killer of college youth.

Let athletes be reported, even in total error, to be involved in scandal, however, and you never hear the end of it. In Bream, New Mexico, for instance, a bumbling district attorney broke a story (as he confessed, he was trying to get into the legislature) on a nonexistent drug ring and announced that among the peddlers he had identified one of the stars of Sunfish State's great tennis team. As it turned out, there not only was no ring, there was not even anybody of that name on the tennis squad and never had been. But the story made the wire services, appeared in papers all over the country and went into clipping files. The correcting facts got grudging play in the Bream papers and made fillers on the back pages of the *State Times*. For years thereafter occasional authoritative references were made to "the drug problem in Sunfish tennis."

Because it happens more or less that way all the time, it proves hard to treat student athlete disciplinary problems with an even hand. If you don't protect them, they'll be crucified. If you protect them too much you will find yourself in danger of becoming an accessory to crime: every once in a while, to be honest, real gangsterism will pop up among athletes, as among other students. But there is always also the danger of overcompensating and getting trapped in the news industry game. I think everybody needs the protection of judicial decision by the ultimate commission. But I think too that advisory to it, referring cases to it for decision when warranted and candidly reporting to it the cases not referred, should be a mixed and balanced committee on student athlete personnel matters made up of student dean and security personnel, students, faculty, athletics administration, and coaching personnel. In such balance is relative safety and justice, and the problems are severer than most people, including most presidents, know. That, too, is academic control.

CONTROL: EXTERNAL

See "Noble Experiments."

The power of competition in American sport and culture exerts the thrust of hydraulic pressure. No institution could long resist it alone. President Theodore Roosevelt acted from clear perception in promoting the founding of the NCAA. A few "independents" manage to get by with diplomatic relations actually but not openly formalized (and therefore always vulnerable).

A conference or NCAA relationship is in essence that very American thing, a social contract. In every such there is that degree of naiveté which Thomas Paine caught to perfection in his charming image of the fine summer's day when mankind met beneath a convenient tree to invent government. Nevertheless, the precedent stands at the center of American good faith—the Constitution of the United States is a self-declared social contract. Furthermore, a contract is a contract: and a college or university ought to be a gentleman in preference to a fink. Finally, as too many presidents in the past have seemed to discover with surprise, conferences, however simple, have teeth. They base themselves on mutual agreement to follow mutually adopted agreements. The ultimate penalty is separation: if you don't obey the rules they won't play you.

The founding fathers supposed any yeoman or shopkeeper rational and moral enough to understand and keep the social contract. A great institution of the higher learning ought to be equal to the same obligation. A squirming, finagling, disingenuous president trying to "stonewall" proved infractions and regularly assessed sanctions may be engaged in "good politics." But he is committing bad citizenship by diminishing the force and credit of academic control everywhere. And experience suggests that the politics seldom really work.

COSTS

Contrary to popular impression, the cost crunch in college sports of which much, if not too much, has been made in recent years, did not catch administrators of athletics programs by surprise. Leading directors, including some of the most prosperous in the country like Dick Larkins of Ohio State and Fritz Crisler of Michigan, had apparently foreseen it for years before they began to sound the alarm during the summer of 1964. The historical roots of the present crisis are worth tracing. There is much to be learned about certain actualities within the world of intercollegiate sport as well as about the present situation.

The Big Game programs with the big stadia, winning traditions, and sold-out capacity rode high in the 1950s. They were economic empires with money to invest by the millions in facilities, in the support of small, expensive sports, in the support of intramural programs and departments of health, physical education, and recreation. Between their access to public enthusiasms and their wealth, they tended to deal from positions of power and privacy, snapping their fingers under the noses of critics, and operating with increasing independence as they drifted away from the merely academic enterprise. Money begets power and power corrupts. They also became increasingly corrupt.

A true history of the matter would show that the present crisis in costs of intercollegiate athletics stemmed directly from necessary reforms to control and reduce those empires and to bring them back toward proper relationships with the academic community. That was a fight, sometimes on the grand scale. And like all struggles for academic control of intercollegiate athletics it does not end. It goes on, a hot, hard fight, at this moment; and everything done in relation to athletics is bound to have its effect for good or ill on that contest.

The steps taken almost everywhere to effect control which also affected costs were various. Some were designed to bring monies "up from under the table" and into the light of open accounting procedures. Others aimed to capture or recapture the athletics empire. Still others came incidentally to the always awkward and sometimes unjust business of trying to treat the intercollegiate athletics enterprise as if it fell, as it never really does, under any of the other categories of activity within the academic institution. Some instances of action: (1) Establishment of declared, open, defined and limited "athletic grants-in-aid" for student athletes. (2) Abolition of "slush fund" accounts, and open pouring of gift monies in support of athletics into "foundation" or other accounts subject to regular institutional procedures of disbursement and reporting and open to Conference or NCAA inspection. (3) Liquidation of separate "athletic association" corporations in favor of departments of athletics in regular line of institutional tables of operation, usually accompanied by abolition or co-optation of the "student athletic fees" which had previously combined with gate receipts to support the corporations. Thus "athletic monies" became "academic monies," plus and minus. Sometimes the "student athletic fee" monies permanently disappeared from department of athletics sight at the moment of this action or shortly after it. (4) Abolition of "fee remission" for athletes in the process of reforming the accounting rationale from one in which the system tries not to "charge and double-charge" itself for internal operations to one in which everybody is "charged" for everything possible.

In the old days the director not only did not have to account for many of his true costs but could not—and dared not if he had been able. "My God, how the money rolled in!" Sponsors and slush funds and the "job program" covered his player and recruiting costs. Sometimes great sponsors sweetened salaries for coaches—and for directors too? On paper his income from student fees and the gate was gravy after he paid the relatively low tariffs for game and travel and office expenses. He became a source of significant investment capital and of numerous small favors in which political advantage figured.

But then things changed abruptly, and fiscal pressures began to advance on him from every direction. In a national mood of exuberant affluence and in a period of chesty expansiveness in the lives of the nation and the universities, everybody and everything seemed to conspire to tax the athletics empire—and at last the very athletics enterprise—to the very edge of their existence.

From nil the expense for grants-in-aid became perhaps the most significant single item in the budget, and inflationary rises in tuition, room, board, and books (the legitimate major items stipulated in the "full ride") multiplied. Two-platoon football and desperately competitive recruiting multiplied the numbers of players and grants-in-aid. Spending on everything jumped way up. The national mood fitted the slogan, "It costs only a little bit more to go first-class." But in fact that "little" is perhaps 15 percent; and the horizon seems always so to fly before it that the rate of increase holds steady. Costs for travel, equipment, services of all kinds kept going up. So did the pressures of competition, leading to ever-increasing staff numbers and recruiting costs, higher salaries and fringe benefits.

For many an administrator the circumstances came to seem bewitched. In the changes from "country store" to "big corporation" accounting procedures, it often became hard to distinguish between "accounting" money and "real" or "spending" money all over the university. But the director seemed caught in the middle. Nobody wanted to give up perquisites or the "soak athletics" mood which had seemed to justify them: student seats, cheap or even free (even after the student fee had disappeared); cut rates for faculty and staff (and more of them with expanding enrollment); free tickets for political, promotional, fund-raising, or just public relations reasons—and lots of little graft. With more students, faculty, and staff all the time, the programs that suffered worst were those which had always sold out the stadium: there were ever fewer seats to sell to the public which paid in "real" money at the gate. You could play more games and raise your prices: but the ceiling on that fell much lower than the ceiling on rising costs.

Almost everywhere, though especially in state-supported schools, the tax of "free tickets" falls heavily on athletics. Conference rules or game contracts necessarily spell out rules of equity about the cost of "freebies." The usual and sensible arrangement is to say, taking a number for instance, that the home team may give out four thousand complimentary tickets without penalty but must pay the visitor the half-price (which represents what might have been the visitor's share) for every ticket given away after that number. That is, if Hopi State, playing at home, papers the house with eight thousand comps, it owes visiting Siwash four thousand times half the ticket price. If the ticket costs eight dollars, Hopi is out thirty-two thousand dollars: sixteen it has given away and, much more painful, sixteen in spending cash money it has to deduct from its half of the net gate receipts. If the ticket went (all real cases) to a legislator's cousin, the editor of a small-town paper, or the chairman of the Department of English at St. Egbert's Little College, tangible returns might accrue to the legislative appropriation, the public relations experts, or the English department when it placed a new Ph.D. at friendly St. Egbert's. But nobody will even blush, much less credit the department of athletics with a penny of its losses.

At five occurrences a year for ten years, not counting interest, athletics at Hopi is out $1.6 million on "freebies" alone. When the treasurer talks budgets with the director, he will of course take that into account. Oh, sure he will! What in fact he will be much more likely to do is to explain that an improvement in accounting policy makes it imperative to charge the department rent for the use of the athletics facilities it built with its own earned funds and that, although the department employs its own business manager to do all its accounting, another new policy requires that everybody in the institution pay 4 percent of its budget to defray the costs of central accounting. Next time the trustees see the budget, pointed questions will be raised about the cost crisis in athletics.

In a world where it is seldom difficult to be disingenuous by solemnly playing it straight and going by the book, there generally appears, to my eye, a gap yawning between fiscal reports on intercollegiate athletics and reality. One of the most candid, realistic exceptions to that generalization I have happened to see is perhaps therefore worth consideration. It was written by Chancellor A. Kenneth Pye of Duke University in reply to the query almost every major athletics program ought at least to know the answer to: What would it cost us directly to drop out of Big Game competition? What would we save? Generally I have left Duke out of the book, partly because I work here now but mainly because I had been here only two years before I took leave to write the book and I have come to know just that little which tells me that, if not unique, Duke's circumstances are different in certain ways from those of almost any other institution. But I think the nail Chancellor Pye hit squarely on the head has the opposite characteristic: it belongs to almost everybody.

What the Pye Report shows is that in 1971 the budget deficit in Duke athletics, though a tidy sum, amounted to less than 1 percent of the general budget of the university—"excluding hospitals" (a significant remark). Of that budgeted deficit, more than 40 percent "returned to the University for tuition" charged against athletics for grant-in-aid athletes. Another 44 percent of the deficit arose from "recent accounting changes" allocating substantial charges against athletics for "Central Administration and Plant Operations Cost." The faculty fringe benefit of reduced tickets came to more than 10 percent of the remaining figure, and even then the now puny deficit carried "the band and certain other items not directly a part of intercollegiate athletics." Never mind the "certain other items," subtracting the faculty benefit and the band cost arrives at a deficit for intercollegiate athletics, computed from (not by) the Pye Report, of twelve one hundredths of 1 percent of the general university budget, excluding hospitals.

But the report leaves such computation to others and presses on to its main task of asking what would happen to costs if some or all sports were eliminated. The Pye Report was done in 1971, though its figures have been kept up to date, and I am assured that most proportions do not change significantly with the numbers. For it the University Business Offices calculated the phase-out costs of dropping intercollegiate sports at:

Cancellation penalties	$ 800,000
Contracts of head coaches	100,000
Student aid on grants-in-aid already given over four years reducing 25 percent each year	1,540,000
Termination pay	100,000
	$2,540,000

After that, the net annual costs remaining to the university figured at 50-66 percent (not counting student loans) of the present budgeted deficit if all intercollegiate sports were dropped. If only "nonrevenue sports" were dropped, remaining costs calculated at about 67 percent. Eliminating football and basketball but retaining "nonrevenue" sports projected costs approximating 100 percent of the deficit figure. Dropping football but keeping basketball and nonrevenue sports would cost more than retaining football or the deficit.

I thought the Pye Report was correct in challenging the justice and wisdom of classifying, for "administrative convenience," intercollegiate athletics "as an auxiliary enterprise . . . expected to generate income to meet its expenses"; for that category reflects the logic of an athletics empire alienated from the academic community and "free" from academic control. The report points out that the athletics enterprise is both more controlled, fiscally and otherwise, than "other auxiliary enterprises such as Dormitories and University Stores" yet is treated less generously than such auxiliary enterprises as scholarly journals, where expense budgets hardly reflect "the true expenses which are carried on academic budgets." It points out that

A number of University activities not directly related to education or research would show substantial deficits if segregated as auxiliary enterprises, instead of being subsumed into other categories—for example, the operation of the Duke Gardens, the Chapel and the Chaplains, the Student and Faculty Health Services, all student extracurricular activities and the operation of the Student Union.

Finally, the Pye Report suggests, most mildly, that it may not be appropriate to deal with the program in intercollegiate athletics as if it were known to be without cost benefits or effectiveness. Before you cut its throat, might it not be well to ask whether anything worse or weaker ought not be liquidated first? Do we not need simply to study the facts, in fiscal and other expense and contribution, to learn more than we know amid the welter of wildly conflicting claims and charges about the worth of college sport? We do.

All this is fairly accurately the ground of the crisis in costs. It tends to make the crisis not unreal but something which means or can be made to mean just about anything an interpreter chooses. People hostile to intercollegiate athletics have leaped at the chance to use it to play the game Dr. Berne calls "Now I've Got You, You Son of a Bitch." Some ill-advised directors have used it to play cute or vengeful games of, "OK, I'll Cut Your Minor Sports and See How You Like That." Some administrators, having thrust athletics to the wall, have found ways to let up on them at least enough to let them carry on. I think that last has happened because college athletics do produce substantial cost benefits which nobody knowledgeable wants to lose, though more of that in its place. But we have to think about other and real if nonfiscal costs; and we have to consider the promise of proposed fiscal solutions. Nobody supposes either that we can go back twenty-five years or that we can go on as we are. Solutions must be found, preferably solutions which do not sacrifice our gains in academic control but advance them.

I think there is merit in each of the following possible solutions to our crisis in costs: (1) better business and promotional practices to make more money at the gate; (2) cutting costs; (3) raising endowments in support of intercollegiate athletics.

Like the recurrent "crime wave" when other news fails, the "costs crisis" was in part perhaps a media spasm. In part it was an object of the crisis mentality of the nation. Rumor has it that, threatened by demotion from Division IA to Division IAA of the NCAA, a number of institutions which had been singing those Big Game blues and threatening to depart that inappropriate realm forever found the morale and means to become miraculously recovered invalids. Still, those are hardly solutions.

Directors rich in promotional and business giftedness like Morgan at UCLA, Canham at Michigan, Cekaj at Penn State, and Hirsch at Wisconsin, among others, have done well at solutions of the costs crisis based on imaginative, insightful practices. But they tend to have winners, and most of them have large nearby populations to draw upon. Solutions need to promise longer terms, more secure margins, and continuity and stability superior to programs which stay too close to the red bottom line for comfort.

Cost-cutting, seriously done, holds more promise, especially since it would cut rates of increase which obviously must stop somewhere short of the mathematically not too distant dates at which entire general budgets would go to intercollegiate athletics and nobody do anything but work for them. Limits on affluent, "first-class," and especially conspicuous expenditure can—and ought by right and propriety, not just need—be made. Sometimes I have thought that directors of athletics ought to have a system like Alcoholics Anonymous, a Spenders, Ltd., perhaps, which would give a man somebody to call up who could talk him out of it when he felt about to buy off a coach's neurosis with a large, inessential expenditure. The pressures and troubles of Coach's life are such that he periodically falls victim to a terrible need to feel loved, appreciated, wanted, a fierce yen for a security blanket represented by the expenditure of a large sum of cash on behalf of *his* program, *his* need to keep up with Siwash, *his* fine family of great young men. After Coach has left the office, the director ought to have somebody who understands to call up and be talked out of it.

Certainly it is not necessary to go back to the days when you hung your trousers on a rusty nail in the boiler-room wall and hoped they would still be there when the game was over. Extravagance and compulsive spending are something else. Nevertheless, cost-cutting of that sort, however appropriate and desirable, will solve few problems for long. There appear to be only two possibilities for real economy in operating the intercollegiate Big Game as we now know it. They interrelate, and they are conservative in several good senses. They are a return to the college game in football, so-called one-platoon, and a return to the ancient, honorable, healthy practice of coaches doubling-up—coaching two or more sports every year.

For reasons I think have to do with the esthetics and authenticity of the game as well as mere economics, I hold with those who, like Coach Joe Paterno, think that college football ought to go back to rules allowing limited and selective rather than "free" and mass substitutions. I don't think the consequences would bear out the nay-sayers and their contention that "one-platoon" football would lose money because nobody would want to come and see it. As Coach Paterno replies, "There's a whole generation out there that's never seen it; they'll be curious . . ., and it could buy us time until the economic crisis is over." It is one of the few possibilities for saving substantial amounts of recurrent, otherwise steadily inflating expense in real dollars.

The functional logic of football with unlimited substitutions evolved the fact of two football teams within the same squad, one for offense, the other for defense, practicing on different fields. The next refinement separated specialists—mainly kickers—from both. From that it takes only a short step to supposing that the three estates unite only on the plane bound for an away game. From that point you can visualize the nightmare of conclusive absurdity which Samuel Yellen imagined in his short story, "How Football Died."

Until recently the least inhibited coaches felt they needed (and they had) 150 men on full grants-in-aid to supply a game in which only 11 may be on the field at once. Proper coaching of such numbers was thought to require perhaps 15 full-time men. Ignoring numerous satellite people and all but the most central expenditures, and trying to keep numbers relatively conservative and round, if grants-in-aid cost $3,000 each and coaches, with their fringe benefits, averaged out at $25,000, your budgetary commitment on the first day of practice would be $850,000 for people. Scaling that down to 100 players and 8 coaches reduces the cost to $500,000. If, on the other hand, college players were once more to "go both ways," play all parts of the game and not be specialized into component segments of it, the maximum useful number of varsity squad members would be on the order of 50, for whom 5 coaches are plenty. Now our number will be $275,000; and we will have returned to something like the figures at which intercollegiate athletics had no crisis in costs.

Budgeted numbers vary from one sort of institution to another, but the proportions would remain about the same. Further, those big, initial savings would represent only a part, perhaps not the greatest part, of the gain. Satellite and service personnel—trainers and managers and equipment men, graduate assistants and tutors and "gophers" would all diminish. Large expenditures and terrible strains would come off the recruiting process, lowering the profile and costs of off-season activities healthily. Coaches' teaching and their abilities to relate properly to players personally would be enhanced. And they would be freer to work with other sports.

When a $25,000 coach expert at the Big Game moves into a "non-revenue" or "minor" or *other* sport, you get a substantial added return on your investment and help your total athletics budget by the amount of the sum not paid somebody else. You often also get a better coach and a finer program in the other sport. One of my freshman football coaches was Ray Dietrick, a superb basketball coach. Though he left us on October 15 when basketball practice began, during the preceding month he gave me some of the best individual coaching I ever got: under the circumstances he had leisure to study and help mere frosh. At Syracuse for many years Roy Simmons held an enviable reputation as boxing coach and lacrosse coach. But in the fall he proved a wizard at the design of pass defenses. Coaches who remember the time when almost everybody doubled or tripled in the sports he coached think the quality of Big Game coaches was heightened by the benefits of moving from one to another, of not being compelled forever to pound at the same rocks.

Cutting down the numbers means reducing the escalation in pressures as well as costs. As Paterno suggests, assistant coaches ought to be tied into nonathletic service to the academic community too: "Let them work in development, admissions or the alumni office in the off-season," he told a press conference. "Or have them go after faculty rank and tenure. Then we won't lose so many young coaches." And then, I hasten to add, we won't callously wipe out so many old coaches, either. In other sports as in other service, Big Game coaches could gain the experience and find the niches in the great reef which would permit everybody gracefully to transfer them, when the time came, from Big Game pressures to other service. The increased stabilities and broader community contacts of such relations would go far toward reconciling the athletic to the academic. Obviously it would tend to perfect academic control.

All of this would give us better, truer, intrinsically more interesting and certainly more collegiate football. To put it without varnish, the professionals do not play football nearly so well as their superb athletes and their knowledge of the game permit. Like a lot of people who have known and loved the game for a long time, many of them far better players than I ever was or could have been, I think the pro's play relatively slow, stereotyped, and corrupt football for reasons essentially cynical. They play not for the game but for the money. Their game is entertainment, not athletic competition. They are in show biz, not the Big Game. The first business of show business is box office. It aims to "take" the customer for a mark, a sucker. It treats its own the same way. Its notion of sport is a rip-off.

None of the immediately foregoing is news or an original discovery. It provides a benchmark for measuring intercollegiate athletics: so far as the Big Game in all its elements departs from show biz and approaches expression of the academic community, its character and traditions, just that far it is collegiate and worthy of preservation. Sometimes I wonder if you can't use Howard Cosell as another benchmark. Let me hasten to add that I perceive Mr. Cosell as a character actor of extraordinary talent, perhaps the best since the late Boris Karloff. Cosell's chosen role he plays brilliantly as that of the loud, brash, street-wise fan who knows everything but understands nothing. For him the media sports exploiters work in spite of the fact that he is on to them. He sees through everybody, sees everything except what is actually going on. For him nothing will do but debased sport and nothing counts but the score. To him esthetics do not exist, only arithmetic.

The *lumpen* fan craves offense that "moves the ball" and scores a lot. In pro basketball they have given him the time clock to force quick shots and have outlawed natural, intelligent, authentic defense. In pro football they have abandoned much of the game for a monotony of "putting the ball in the air" with forward passes. But in order to do that passing they have had to corrupt one of the most essential rules of the game. To illustrate by analogy: much of the balance of baseball depends on the geometrical niceties of the ninety feet between the bases. Make it eighty feet and the scores would shoot up. Much of the balance in football depends on the rule that, except for the ball-carrier, the players on offense cannot use their hands against defenders—they can block but not tackle, they can interfere with their bodies but not their hands and arms. But in "pro offense" you see holding and shoving and even tackling on every play, especially the passing plays on which the backs and flankers need time to execute the also illegal picks and screens against defenders which will set them free. It may be "offense" but it is not football. It serves for show biz, but it adds to other factors to make entertainers out of marvelous athletes who do not play football—as in the NBA they do not play basketball—nearly so well as they know how. With the games sophisticated, impoverished, counterfeit, ersatz, and with the great players cheated out of the full, free exercise of their gifts, no wonder the athletes like the entrepreneurs and gamblers and parasites think about money: what else is there?

On the collegiate side there is integrity and authenticity for the games and for the relationships to community and to the culture. On that side I find it hard to believe that the two-platoon or unlimited substitution rules really give us a better game, much as I respect many of the people who do think that. Two-platoon football is easier to coach because you can do the job with *quantity*, analysis, task-breakdowns, relatively inexpert instruction and evaluation governed by generalship rather than with *quality* of total and organic perception and with personal teaching, personal relationships. It is a game which as it is more easily controlled by coaches provides them more exposure and greater rewards. When the coach has to send his team onto the field and let them play, the game belongs to the players. They must work out its rhythms and dynamics of domination and defeat. Then it belongs to them and the students they represent. The players achieve their team character and identity as their season builds. There arise situations in which their multiple talents and personal powers of perception and adjustment turn the tides, and the game becomes more its true self.

That it is important to establish identity for the college game might justify taking long risks for that identity even if it were not a better game and more suited to its circumstances. And it is important at least to notice that there are also cost considerations in which dollars do not initially figure. For the colleges, a reliance on box office is a relative evil in itself. It gives us too quickly to think of public relations, to have too ready an eye for the "gate," to become reluctant to put first things first. What first things? Well, the welfare of students, especially athletes; institutional relationships; moral values and our reputations, our good name.

To avoid costs like that, to avoid loss of the benefits of intercollegiate athletics, to strengthen academic control, trustees and presidents, administrators and faculty, might find it best to do as the Ivy League has done and take intercollegiate athletics into full budgetary membership in the academic family. That means too to make general institutional funds available, as necessary, to support their proper conduct.

Is that too painful? There is emerging a new and potentially very promising solution to the costs crisis and certain painful difficulties in academic control. It is to raise permanent endowments to free the Big Game and all intercollegiate athletics from fear of the "gate" and from need to emulate show biz. Right now the movement to raise such endowments moves apace at a number of colleges and universities, and it is hard to see why it should not succeed.

COSTS/BENEFITS

The economics of a college more nearly resemble "Economy" in Thoreau's *Walden* than economics in the Exxon Corporation: academic economics, like *Walden*, prize intangibles most. By any count, the costs of the Big Game are as importunate as the demand for it. But the benefits demanded and paid for seem less evident to some of the taxed than to others. It is fair to ask of the Big Game that it answer the query of Benjamin Franklin's famous bagatelle: "Do we pay too much for the whistle?" What benefits do we buy with the costs we pay for the Big Game?

I make no doubt that the Big Game serves all the positive humane ends of play, intensely and effectively. These humane ends, inseparable in experience, are classifiable as personal, as cultural, as academic. Turning to a list of key words I have kept taped to the wall above the desk at which I stand to write, I may say in seriousness that the Big Game serves ends which are intrapsychically bonding and bounding, cathartic, egosyntonic, sublimating, transforming. Enculturative, they provide us symbolic tools, even serve for language, communicating, forging community. Communally they provide us with culture texts, in which to read the natures of self and group. Their esthetic effects are potent. They are festal and fraternal, ritual and perhaps religious, certainly synergistic.

The powers lent an academic institution by its possession of such an instrument are exhilarating and frightening, like owning a genie or a nuclear power plant. However wonderful, it might as easily wreck as bless us; it might come to own us, not we it. Nevertheless, the games belong peculiarly to the academic community of students whose powers of *virtu* and whose characteristic relations to the culture at large they express. Therefore they present vital, often unique, experiences of community to academe. They inspire pride, morale, belief, devotion, the concentration, multiplication, and release of energies in the members and citizenry of that commune. And they do these things as well from good losing as good winning.

The costs, however, are also tangible. What about tangible benefits?

What does the Big Game do practically for its hosts? I should list the benefits of a sort for which corporations like Exxon spend money as: (1) exposure—of the media sort for which corporations pay massive public relations and advertising costs, if only for "brand recognition"; (2) recruitment—for the corporations, customers; for the colleges, students; (3) contacts—with alumni and "subway" alumni (like stockholders?), with crowds of the public (like people drawn to a shopping mall?); (4) reputation and influence; (5) public (translate political) support; and (6) giving—of money and its equivalents.

About some of these alleged benefits debates rage which are not easy to resolve factually, though there exist mighty suggestive indicators. Talking about appeals from universities to be included in Division IA of the new NCAA classification, Walter Byers told me recently, "The difference in the way college presidents talk now from twenty years ago is hard to believe. I was amazed to hear them tell what they thought it would cost them to lose firstclass football standing. One of them said he might as well lose his academic accreditation." In James Michener's marvelous book *Sport in America* he gives a list of something like thirteen universities he thinks "not hurt" by dropping football. Perhaps there is no correlation, but three of them have gone through effective bankruptcy since they dropped the game.

One of my favorite places to go to a football game is the University of Tennessee at Knoxville, especially at night when you can watch the dozens of lighted launches dropping down Lake Loudoun, partying, and tie up at the piers to deliver their passengers for the game. What a party! The stadium is a sea of orange—eighty thousand maniacs. You see why the bumper stickers stream by on the highway all day long, announcing: "This is Big Orange Country." Now, Tennessee is a state relatively small in population and thin in resources. It is not many years since major national investments were made to rescue Tennessee. Yet UT is supported academically at levels of influence, affluence, and significance which the ancient Universities of Paris or Bologna or Göttingen would turn green with envy to contemplate. Why? Because of the superb athletics program centering on the Big Game sports?

I would be reluctant to say so because I should not know how to prove it objectively beyond a reasonable doubt. And yet I should think the proponent of an opposite thesis might find his side of the argument more difficult. Do away with the games, the teams, the mythology, the glamor, the exposure, and the contacts. Take down those proud, affectionate signs. Deprive those people of their parties and cut the chains of connection between the citizenry of the state in all directions and the university, and what would happen? Where would all those zealous, wild, and loving constituencies go? Right or wrong, many universities have decided that they would rather not break those golden but magnetic chains. One private university I used to know long ago announced that it had decided to deemphasize and divest itself of the Big Game. It discovered so many kinds of trouble that it turned around and reinvested vigorously and felt its investment well rewarded.

A prominent businessman and politician ardently engaged in raising money for his university told me, "I can get four or five dollars for athletics to every one I can get for anything else." Yale fund raisers think that disillusion with athletics has caused them to lose many millions of dollars in gifts foregone. Outside the United States with its unique pattern of intense public concern for intercollegiate athletics, with few exceptions the great universities are supported by the equivalent of the federal government. Professional fund-raisers in state-supported as well as private universities think and feel that giving often begins in giving for athletics, and relatively small sums, but flowers into the giving of substantial funds for academic goals. The fund-raisers, in my experience, unfailingly tell you that. One famous president, having recruited a Nobel Prize winner to the faculty, was asked what it meant to the university. His reply, according to faculty folklore, was: "It's next best to going to the Rose Bowl." The ultimate test, I suppose, for the Regulars and Irregulars of intercollegiate athletics alike, will be whether the requisite endowments in their support can actually be raised.

THE MEGALOPOLITAN MYSTERY; OR, NEVER IN NEW YORK

In a matter of days from this writing it will be forty-five years since, an uncoordinated thirteen-year-old, I turned out for my first organized football team and got cut. The next year I won a uniform because, still uncoordinated, I was bigger. That the next two years after that I played regularly was a greater achievement than I understood; for it was on a good team in an area prominent for intensity in its football tradition and significantly productive of college players. Professor John F. Rooney, Jr., listed it sixth in the nation in per capita rate among "The Leading Cities or Urban Counties in the Total Production of College Football Players"—just behind Cleveland, Ohio, and ahead of Dallas, Texas.

That was at Tenafly High School, Bergen County, New Jersey, first exurb, then suburb, now in effect part of Greater New York. When I played where I come from, New York presented the grandest stage for the Big Game in the nation—and had long done so. Princeton's answer from the pioneering days of the art to Yale-Harvard in New England was Yale-Princeton in New York. In the twenties and thirties Columbia and Fordham and New York University had great teams, and it was taken for granted that teams with something exciting to show would come to town and try it. Army in its great days became an adoptive home team, and nobody who played ball around New York was nearly so shocked as the "smart money" when Columbia won at the Rose Bowl. We knew how the game was played under Little, or Cavanaugh and Crowley at Fordham, or under Meehan at NYU: close, and tight and fundamental—but smart and Big.

The like was true, of course, but even more so, of basketball. We thought it *was* the City game, hardly understood elsewhere, and that what Nat Holman did not know about it Clair Bee did. The shocks of Luisetti and of Mid-East, Mid-West, and Coast basketball were unthinkable when teams from CCNY and Manhattan and Long Island or St. John's stood off the nation in the National Invitational—the only big tournament in the world.

Then, as it seemed, like everything really worthwhile in America, the Big Game was and long had been best in New York. Where is it now? Where are the Polo Grounds? It is never in New York. Stranger still, it is almost never in that extended New York (if you please), that famous megalopolis which stretches all the way from north of Boston through the District of Columbia. One of the most colorful, intense, and satisfactorily American experiences has vanished from the area in which it was invented. Though student athletes come significantly from megalopolitania, they have to go elsewhere to play the Big Game. It is played in every other quarter and region of the country, from Seattle and Portland and Palo Alto and Los Angeles to East Lansing and Columbus and Morgantown and Raleigh, from Tallahassee to Lubbock, from Minneapolis to Waco, from Ann Arbor to Phoenix. But never in New York. It is played around the "Bos-Wash" perimeter from Syracuse to Penn State to Maryland; but never in New York—not in the memory of any child born since Fordham packed it in and Notre Dame stopped playing Army in New York. It's the Megalopolitan Mystery, a puzzle of locus for which I can find no sensible answer.

Even interior to megalopolis as a demographic concept the situation seems confusing. Usually the notion of the one, great continuous city has been imagined as a "T" shape lying on its side, with the top element running along the coast, Boston to Washington, and the East-West shaft running from New York to Chicago. But on the East-West axis the Big Game retains and has even come back into its power. On that axis the patterns are, in NCAA geographical terms, Mid-East and Mid-West. To put it another NCAA way, the whole area lies in or across eight geographical districts. From District 1 , New England, the Big Game is gone. But if, leaving Puerto Rico out of consideration, you draw a line through District 2 along the Catskill and Allegheny Mountain chain's fall line, historically an ancient and significant boundary, you will delineate vertically on the map the area where the Big Game is, in effect, never. It is the old eastern but not southern colonial area, "Over the Mountains" to the early frontiersmen. Beyond that line Penn State plays the Big Game in its Nittany fastness, Syracuse in its Onondaga castle, and both are backed by Pitt. The South begins with Maryland and Virginia. A continental experience begins at those somehow cultural borders.

What happened to the East? You can hear a number of uncomplimentary, even sinister, explanations which, as a native of the region, I reject. You can hear self-serving rationalizations at which, as a native, I feel privileged to scoff. Long a student of the Big Game and one who remembers how it used to be there, I cannot help feeling that forty or more millions of Americans are deprived by their region's loss of the opportunity for intense, rewarding experience. It is not true that in the East they are too moral, too tasteful, too preoccupied with "high culture" for mere college games: the profusion there of less moral, far tawdrier activities denies the one claim; as for the other, where now, really, in proportion to population, *is* the Great American Desert of the Bozarts? For popular culture not to possess it locally, for it to have to look to Columbus or Norman or Pasadena for the Big Game, is a variety of impoverishment.

Furthermore, I suspect that its absence tends to impoverish higher education in the East. It deprives the student of intensities familiar to his contemporaries elsewhere. And it may be a factor in the relatively starved and orphaned condition of the state university in the East. The realities have never somehow dawned on the region. Of the eight Ivy League institutions, six would generally be thought competitive in the big leagues of American universities. But they are national, not regional, by effective intent; and the percentage of eastern students who can get into one is minuscule. Is there, beyond them, any university in the region competitive in quality with the national best? I could not name it, and it does not seem to appear in lists of the national rankings. Per capita expenditures for higher education by eastern states are disgraceful. They export college students by the hundreds of thousands every year to profit from the expenditures of obscure, distant, provincial states—and the East suffers a steady hemorrhage of young talent.

It is easy to recall when love for and pride in CCNY were fierce. Who loves CUNY? or SUNY? And who will give, much less sacrifice, anything to or for them? These are questions made the more interesting by the fact that, in contrast to the national mood, that of the East is largely one of alienation from, even disgust with its public universities. As illustrated in the work of megalopolitan sports media people, the Big Game is not understood in their region because it has ceased to happen there; and they seem not to know how to experience it esthetically, festally, folklorically, communally. Knowing only the pro's, they seem to insist, provincially, that there is nothing else to know. But knowing only the pro's seems also to lead many of them to disgust, a radical alienation which appears to extend to higher education in general. It is, for the region, a sort of calamity.

The Church Fathers, I have heard, long ago concluded that some saintly heretics would be saved because the error they could not renounce was something they could not help: it was based upon "invincible ignorance." I suppose the strategy aimed to disarm examples of erroneous good, and so I should be inclined to deal with the ignorant megalopolitan idealist in his innocence of the American college game. He is probably right in his suspicion that, members of academic communities aside, the constituency for the Big Game hails from the towns and the "sticks" more than from centers of metropolitan sophistication. But that does not guarantee that they are not missing something where he comes from any more than it warrants supposing that James Reston, who does understand the nation, was wrong when he wrote a decade ago in the *Times:*

> Nobody in America has really analyzed the positive effects of sports on the remarkable growth and development of state university education in America. No doubt state university sport has been professionalized and corrupted, but it has done something else. It has produced football teams which have become symbols of state pride. It has kept the alumni in touch with the university. More important, it has held the interest and the allegiance of legislators in the state capitols, and has in the process helped produce educational appropriations for all these institutions on a scale that

would never have been possible without the attraction and the pride engendered by these sporting events at the universities on autumn Saturday afternoons.

In short, there appears to be somehow a degree of correlation between the Big Game and a certain excellence in higher education. The correlation is obscure, not a sure thing in any individual case, but somehow there. Or, at any rate, the assumption that there is nothing there, nothing in it, seems less than reliable. Reston's "professionalized" is, obviously, a term I would want to explore, mitigate, perhaps confront with other principles of reality. Certainly I could not respect it as an offhand or knee-jerk condemnation. The proper response to his "corrupted" is one of the aims of this book. So far as "corrupted" is true of the Big Game it calls for reform: continuous, elastic, tireless war.

There may be something artificial about the exile of the Big Game from East Megalopolitania. Evidences exist of a true appetite, a real, unforgotten demand for it. When on 15 September 1975 Boston College played Notre Dame in a sold-out Foxboro Stadium, ABC and the institutions made a grand fuss about an event of "major significance to amateur athletics and Catholic education and the whole Boston area." ABC stressed the point that the crowd of sixty-one thousand was "the biggest ever assembled for any event in the history of Massachusetts." Crowd enthusiasm was intense. Luminaries of the Church abounded. Much time was devoted to the tradition of the late Frank Leahy. Similar feelings revived for the undefeated Rutgers basketball team in 1975-76 and its climax game with Princeton.

It was clearly a media mistake to put down Boston College for losing to Notre Dame and Rutgers for not winning the NCAA. The news really was the reality of the regional joy in the Big Game when, for a moment or two, it came alive again in the East.

THE SPORTS MEDIA

Hire a real pro for a director and let him hire another for sports information. Pay them well. Keep your profile as low as you can. And let them worry.

"AMATEURISM"

An almost impenetrable language problem, it represents the dead hand in American culture. We probably ought to abandon the word. Like certain other aspects of the antique ideal of the gentleman, "amateurism" was killed by the democratization of the culture. It is now mainly a source of frustration and misplaced rage as applied to American intercollegiate athletics. A.O. Lovejoy, the genius who systematized intellectual history, thought it essential to call attention to *"the role of semantic transitions and confusions, of shifts and of ambiguities in the meaning of terms, in the history of thought and of taste.* That 'man lives not by bread alone, but chiefly by catch words,' is not precisely the whole truth, but . . . nearly all of the great catchwords have been equivocal—or rather, multivocal." Further, he said, "since the word is one and the ideas it may express are prodigiously numerous and various, it is, for the historian, often a task of difficulty and delicacy to determine what . . . the idea behind the word is."

So muddled has the situation of "amateur" become that the word may have passed beyond redemption. A first-class book lies ready for the historian of its misadventures. Things have come to such a pass that discussion is more apt to focus on its violation than its character: witness the subject index card of one great library's catalog. "Amateurism in Sports," it reads, "See Professionalism in Sports." That reverberates to the beat of the drums at faculty meeting. Moreover, at the highest levels of national policy-making, matters have become still worse. In a context full of implied approval, the *Chronicle of Higher Education* on 17 February 1976 printed a story by Larry Van Dyne summarizing a preliminary report by the President's Commission on Olympic Sports which, he said, "issued a stinging critique of this country's whole approach to amateur sports," continuing:

> Nothing less than a "thorough reorganization" of our amateur-sports system is required to improve our declining performance in the Olympics, to protect the rights of college and other amateur athletes, and to increase public participation in a wider range of so-called "minor" sports, the commission said.
> Absolutely essential, it said, is a new national organizational structure in which a single, comprehensive "highest sports authority" would be clearly in charge of all amateur athletics.

An "amateur-sports system"? Institutionalized, bureaucratized, centralized, nationalized—but "amateur"? Were they joshing?

No, I suppose not. The Olympic situation is close to unspeakable, anyway. An American college basketball coach, who must and does recruit, for instance, with the nicest attention to NCAA rules which I don't myself quite understand though I helped write some of them, came home from a tour of duty helping Israelis master his game to report that "many amateur athletes in Europe are making more money than professionals. They call it compensation for the time the players are away from their jobs, but it's pay. And they still retain their amateur standing and eligibility for the Olympics. . . . [Some] get a car, an apartment, and up to $200 a month."

Bob Fleischer, who had just finished a year of professional competition in Italy, was declared eligible for the American Olympic squad when Americans who had ever competed, or merely signed an agreement to do so, for an American professional team were ineligible. The logic? Apparently that the Italian members of the same Italian team and league were eligible and would doubtless compete. But Michael T. Harrigan, executive director of the President's Commission on Olympic Sports, told the *New York Times*, "The amateur rules allow subsidization of athletes, so, if we want to subsidize, let's just do it." What he then proposed was what the basketball coach found abroad, what has for decades been a rather general practice worldwide, what is now the official policy and practice of the United States Olympic Committee.

To clarify these matters, so difficult and delicate of interpretation, Lord Killanin, President of the International Olympic Committee, took the naughty word out of the Olympic Rules. "This reflects," he noted, "the positive effort to modernize the terms under which one person may compete in the Olympic Games, yet another making his living from sports should be barred." One needs a decent cover, you see. It's all in how you say the thing—a language problem.

For purposes of grasping answerable reality principles in American intercollegiate athletics I should follow Lord Killanin's method and drop "amateur" from the current vocabulary. It was probably a mistake born of an oddly American set of concerns which entered "amateur" upon our consideration in the first place.

The *Oxford English Dictionary*, the standard historical authority on English usage, lists essentially two meanings for "amateur": (1) hobbyist; (2) incompetent. It does not mention athletics, and its citations regularly connote want of seriousness. It is the American "Merriam-Webster Second," by contrast, which adds a third category, cannily stated: "In sports and esp. athletics, one who is not rated as a professional." The writer of that definition understood the situation. An amateur is one so rated, defined, certified, no matter how arbitrarily or absurdly, by some agency, usually one more or less self-appointed and self-perpetuating.

In the beginning, which appears to have come with eighteenth-century cricket matches in England, they distinguished between the "gentleman" (who not only had status but could afford to pay to play) and the "player" (who lacked status, was poor enough to have to be paid to play, and ranked as a servant). If the idea of the amateur had prevailed (did it exist?), the players would have been ringers. But it did not. The players were there because they played so well they made the side a more attractive bet. With that fine, brutal candor typical of English distinctions, they were rated servants because they were paid to serve the gentry's play: agonistic game action, gambling action. On neither side any nonsense about "avocation." If you are going to take athletic endeavor seriously you can't also really make a living at something else: the full-time athlete, like his counterparts the full-time artist or scholar, will outperform you.

In our very times the "grand old name of English gentleman" has largely extinguished itself by an act of conscience against its anomalies. The difficulty always was that a class of landed gentry, the tradition, clashed with the ideal of the gentleman *sans peur et sans reproche*. At his best and highest that gentleman lived, worked, spent, burned himself like a candle transforming its substance into light, entirely for others. He gave without thought of self, a model of disinterestedness. But to do so the gentleman had to be rich beyond considerations of prudence. And his social relations were such that he was surrounded by worshipful deference except in those rare moments when he paid the like to his own superiors. Such conditions corrupted saints.

So that in fact "fine gentlemen," wasteful, arrogant, dissolute, and callous, rejoiced in privilege and wielded snobberies like a psychic sword over a bleeding populace. For such a situation no defense could be found against the American cry for democracy or the Marxian cry for social justice. The class of gentry undertook to put itself down for reasons of conscience, and it has succeeded.

No matter what the late Avery Brundage thought he meant when he fought so long and stubbornly and unfairly for "amateurism" while the world changed about him and beneath his feet, in truth by "amateur" he could only mean "athlete so rich he can pay to play." All else compromised, sophisticated, betrayed his cause. His successor, a British peer, took the word out of the Olympic rules; and most properly: it is a fossil.

There need here be no rehearsal of the class and racial injustice done the great Jim Thorpe when he was stripped of his Olympic medals for doing what Yale and Harvard men did, with impunity, on the same summer baseball teams. No need to recite the interminable litany of hypocrisies in national and international tennis or golf, or in AAU sponsored track and field, basketball, weight-lifting, in women's athletics, wrestling and boxing, and so forth. Because it is, at weary last, about over. The fossil keeps a stiff semblance of life only in certain academic illusions about intercollegiate athletics.

That is the real contemporary condition, the only way out toward a viable future for postfeudal humanity. Where does it leave the antique distinctions between the gentleman and the player, the "amateur" and the "mucker"? It leaves them exactly where we place all distinction based on wealth or class or snobbery: without respectable standing with the American idea of things. Pay or be paid. The English once made invidious moral distinctions between rich-upper and poor-lower classes. We cannot; and in sports, trying to deal with "amateur," we have engaged in a great deal of obtuse discussion, messy legislation, and unjust action.

Every lover of the human comedy should take one good look at the *Manual of the National Collegiate Athletic Association*. It is a logical phantasmagoria which represents the collective effort, over decades, of earnest, intelligent men, men of deep professional dedication and good will, to design workable sense for "amateurism." As a jungle of contradictions, obfuscation, and absurdities, its achievement surpasses the memorable. It would make an instant atheist of anyone who doubted that the Creator of the human mind lacks a sense of humor. The time has come in college sports to place "amateur" on the high shelf with other cracked treasures of antiquity like gentility and knighthood.

Patterns of nervous anglophilia, paranoiacally provincial, eagerly snatching at power and snobbery, have been observed to run naturally deep in the American grain since colonial times. Walter Camp, for all his talk about democracy, held firmly to British distinctions in his *Book of College Sports*. The effects, nationally and historically displaced, bedeviled American sports with irrelevant issues of social class, status, and snobbery. Like Santayana's, Camp's college athletes "had leisure." Like the protagonists of Henry James, the sports heroes of middlebrow myth in *St. Nicholas*, *Boy's Life*, and *Youth's Companion*, to say nothing of Frank Merriwell, had money to set them morally free.

Nobody worked. Thorstein Veblen had them right. Amateurs, gentlemen, good guys belonged to the "leisure class." Certain British observers have acutely seen through the resultant absurdities, perhaps because nonsense lends itself to the English sense of humor.

A nice example of that humor at work popped up in an unlikely place during the autumn of 1964, when George R. Clay of Princeton could not resist sharing and wrote a letter to the editor of the *American Scholar* about luncheon talk with a distinguished British writer. As the conversation drifted, the "subject of American versus European education was discussed briefly but masochistically"; and the visitor objected: "Have I ever told you about the All-England rugby player who was at Oxford while I was there? No? Then let me—it may convert your reverse snobbery into healthy, red-white-and-blue-blooded chauvinism."

For three years, the story ran, the rugger star was quietly carried by the faculty so he could play. But in his last year "—and on the eve of the most important game—he was flunked, Sent Down, expelled" for failing a gut course in "Divinity." When the news transpired, that evening in Commons the traitor professor found himself indignantly surrounded by "livid colleagues," demanding tacitly why he had "taken it upon himself to flunk the fellow and humiliate them all?"

"Gentleman," stammered the Divinity Professor, "I—I know exactly what you're thinking, believe me I do, and I don't blame you, don't blame you a bit, but you must believe me when I tell you that I wrestled with my conscience, I searched my soul, but I could not bring myself, it was simply not within me, to give a passing grade to any student who spells 'Jesus' with a small *g*!" Was that a put-on? Possibly. But I am assured by a distinguished professor at Cambridge that at least one college there has, and regularly awards, scholarships for rugby.

Confusion sprang from multiplicity in the American Dream, one of the brightest yet most complex parts of which has been the Dream of College. For of course from the start Dreams of College shifted their shapes and proliferated with the swift growth and slow democratization of the national life. We are still in the grip of multiplicities so great about American education as to need perhaps to settle, at least as far as eye can see into the future, for the relative comforts of pluralism and competition among aims, forms, and styles. From the multiplicity of their dreams the people support many sorts of colleges and universities richly; and the same factors must affect collegiate sports. They will be multiple too. But after Mr. Jefferson, as after Lincoln, and especially after Justin Morrill, the actualities can never return to the Yale of Camp or Dink Stover, the Harvard of Owen Wister. The obvious pun is nevertheless too fine to pass up: Morrill was moral; he put the masses into the universities.

In a moment like the present of profound, obscure but swift culture change, surely the least useful posture is that of rigidity in defense of dead snobberies. In colleges and schools in this century we have regularly subsidized training tables, travel, equipment, medical care, and awards for athletes. And as soon as we began to extend the opportunity for collegiate competition to boys from lower middle-class and poverty levels of the population, there had to be support for their college attendance. After decades of deceit and hypocrisy, we came generally, for purposes of control, to regularize that in the "grant-in-aid." The alternative is and was to say: Pay or don't play. You *have* to cross that line; and as soon as you do the rest of it is a matter of control.

One result of change already established is that the savaging of Jim Thorpe, like the absurdities of the late Avery Brundage, are now rather universally condemned. We see that the multiplicity of standards, still too often rigid, is inconsistently enforced. We have not quite repented and ceased to practice contradiction and injustice, but we are groping toward better standards and procedures. What holds us back? Too often your true hypocrite, or Pharisee, is a desperate, untimely idealist stranded on an atoll of ancient good no longer couth. Brooding isolation transforms him into an outraged reactionary, and the rest follows. It is a representative problem of American culture at least as old as Cotton Mather. Even the AAU in a new dispensation has launched its boat on seas of change. Where, then, are the faculties?

Though there is nothing (as is proved by decades past of painful repulse) the colleges can do about the "amateur" debacle, they can at least get clear of it. It might be argued that a radical revival of the word is feasible. The true amateur might be defined *de novo* as the competitor who for the love of the esthetics of his game devotes himself to it. Roger Bannister, justifying his thing, answers that you do it for joy and freedom: "The sportsman is consciously or unconsciously seeking the deep satisfaction, the sense of personal dignity, which comes when body and mind are fully coordinated and they have achieved mastery over themselves. For a young man there are still few fields in which perfection can be approached and with such momentary if transient finality." These tests are intrapsychic and esthetic. But what have they to do with "pay"? Who is to say that the athlete cannot know them purely if anybody but his family pays, if institutions or even the box office pays? We say no such thing of the artist, the scientist, the scholar. How shall we say it of the athlete? It is an intolerable snobbery.

Does the situation so sketched leave intercollegiate athletics, then, with no ground of distinction between themselves and professional sports? Not at all. The real distinction is worse confounded by those who would insist on the money test. That test says, "If you can't pay to play you are a professional." Or worse it says, "Well, if you can't pay to play and we need you, we will arbitrarily decide what expenses you may be allowed; but if you get anything more, we will declare you 'dirty' or 'tainted' and cast you into professional darkness." The presumption is morally monstrous. In operation, the system has proved itself practically monstrous by a history of injustices so incongruous it is now doubtful that much of it will bear judicial review. The right alternative tests, I am convinced, look not to class status or economics. They look to authenticity. What we must and can do is where necessary to reform and where possible to conserve: we can make and keep the Big Game collegiate.

NOBLE EXPERIMENTS

All experience combines to show that you cannot have academic, internal control of intercollegiate athletics unless you also have external, federal control. By "federal" I mean the federated, mutual control contemplated by the charters of the eighty-odd conferences ranging from the Arkansas Intercollegiate and Atlantic Coast at one end of the alphabet to the Western State and the Yankee at the other end. Or as in the charters of the great associations like AIAW and NCAA. Very American devices, such federations are almost as old as formal college sports, dating from the 1880s. As instruments they are inevitable and necessary—and they do not presently work. Therefore they present a challenge of major proportions and significance to the trustees, presidents, athletics administrative professionals, and the faculties. We live in the presence of a constitutional crisis in the instruments of federal academic control.

It gives me no pleasure to be forced to recognize the fact and still less to feel compelled to say it. In my small way, I am in part to blame for their failure together with a number of people for whose abilities and personalities and characters I feel great respect and, in many cases, affection. I know how heartbreakingly hard they have labored, how much they sacrifice and endure. But I am forced to the conclusion that the present structures, in their discontinuities and inadequacies, cannot be made to work. The record of the past fifteen years proves it. We need a fresh start.

At the best levels we have in fact lost a great deal, especially in the wrecks of hope, during the past decade. In the years of the early to middle 1960s, experiments, launched in the middle fifties with dedication and good will, even readiness to sacrifice, promised real advances. The road back is littered with their debris. They have become, in the grand rhetoric attached to Prohibition, "Noble Experiments"—the national irony's traditional tag for failed dreams.

As it insists on its present shape, this essay surprises and disconcerts the writer, who began with different plans and a couple of running feet of file materials for carrying them out. Perhaps they may yet make a different book. But the main conclusion to which long research, a number of interesting conversations, and hard reflection have brought me displaces earlier intentions. Though there are a lot of interesting and significant things to say about the history and present condition of the best of the Noble Experiments, now I feel it only important to say that they have to be renewed, rethought, restored to vigor and point, perhaps replaced. Even the best and most promising of the instruments from the past no longer perform the offices for which they were designed. What holds true for them holds doubly for the rest. Perhaps they always needed to be nobler and more experimental, perhaps it is only that they have lost resiliency, inspiration, courage, clarity, applicability, the capacity to do the job. Perhaps they have become too dominated by parochial and shortsightedly selfish concerns. Perhaps they should be absorbed into larger, more functional and organic forms.

We need a new start with a powerful creative thrust behind it. If, as I think, every experiment in federal control, national or conference, stands a present failure no matter what it once accomplished in the past, we have a challenge to which we must respond successfully. Arnold Toynbee's theory of the life and death of cultures and civilizations applies to us. Challenged severely, we must respond creatively or be frozen to the cliff of history. Analogy with the history of the American Constitution applies to us. Loose and halfhearted federation having failed us, we need to go to work. We need a lot of hard, answerable thought—our own Federalist Papers—and a new commitment to making federalism work. "Join or Die!" said the motto of the Revolutionary banner.

The call to renewal has been a main theme of American yearning, experiment, law, education, and action in every generation. It remains powerfully so at this moment in the national life. But the moment is too long overdue in college athletics. In the face, then, of our present confusions and paralysis, what must we do? Some suggestions:

1. We have to clarify our intentions to ourselves. The original impulses behind the Big Ten, the NCAA, the Ivy League (to take them in historical order) were essentially American: to set a city on a hill, a light to lighten the darkness, the beacon of a good, right example. Their principles were sound, but they need to be rethought, enriched, and brought into living consonance with the realities of the final quarter of this century. If, as I think, the justification for our games is that they express the traditions and characters of our academic communities, we have to search out and recognize the points at which what we do no longer represents realities and go to work to experiment and discover what will express the realities we have.

2. We have to find talent and free it to work. Almost any commissioner or director or faculty representative can tell you honestly that he is stretched out as tight as he can be and still has neither time nor strength enough to get the job done. The truth is that most of those most precious of commodities goes into frantic stamping and beating to put out grass fires before they can get into the woods.

There is not enough first-rate talent in the field, and that is for lack of care and support. It is unbelievably difficult to locate or recruit a first-rate commissioner or director. We need to be training a lot more, and something of the same thing goes for the right faculty committee members and chairpeople.

Again, almost any commissioner, director, or faculty representative will tell you, "My toughest problem is getting the president's attention until I have a desperate crisis." By definition we cannot and must not have much of his attention most of the time, but the job of renewal will require mobilization of the best talent—presidential, professional, and faculty—all the know-how, know-what, creativity, and moral leadership we can amass. The one sure thing is that it will not do itself.

3. I would start by sending all the books of rules for the conduct of intercollegiate athletics, including the NCAA's, to archives and beginning again. I would have a well-written, unmistakable text for Rule I, providing that nobody shall compete who is not a bona fide student. It

might take two and a half pages to spell that out. Then I would let the rules rest until the new constitutional process was complete.

4. I do *not* mean that I would destroy or even disable the present structures of people and operations through which the NCAA, for instance, provides indispensable services to the Big Game and all the lesser games. In the not too long run I should wish to see some of their bureaucratic confusions unsnarled. But while I kept them in place— and perhaps working a little harder than ever—I would have them presented with a new, shorter, more realistic, and (above all) a readable constitution.

I don't know whether right solutions to present problems can be "universal"—applying indiscriminately to Brown, Notre Dame, Texas, Slippery Rock, and Simpson College. It is more important that the instruments of federal control express and be answerable to realities. An ultimate federation might join variant leagues at a rather high level of abstraction from the details of practical governance. What I'd ask would be structures that would take sensible account of the actual relations of our sports, and especially of the Big Game, with academic and national life as they now are. Whatever we created would have to work. A committee of one hundred presidents ought now to prepare to put the process of constitutional renewal in motion.

Conclusion

In what has become an ordinary part of the daily news, the paper on the morning of this writing carries a *Washington Post* wire service story reporting that investigating teams from the General Accounting Office have gathered evidence to support the finding that physicians nationwide are "overcharging Medicare and Medicaid patients by as much as 100 to 400 per cent on tests." A federal official "who declined to be named" estimated "that doctors nationwide may be cheating the government out of 'a billion dollars a year, and all their patients out of much more.'" As the most casual citizen knows, however, it would be unfair to single out the M.D.'s as the nation's outstanding rip-off artists. Imagine trying to award the gold in that competition.

I cite the case to illustrate the ground of a riposte from coaches, athletes, and Baker Street Irregulars which, though not unanswerable, I find formidable. Indeed, I am in danger of being skewered on one of my favorite weapons. I insist, helplessly, that academic life in general and its athletics in particular stand in grave need of answerable principles of reality. I also insist that these must be honorable because it is wrong for the university to constitute itself a school of crime. But, comes the reply, is that latter point realistic? Is this a world, a culture, in which principles of authenticity, integrity, and honor are in fact answerable?

"Oh, you're just an egghead!" said one distinguished gentleman. I took him to mean that he thinks a realistic education would teach the students what life, the world, the culture really are—crooked, rapacious, false, and mean. There winning really is the only thing, and it makes no difference how so long as you win—except perhaps that you ought to enjoy doing it as much as possible. "All men have their price," said wicked old Walpole. "In this world," observed Poor Richard, "we are saved not by faith but by want of it." Such being the situation, what is there to teach young persons except, "The name of the game is Win?"—perhaps, the faintly more sophisticated: "We win. Spare me the details."

Not long before Centennial time, that prince of American optimists Walt Whitman was writing in *Democratic Vistas*:

> I say we had best look our times and lands searchingly in the face, like a physician diagnosing some deep disease. Never was there, perhaps, more hollowness at heart than at present, and here in the United States. Genuine belief seems to have left us. The underlying principles of the States are not honestly believ'd in. . . .
>
> An acute and candid person, in the revenue department in Washington, who is led by the course of his employment to regularly visit the cities, north, south and west, to investigate frauds, has talk'd much with me about his discoveries. The depravity of the business classes of our country is not less than has been supposed, but infinitely greater. The official services of America, national, state, and municipal, in all their branches and departments, except the judiciary, are saturated in corruption, bribery, falsehood, mal-administration; and the judiciary is tainted. The great cities reek with respectable as much as nonrespectable robbery and scoundrelism. In fashionable life, flippancy, tepid amours, weak infidelism, small aims, or no aims at all, only to kill time. In business, (this all-devouring modern word, business,) the one sole object is, by any means, pecuniary gain.

Lincoln Steffens concluded his studies of political corruption in the United States by deciding that all wealth, civilization, learning, organized religion, even reform movements depended for their affluence and power upon the necessity of business systematically to corrupt politics for profits gained through privilege. He came to believe that the very ideals of the reformers were fountains of vice. Neither, of course, have such troubles been limited to business and politics. The summer 1976 number of the *American Scholar* printed a symposium on "Social Science: The Public Disenchantment." Among the topics set they raised the question: if there has been disenchantment, "Do you think this loss of confidence is merited by the behavior of social scientists over the past ten or so years?" They queried a number of greatly distinguished scholars and gathered some shattering opinions: (1) "The social sciences have lost prestige because they have claimed to be able to deliver more than they possibly can deliver." (2) "It is entirely wholesome that social scientists now are marked-down gurus, both because they deserve their fate and because adversity may guide them toward serious reconsideration of their tiresome pretensions to ethical neutrality and ideological purity." (3) "The follies of social science are rooted in its founders' search for immutable, infallible truths about mutable, fallible men. . . . It is neither possible nor desirable to extirpate all spurious, vulgar, commercial, partisan, slovenly, and popular forms of science and scholarship; pollution control will remain a serious problem in most disciplines." (4) We have had "years of extravagant promises, disastrous results, and trendy, self-indulgent gobbledygook. . . . It is not *knowledge* that has been dethroned but *fraud* that has been exposed." (5) "Many scholars who should have known better acquiesced in the process of allowing eager politicians to convert bad ideas into dubious policy."

I'm afraid I can say from observation that during the same years it has been demonstrated that you should seldom permit humanistic scholars control over power or money—not if you want humane relationships or value in return for dollars spent. If, however, I were asked to say what had most dismayed me about my profession since 1960 I should have to answer that it was the discovery of the tyranny within it of the conviction that nobody ought to do anything of value for nothing—indeed, without ample pecuniary return. As a class, that is to say, academics are morally better than business men or politicians in perhaps one regard: they operate on pettier levels.

From the point of view of men and women "of the world," devoted to status and privilege, to small pleasures and brief security, to safely fenced-in exploitations of the ego, there is not a little to be said for a mild immorality. We do, after all, teach things like advertising in academe. But from that worldly standpoint, whether it countenances intellectual fraud, small peculation, or instruction in worship of William James's Bitch-goddess Success, no moral ground exists from which to level condemnation against even corrupt intercollegiate athletics. Coach and the Irregulars may reply that at least they cheat in favor of a Big Game. What's Big about the rest?

As Damon Runyan's narrator observed, "In anything between human beings, the odds are 6-5 against." He recalled us to a bedrock American issue, the last, most creative tension between John Adams and Thomas Jefferson, for instance. Six to five against what? Given the prevalence of folly, are the odds 6-5 for or against the probability that the people and their culture will opt in the long run for ruin or survival? The odds are at best narrow; and your capacity to opt for either faith may hinge, as William James thought, more upon temperament than upon intellect or even experience. Of course it is possible that the values in human, American, and academic life to which this book addresses itself are idle. Perhaps the dreams of community and personal wholeness are really empty, Utopian, even dangerous. Very likely they are at best a sometime thing, in contemplation a ground for momentary stays against confusion, only as good as the next game.

Certainly the argument can be made that cheating, exploitative collegiate athletics mirror much in American life. But is it six or five? You feel an edge of foregone disgruntlement in much recent writing about sport which suggests the emotions, traditionally absurd, of a baffled romanticism. "The abdication of Belief," said Emily Dickinson, "Makes the Behavior small—." Every deadpan, cutthroat suspicion and ironic rejection of activity as such becomes a way of death. Uneasy questions arise. Henry Adams is one thing, but should sports writers sound like him? Is there abroad here a habit of gaining psychic income from a snobbery of reflecting upon how awful those subhuman slobs must be, those poor things who play sports where there rest no sufficient millions of dollars to subsidize their detachment from a sordid world? To what do we owe these customs of ideological rhetoric and Mandarin self-distancing from the behavior of the people in their culture? Shall these dry bones live?

Or, when we try to talk realities, are we only dealing with the ageless riddle of the painful earth, the problem of evil? Nobody solves it to everybody's satisfaction or ever has. It is the mystery of Job and Genesis and of all that's tragic, the moment of its perception perhaps coeval with the achievement of human mind. The solemnest of mysteries, it is scarcely apt to be dissipated by fretting, misrepresentation, the stiff refusal of human complicity or solidarity. It will even survive chic. I do not, of course, propose not to take seriously the problem of evil—in sports or anywhere—but I might make an exception for the sort of people who cannot contemplate allowing life to go on before they abolish it.

What I believe to be a major source of much morally ambiguous and inchoate behavior is a motive almost pathetically interesting and suggestive. People rage against the Big Game out of exasperation at their sense of a sanctuary betrayed. Because it seemed perfectly to express the commonplace agonies of our times, a sentence by Skip Rozin from an article in the *Audubon Magazine* for July 1975 caught my eye. Inside Fort Tryon Park, he said, lives the air, appreciated by old persons, of "A Morning in Another Time," regardless that "corruption and inflation still rage outside the gate." Though the times have seemed to insist on soilure and death, the heart cries out for sanctuary, remembering the good, if only the values of good intention, of the past. We must press back to preserve the sanctuaries, like the incredibly beleaguered yet potent, wisely guarded shrines of old beauty kept in the midst of the wastelands of modern Japan. The Game is itself a sanctuary, and its complex esthetics are more. They are threatened by the hollow-heartedness, the actual fiduciary as well as intellectual corruptness of the world and academe. Yet we cannot preserve them or any other sanctuaries unless we empower them, by acts of moral creativity, in the present.

The problem is to find the best available ways to live on in spite of evil, and I suppose those ancient wisdoms to be best which advise us to shun and fight it. And in doing so I think we are not without help. One advantage for good against all worldliness and corruption is that they become ways of death, of nothingness, and at last of terror. I remember with affection and gratitude the little old man from a deeply beleaguered college athletics situation who, glaring round the floor of a great convention, said to me in friendship, "This is the biggest roomful of hypocrites in the entire U.S. of A." It was pure moral revulsion. Therefore the situation is not without hope.

That the parties of despair fall measurably short of commanding the whole situation can be demonstrated from sources as broad as the national mood to instances as particular as the following, perfectly current memorandum from its president to all decision-making personnel of a great and far-flung international corporation which wishes to be modest about its name. It reads, in major part:

> There is much discussion in many circles today about ethical standards in U.S. corporations. The following discussion and attached policy is an elaboration of our traditional policy for your guidance, as well as a description of a mechanism for problem resolutions.
>
> "Ethical standards" is a phrase which has been badly misused, and we feel the need to define it as it is useful to apply it to [Our Company].
>
> For [Our Company] it means simply:
>
> 1. Obeying the law—in every community, in every country in which we operate, and obeying the law in spirit as well as letter; never taking advantage of a loophole in the wording to avoid complying with the intent.
>
> 2. Being honest—unqualified honest; telling the whole truth.
>
> 3. Being fair—treating the customer, wherever he is, as we would want to be treated if we were in his shoes.
>
> 4. Being concerned—Individuals who work for the company and communities in which the company is located are affected by the company's

policies and actions; this company must have a concern to act always in such a way as to be helpful and beneficial to those affected by its acts, and never harmful to them.

5. Being courageous—a willingness to follow the pattern just laid out, even if it may mean losing business. (It seldom does. Over the long haul people trust and respect this kind of behavior, and wish more of our institutions embodied it.)

The reason for such behavior is that, in the long run, *nothing else works*. Read the paper, and see for yourself.

In his effective way, that president has put the same point about the horror of corruption which Emerson argued and Henry James confirmed in some of the greatest of his art: that it makes nothing out of something, obliterating life. It delivers us to privation, the emptying out of light, warmth, being. It leaves us in the fright of utter darkness, cold, nothingness. Whitman had it right, "hollowness at heart." In "Respondez!" one of his most interesting but least known poems, he proclaims: let people, let the nation, let the culture go on and be corrupt utterly; then he asks, in abrupt ending, "What do you suppose death will do, then?"

Fascinating corroboration offers itself in a volume of psychocultural analysis by Dr. Herbert Hendin, *The Age of Sensation* (1975). Attempting what he calls "an open-ended psychoanalytic study of college youth in America," Hendin proceeds to wholesale condemnation of the present state of the culture. Having studied about five hundred students, mostly at Columbia, he concludes that "this culture is at war . . . a war of qualities, of difficulties in which there is no one who is not a casualty." He finds young people in their sexual relations full of anger and hostility, bent on hurting and humiliating one another emotionally, terrified of intimacy, involvement, tenderness—"a fear of being totally wiped out, of losing the fight for self-validation." They are consumed with rage. Afraid of competition yet desperate for success, Hendin's young people wish they could be machines. They actively pursue only "disengagement, detachment, fragmentation, and emotional numbness." They are not headed for disaster, they live there. "Why this is hell, nor am I out of it," said Marlowe's Mephistopheles.

Though Hendin thinks sport was a last, lost barricade for his generation of losers and rather wishes it could have been held, I am not sure he believes, or wishes to, that anything will work. *The Age of Sensation* says, "Mene, Mene. . . ." I would think it foolish to say that intercollegiate athletics could cure Hendin's zombies. But, then, I do not believe his unitary generalizations about the generation or the culture, either. I think the tragedies and disasters and conflicts he describes really are there, but I do not believe he grasps the whole of things by a luckily long shot indeed. It does, however, seem to me that he graphically illustrates what the achievement of nothingness—*nada y pues nada y nada*, as Hemingway's waiter saw—psychically and culturally can be.

Because "realism" in any art form is the achieved illusion of a shared, a common reality, it does not matter inside the charmed circle of artistic success whether outside reality is single or multiple. At the Big Game, all evidently, many realities obtain. Does that matter? Only when participants lose their grip on the difference between "art" and "life," the differences among orders of reality. And, again, only in proportion as one sort of reality, taken as a warrant for behavior, produces good or bad effects. If certain effects, temporarily bad, come to good ends—cathartic, for instance, well and good. If that behavior is contained in the stadium and controlled outside it by decorum, very well. But an institution of higher learning and education involved with the Big Game had better keep its vision whole, lucid, and rational. It must act to prevent and to control effects which spill over into unacceptable behavior outside the arena, especially that which happens within its academic pale. What shall be its warrant for action? The welfare of the whole. What can be, must be, its test and standard of control? Authenticity.

Whatever of authenticity and satisfaction and commonality could be created in American culture to place palpable human existence in the worlds of Hendin's or anybody else's folk would, on the other hand, constitute one sort of positive good. It is no joke, in the face of all that agony and horror. And that is why, not as panacea but as something of positive cultural achievement toward authenticity and community, I should pursue the Big Game and defend it from corruption. In short, I feel prepared for positive reasons to reject the famous statement, and what I think its implications, of Xenophanes of Colophon (ca. 480 B.C.) about the Games: "These things do not make fat the dark corners of the city." On the contrary, for the culture, failing which the people descend into Hendin's Hell, they form a part of the bread of life.

Something beats nothing all the time. To believe that life is better than death may be a prejudice, but with me it is inveterate. Form and its satisfactions, like home and its humanities, may be transient; but they are better than anomie. If nothing is here to stay, in the life of *homo viator* the momentary stops and stays are precious, the best things available. What is there to rail against? The games sing in C-major, the up-key in culture, and have only to resolve, faithfully and triumphantly, to it. Treachery, delusion, cheating, selling out, and all the horns of egotistical vice, like bad losing, may sound their notes without real harm if they are resolved into the major at last. Defeat, like tragedy, there must be: no losers, no winners. But they may resolve too in redemption and renewal.

As Santayana half foresaw, the great lion in the path of Hendin's victims, post-Freudian egotists, is the temptation never to let go of "self-validation," never to submit to Santayana's spirit of English liberty—or of American democracy or our team sports with their traditions of self-sacrifice, the investment of the ego in love or duty, the social contract, the general welfare, the team. Yet as I write, the Big Game has once more nationally, internationally played its music. It's a lot more fun, there's joy, esthetic return, synergy, there's abundance in playing it straight. Quinn Buckner, captain in the same year of NCAA and Olympic championship teams both famous for teamwork and "sacrifice," saw the victories as equally satisfactory because they were achieved by players united in teams of joint prowess greater than the sum of individual potentialities. His truth revises the hasty notion of basketball as a jazzy, "one-on-one" sort of exhibitionism. His joy was of the moment, and even now it is gone; but I do not expect to see him in Dr. Hendin's Hell.

Anywhere integrity and authenticity exist or a motion is made to gain or restore them, anywhere those standards are raised in American culture in our time, that is important. The Big Game calls for care, for renewal and redemption. Without impropriety, I think, you can say: "Where it is corrupt, purify it; where it is in error, direct it; where in any thing it is amiss, reform it. Where it is right, establish it; where it is in want, provide for it; where it is divided, reunite it." For without vision the people perish. And the Big Game, perfectly one of Geertz's "culture texts," enacts before our eyes what in turn our responses enact among and within us, the sight and feel, the otherwise inexpressible *gestalt* of what the American dreams would be were they realized more often and broadly. How many of the things we do really have more value?

As in the governance of democratic life generally, reform of the Big Game can take no other effective shape than that of a steady state. Many, subtle, and strong, the impulses toward corruption never slacken. They must be met equally. Reform must become everybody's good. Though it cannot be radical and be reform, it must be determined; it must be imaginative, tireless, based firmly on answerable principles of reality.

The real odds being what they are, in moral behavior it is the rigid millenarian demand—whether from the Right or Left—for perfect purity, a platonic chastity, which living culture must resist. Honor is not forever, not the motive of anything one does for eternity. It always concerns something between human beings, and it expresses integrity, authenticity. It tells one what is the right thing to do for the present moment, in the knowledge that nothing will be permanently settled. Not "Chastity or Death!" but, inevitably, "just a little bit pregnant" represents the human condition. Reform, reconciliation, atonement must be our aims: restoration of the means to go on better, the establishment of continuities so sound they can survive. These can be lived, where the ways of despairing wickedness or delusive purity can only be died. Wrong stays wrong and goodness right; and wrong seeks nothingness where right finds health: "It is that in nature we are from," said Frost. There are always next time and next year, and it is for every next one that health must be sought.

The Big Game we know needs a general, sensitive bringing up to date in response to the culture and subcultures it serves. It needs to be liberated from the "gate" and made independent of the things for which the media and show biz hate themselves. It needs a fresh reconciliation with academe. These are aims which cannot be reached suddenly or by great, simple leaps. They will require untiring acts of daily renewal and redemption. But that can be done. And as it happens, with it, in detail, the same renewal and redemption can be worked in the patterns and other culture texts of our academic and national life. It is, after all, the business of the Big Game to be symbolic and exemplary.

References

Adams, John, to Thomas Jefferson, 15 Nov. 1813, from Edwin H. Cady, ed. *Literature of the Early Republic*. New York: Rinehart, 1969.

Adams, Samuel Hopkins. *Grandfather Stories*. New York: Random House, 1955.

Adatto, Carl. "Golf," in Slovenko and Knight.

Allardt, Erik. "Basic Approaches in Comparative Sociological Research and the Study of Sport," in Lüschen.

Ashworth, C.E. "Sport as Symbolic Dialogue," in Dunning.

Auguet, Roland. *Cruelty and Civilization: The Roman Games*. London: Allen and Unwin, 1972.

Avedon, Elliott, and Sutton-Smith, Brian. *The Study of Games*. New York: Wiley, 1971.

Bannister, Roger. "The Meaning of Athletic Performance," in Talamini and Page.

Barber, C.L. *Shakespeare's Festive Comedy*. Princeton: Princeton Univ. Press, 1959.

Bardacke, Theodore. "Break Up Robin and Her Merry Men." *San Diego Magazine*, May 1974.

Beisser, Arnold R. *The Madness in Sports*. New York: Appleton, 1967.

Bend, Emil. "The Impact of Athletic Participation on Academic and Career Aspiration and Achievement." Pittsburgh: National Football Foundation [1968].

Benedict, Ruth. *Patterns of Culture*. New York: Pelican, 1946.

Bent, Silas. *Ballyhoo: The Voice of the Press*. New York: Boni and Liveright, 1927.

Bergler, Edmund. *The Psychology of Gambling*. New York: Hill, 1957.

Berne, Eric. *Games People Play*. New York: Grove, 1964.

Bettis, Stan. "The Unmaking of the Coach, 1972." *Old Oregon*, Spring 1972.

Biddulph, Lowell G. "Athletic Achievement and the Personal and Social Adjustment of High School Boys," in Sage.

Big Ten Records Book, 25th Edition, 1972-1973. Chicago: Big Ten, 1972.

Blake, Kathleen. *Play, Games, and Sport: The Literary Works of Lewis Carroll*. Ithaca: Cornell Univ. Press, 1974.

Boorstin, Daniel J. *The Image: A Guide to Pseudo-Events in America*. New York: Harper, 1964.

———. *Democracy and Its Discontents*. New York: Random House, 1974.

Bowen, Ezra. "I Finally Got the Point." *Sports Illustrated*, 10 Feb. 1969.

Boyle, Robert H. "The Bizarre History of American Sport." *Sports Illustrated*, 8 Jan. 1962.

———. *Sport–Mirror of American Life*. Boston: Little, Brown, 1963.

Bradford, William. *History of Plimouth Plantation*. Boston, 1899.

Bradley, Bill. *Life on the Run*. New York: Quadrangle, 1976.

Brailsford, Dennis. *Sport and Society: Elizabeth to Anne*. London: Routledge, 1969.

Brogan, D.W. *The American Character*. New York: Knopf, 1944.

Brondfield, Jerry. *Woody Hayes and the Hundred-Yard War*. New York: Berkley, 1975.

Brown, Roscoe C., and Cratty, Bryant J. *New Perspectives of Man in Action*. Englewood Cliffs, N.J.: Prentice-Hall, 1969.

Browne, Evelyn. "An Ethological Theory of Play," in Sage.

Bryce, James. *The American Commonwealth*. 2 vols. New York: Macmillan, 1899.

Cady, Edwin H. *The Gentleman in America*. Syracuse: Syracuse Univ. Press, 1949.

———. " 'The Strenuous Life' as a Theme in American Cultural History." *New Voices in American Studies*, ed. Browne, et al., West Lafayette, Ind.: Purdue Univ. Press, 1966.

———. "Athletics and the Academic Community." *Review*, Fall 1969.

Camp, Walter. *Walter Camp's Book of College Sports*. New York: Century, 1895.

———. "Should a Boy Play Football?" *Collier's*, 19 Nov. 1904.

Capell, Martin D. "Games and the Mastery of Helplessness," in Slovenko and Knight.

Carew, Richard. *A Survey of Cornwall*, London, 1602. F.E. Halliday, *Richard Carew of Antony*, London: Melrose, 1953, is a good edition, but I have preferred to modernize the English myself.

Carthy, J.D., and Ebling, F.J., eds. *The Natural History of Aggression*. London: Academic Press, 1964.

Clay, George R. "Letters to the Editor." *American Scholar*, Autumn 1964.

Cohane, Tim. *Great College Football Coaches of the Twenties and Thirties*. New Rochelle, N.Y.: Arlington, 1973.

Coleman, James S. "Athletics in High School," in Sage.

———. "Sports and Studies as Paths to Success," in Loy and Kenyon.

Cooper, James Fenimore. *Home as Found*. Philadelphia, 1838.

Coover, Robert. *The Universal Baseball Association.* . . . New York: Signet, 1969.

Cope, Myron. *The Game That Was* . . . . Rev. ed. New York: Crowell, 1974.

Cousy, Bob. *The Killer Instinct*. New York: Random House, 1975.

Crèvecoeur, St. Jean de. *Letters of an American Farmer*. London, 1793.

Cutler, John L. *Gilbert Patten and His Frank Merriwell Saga*. Univ. of Maine Studies, ser. 11, no. 31 (Orono, 1934).

Danzig, Allison. *The History of American Football*. Englewood Cliffs, N.J.: Prentice-Hall, 1956.

———, ed. *Oh, How They Played the Game: The Early Days of Football and the Heroes Who Made It Great*. New York: Macmillan, 1971.

Deford, Frank. "No Death for a Salesman." *Sports Illustrated*, 28 July 1975.

Denlinger, Kenneth, and Shapiro, Leonard. *Athletes for Sale*. New York: Crowell, 1975.

Denney, Reuel. *The Astonished Muse*. Chicago: Univ. of Chicago Press, 1957.

Deutsch, Helene. "Some Dynamic Factors in Sport," in Slovenko and Knight.

Dickinson, Emily. *The Poems of Emily Dickinson*. 3 vols. Cambridge: Harvard Univ. Press, 1955.

Dodds, E.R. "Introduction" in Euripides. *Bacchae*. 2d ed. Oxford: Oxford Univ. Press, 1960.

Dolan, Joseph P. "Parents of Athletes," in Slovenko and Knight.

Dulles, Foster Rhea. *America Learns to Play*. New York: Dutton, 1940.

Dunning, Eric. "The Development of Modern Football," in Dunning.

——, ed. *Sport: Readings from a Sociological Perspective*. Toronto: Univ. of Toronto Press, 1972.

Durant, John, and Bettmann, Otto. *Pictorial History of American Sports from Colonial Times to the Present*. Rev. ed. New York: Barnes, 1965.

Durso, Joseph. *The All-American Dollar: The Big Business of Sports*. Boston: Houghton Mifflin, 1971.

——. *The Sports Factory*. New York: Quadrangle, 1975.

Edwards, Harry. *Sociology of Sport*. Homewood, Ill.: Dorsey, 1973.

Eggleston, John. "Secondary Schools and Oxbridge Blues," in Loy and Kenyon.

Eiseley, Loren. "The Poignant Work of Tampering with Prehistory." *Smithsonian*, Oct. 1975.

Elias, Norbert. "The Genesis of Sport as a Sociological Problem," in Dunning.

——, and Dunning, Eric. "Dynamics of Sport Groups with Special Reference to Football," in Dunning.

——, "Folk Football in Medieval and Early Modern Britain," in Dunning.

——, "The Quest for Excitement in Unexciting Societies,"in Lüschen.

Ferril, T.H. "Freud on the 50-Yard Line," in Newcombe.

Fishwick, Marshall. *Parameters of Popular Culture*. Bowling Green, Ohio: Popular, 1974.

Flath, Arnold, ed. *Athletics in America*. Corvallis: Oregon State Univ. Press, 1972.

Fox, J.R. "Pueblo Baseball: A New Use for Old Witchcraft," in Loy and Kenyon.

Frazer, James G. *The Golden Bough: A Study in Magic and Religion*. Abridged. New York: Macmillan, 1940.

Freeman, Derek. "Human Agression in Anthropological Perspective," in Carthy and Ebling.

Friedenberg, Edgar Z. "Foreword," in Slusher.

Fromm, Erich. *The Art of Loving*. New York: Bantam, 1963.

Froncek, Thomas, ed. *Voices from the Wilderness*. New York: McGraw-Hill, 1974.

Robert Frost: A Descriptive Catalogue of Books and Manuscripts in the Clifton Waller Barrett Library, comp. Joan St. C. Crane. Charlottesville: Univ. Press of Virginia, 1974.

Frost, Robert. "The Trial by Existence." *Independent*, 11 Oct. 1906.

———. "The Figure a Poem Makes." *Collected Poems*. New York: Holt, 1939.

———. *Selected Letters*, ed. Lawrence Thompson. New York: Holt, 1964.

Frye, Northrop. *Anatomy of Criticism: Four Essays*. Princeton: Princeton Univ. Press, 1957.

Furlong, William. "Danger as a Way of Joy." *Sports Illustrated*, 27 January 1969.

Gahringer, Robert E. "Can Games Explain Language?" *Journal of Philosophy*, 30 July 1959.

Galpin, W. Freeman. *Syracuse University*. Vol. I: *The Pioneer Days*. Syracuse: Syracuse Univ. Press, 1952.

Gardiner, E. Norman. *Greek Athletic Sports and Festivals*. London: Macmillan, 1910.

Geertz, Clifford. "Deep Play: Notes on the Balinese Cockfight." *Daedalus*, Winter 1972.

Gregory of Nyssa. "Concerning True Virtue," *The Life of Moses*, trans. B. Gregg.

Griffith, John L. "A Philosophy of College Athletics." *Athletic Journal*, Jan., May 1931.

———. "Do Athletics Contribute to Education?" *Athletic Journal*, Jan. 1932.

Grobani, Anton, ed. *Guide to Football Literature*. Detroit: Gale, 1975.

Guthrie, W.K.C. *The Greeks and Their Gods*. Boston: Beacon, 1955.

Hamilton, Edith. *The Greek Way to Western Civilization*. New York: Mentor, 1942.

Harris, H.A. *Greek Athletes and Athletics*. Bloomington: Indiana Univ. Press, 1966.

Hart, M. Marie, ed. *Sport in the Socio-Cultural Process*. Dubuque: Brown, 1972.

Hartogs, Renatus, and Artzt, Eric. *Violence: Causes and Solutions*. New York: Dell, 1970.

Hays, H.R. *From Ape to Angel: An Informal History of Social Anthropology*. New York: Capricorn, 1964.

Hendin, Herbert. *The Age of Sensation*. New York: Norton, 1975.

Hesburgh, T.M. "The True Meaning of the Game." *Sports Illustrated*, 12 Dec. 1966.

Hoffman, Frederick J. *Samuel Beckett: The Language of Self*. New York: Dutton, 1964.

Hofstadter, Richard, ed. *American Violence: A Documentary History*. New York: Knopf, 1970.

Hogan, William R. "Sin and Sports," in Slovenko and Knight.

Howells, W.D. *A Boy's Town*. New York: Harper, 1890.

———. "Bibliographical." In *The Landlord at Lion's Head*. New York: Harper, 1909.

———. "Matthew Arnold." In Cady, ed., *W.D. Howells as Critic*. London: Routledge, 1973.

Howells, William W. *Back of History: The Story of Our Origins*. Rev. ed. New York: Anchor, 1963.

Hubbart, Henry C. *Ohio Wesleyan's First Hundred Years*. Delaware, Ohio: Ohio Wesleyan Univ. Press, 1943.

Hughes, Thomas. *Tom Brown's School Days*. London, 1857.

———. *True Manliness*. (Selections by E.E. Brown.) Boston, 1880.

Huizinga, Johan. *Homo Ludens: A Study of the Play Element in Culture*. Boston: Beacon, 1955.

Jaeger, Gertrude, and Selznick, Philip. "A Normative Theory of Culture," in Meredith.

Jeffers, Robinson. "Science" and "Shine, Perishing Republic." *The Selected Poems of Robinson Jeffers*. New York: Random House, 1959.

Jenkins, Dan. *Saturday's America*. Boston: Little, Brown, 1970.

Johnson, William O. *Super Spectator and the Electric Lilliputians*. Boston: Little, Brown, 1971.

———. "The Day the Money Ran Out." *Sports Illustrated*, 1 Dec. 1975.

Jokl, Ernst. *Medical Sociology and Cultural Anthropology of Sport and Physical Education*. Springfield, Ill.: Thomas, 1964.

Jones, Marilyn. "Perceptual Characteristics and Athletic Performance," in Whiting.

Kavanaugh, Aidan. " 'I Shall Not Live Forever If I Cannot Make It through Tomorrow Morning.' " *Yale Alumni Magazine*, Dec. 1975.

Keating, James W. "Paradoxes in American Athletics," in Flath.

Kelley, Brooks M. *Yale: A History*. New Haven: Yale Univ. Press, 1974.

Kelly, John B., Jr. "Amateurism in Sport as a Viable Ideal in the 1970's," in Flath.

Kenyon, Gerald S. "Attitude toward Sport and Physical Activity among Adolescents from Four English-Speaking Countries," in Lüschen.

——. "A Conceptual Model for Characterizing Physical Activity," in Loy and Kenyon.

——. "Sport and Society: At Odds or in Concert?" in Flath.

——, ed. Contemporary Psychology of Sport. Chicago: Athletic Institute, 1968.

Kieran, John. "Sports." In America Now, ed. Harold Stearns. New York: Scribner's, 1938.

Kingsley, William L. Yale College: A Sketch of Its History. 2 vols. New York: Holt, 1879.

Klapp, Orrin E. Currents of Unrest: An Introduction to Collective Behavior. New York: Holt, 1972.

Krout, John. Annals of American Sport. New Haven: Yale Univ. Press, 1929.

Lahr, John. "The Theatre of Sports," in Hart.

Langer, Susanne K. Philosophy in a New Key. New York: Mentor, 1958.

Lardner, Ring W. "Sport and Play." In Civilization in the United States, ed. Harold Stearns. New York: Harcourt, 1922.

Larrabee, Eric, and Myersohn, Rolf, eds. Mass Leisure. Glencoe, Ill.: Free Press, 1958.

Leonard, William Ellery. Two Lives: A Poem. New York: Huebsch, 1925.

Lever, Janet. "Soccer as a Brazilian Way of Life," in Stone.

Levy, Bill. Three Yards and a Cloud of Dust. Cleveland: World, 1966.

Lewis, Guy. "The Beginning of Organized Collegiate Sport." American Quarterly, Summer 1970.

Lipsite, Robert. Sportsworld, an American Dreamland. New York: Quadrangle, 1975.

Lorenz, Konrad. On Aggression. New York: Harcourt, 1966.

——. "Ritualized Fighting," in Carthy and Ebling.

Lovejoy, A.O. Essays in the History of Ideas. Baltimore: Johns Hopkins Univ. Press, 1948.

Loy, John W. "Game Forms, Social Structure, and Anomie," in Brown and Cratty.

————, and Kenyon, Gerald, eds. *Sport, Culture, and Society*. New York: Macmillan, 1969.

Lüschen, Günther. "The Interdependence of Sport and Culture," in Lüschen.

————, ed. *The Cross-Cultural Analysis of Sport and Games*. Champaign, Ill.: Stipes, 1970.

McCormick, Richard P. *Rutgers: A Bicentennial History*. New Brunswick, N.J.: Rutgers Univ. Press, 1966.

McCraw, L.M., and Tolbert, J.W. "Sociometric Status and Athletic Ability of Junior High School Boys," in Sage.

McIntosh, Peter C. "Theories of Why and How," in Hart.

McLuhan, Marshall. "Games: The Extension of Man," in Hart.

McPhee, John. "A Sense of Where You Are." *New Yorker*, 23 Jan. 1965.

Maheu, René. "Sportsmanship and Self-Respect." *UNESCO Features*, May 1970.

Malina, Robert M. "An Anthropological Perspective of Man in Action," in Brown and Cratty.

Martinez, Thomas M., and LaFranchi, Robert. "Why People Play Poker," in Stone.

Matthiessen, Peter. *Under the Mountain Wall: A Chronicle of Two Seasons in the Stone Age*. New York: Ballantine, 1969.

Mead, Margaret. *Cooperation and Competition among Primitive Peoples*. Boston: Beacon, 1961.

————. *And Keep Your Powder Dry*. New York: Morrow, 1965.

Menninger, Karl. "Preface," in Slovenko and Knight.

Merchant, Larry. *The National Football Lottery*. New York: Dell, 1973.

Meredith, Robert, ed. *American Studies: Essays on Theory and Method*. Columbus, Ohio: Merrill, 1968.

Miller, David L. *Gods and Games: Toward a Theology of Play*. New York: World, 1970.

Minuchin, Salvador. "Adolescence: Society's Response and Responsibility." *Adolescence*, 16 (1969), 455-476.

Mizruchi, Ephraim Harold. *Success and Opportunity: A Study of Anomie*. New York: Free Press, 1964.

Montagu, Ashley, ed. *Man and Aggression*. 2d ed. New York: Oxford Univ. Press, 1973.

————. *The Nature of Human Aggression*. New York: Oxford Univ. Press, 1976.

Moore, Robert A. *Sports and Mental Health*. Springfield, Ill.: Thomas, 1966.

———. "Injury in Athletics," in Slovenko and Knight.

Morgan, William P., ed. *Contemporary Readings in Sport Psychology*. Springfield, Ill.: Thomas, 1970.

Morison, Samuel E. *The Development of Harvard University since the Inauguration of President Eliot*, 1869-1929. Cambridge: Harvard Univ. Press, 1930.

Murray, Gilbert. *Five Stages of Greek Religion*. New York: Anchor, 1955.

Natan, Alex. "Sport and Politics," in Loy and Kenyon.

Newcombe, Jack, ed. *The Fireside Book of Football*. New York: Simon, 1964.

Niebuhr, Reinhold. *The Irony of American History*. New York: Scribner's, 1952.

Nilsson, Martin P. *Greek Folk Religion*. New York: Harper, 1961.

North, Helen. *Sophrosyne: Self-Knowledge and Self-Restraint in Greek Literature*. Ithaca: Cornell Univ. Press, 1966.

Nye, Robert D. *Conflict among Humans*. New York: Springer, 1973.

Ogilvie, Bruce, and Tutko, Thomas. "Success Phobia," in Sage.

Orpingalik. See Radin.

[Office of Strategic Services]. *Assessment of Men*. New York: Rinehart, 1948.

Page, Charles H. "The Mounting Interest in Sport," in Talamini and Page.

———. "Pervasive Sociological Themes in the Study of Sport," in Talamini and Page.

———. "Sports and 'Sport': The Problem of Selection," in Talamini and Page.

Paxson, Frederic L. "The Rise of Sport." *Mississippi Valley Historical Review*, Sept. 1917.

Phillips, Henry Wallace. *Red Saunders, Pets and Other Critters*. New York: McClure, 1906.

Phillips, Richard H. "Children's Games," in Slovenko and Knight.

Plimpton, George. *Mad Ducks and Bears*. New York: Bantam, 1974.

Polsky, Ned. "Of Pool Playing and Pool Rooms," in Stone.

Porter, Robert T. "Sports and Adolescence," in Slovenko and Knight.

Radin, Paul. "The Literature of Primitive Peoples." *Diogenes*, Winter 1955.

Rahner, Hugo. *Man at Play*. New York: Herder and Herder, 1967.

Raiborn, Mitchell. *An Analysis of Revenues, Expenses and Management Accounting Practices of Intercollegiate Athletic Programs*. Kansas City: *NCAA*, 1970.

Rappaport, Roy A. *Pigs for the Ancestors: Ritual in the Ecology of a New Guinea People*. New Haven: Yale Univ. Press, 1967.

Rehberg, Richard A., and Schafer, Walter E. "Participation in Interscholastic Athletics and College Expectations," in Sage.

Reston, James. "Sports: An Antidote to Trends of Our Time." *Louisville Courier-Journal*, 11 Oct. 1966.

———. "Sports and Politics." *Louisville Courier-Journal*, 15 Sept. 1969.

Riesman, David. *Individualism Reconsidered*. Glencoe, Ill.: Free Press, 1964.

Roberts, John M.; Arth, Malcolm J.; Bush, Robert R. "Games in Culture." *American Anthropologist*, Aug. 1959.

Rochlin, Gregory. *Man's Aggression: The Defense of the Self*. Boston: Gambit, 1973.

Rooney, John F., Jr. "Up from the Mines and Out from the Prairies. Some Geographical Implications of Football in the United States." *Geographical Review*, Oct. 1969.

Rosenthal, Sol Roy. See Furlong.

Ross, Murray. "Football and Baseball in America," in Talamini and Page.

Roszak, Theodore. "Forbidden Games," in Hart.

Rozin, Skip. "A Morning in Another Time." *Audubon Magazine*, July 1975.

Russell, Claire, and Russell, W.M.S. *Violence, Monkeys and Man*. London: Macmillan, 1968.

Russell, William F. "Success Is a Journey." *Sports Illustrated*, 8 June 1970.

Sage, George H., ed. *Sport and American Society: Selected Readings*. Reading, Mass.: Addison-Wesley, 1970.

Santayana, George. *A Hermit of Carmel and Other Poems*. New York: Scribner's, 1901.

———. *Character and Opinion in the United States*. New York: Scribner's, 1920.

———. *The Middle Span*. New York: Scribner's, 1945.

———. *Persons and Places*. New York: Scribner's, 1944.

———. *George Santayana's America: Essays on Literature and Culture*, ed. James Ballowe. Urbana: Univ. of Illinois Press, 1967.

Schafer, Walter E., and Armer, J. Michael. "Athletes Are Not Inferior Students," in Stone.

——. "On Scholarship and Interscholastic Athletics," in Dunning.

Schimel, John L. "Sports Games and Love," in Slovenko and Knight.

——. "The Sporting and Gaming Aspects of Love and War," in Kenyon.

Schneider, Herbert W. *A History of American Philosophy*. New York: Columbia Univ. Press, 1946.

Shaara, Michael. "Colleges Short-Change Their Football Players." *Saturday Evening Post*, 5 Nov. 1966.

Shaughnessy, Edward L. "Santayana on Athletics." *American Studies*, 10, 2, 173-183.

Sheed, Wilfred. "My Passport Was at Shortstop." *Sports Illustrated*, 11 Nov. 1968.

Simpson, Alan. Memeographed press release from University of Chicago.

Singer, Robert N. *Coaching, Athletics, and Psychology*, New York: McGraw-Hill, 1972.

Sisk, John P. "The Promise of Dirty Words." *American Scholar*, Summer 1975.

Slovenko, Ralph, and Knight, James A., eds. *Motivations in Play, Games and Sports*. Springfield, Ill.: Thomas, 1967.

Slusher, Howard S. "Personality and Intelligence Characteristics of Selected High School Athletes and Nonathletes," in Sage.

——. *Man, Sport, and Existence: A Critical Analysis*. Philadelphia: Lea and Febiger, 1967.

Smith, Bradford. *Why We Behave Like Americans*. Philadelphia: Lippincott, 1957.

Smith, Leverett T., Jr. *The American Dream and the National Game*. Bowling Green, Ohio: Popular, 1975.

"Social Science: The Public Disenchantment. A Symposium." *American Scholar*, Summer 1976.

Stade, George. "Game Theory." *Columbia Univ. Forum*, Fall 1966.

Stein, Maurice R.; Vidich, Arthur J.; White, David M., eds. *Identity and Anxiety: Survival of the Person in Mass Society*. Glencoe, Ill.: Free Press, 1960.

Stokes, Adrian. "The Development of Ball Games," in Slovenko and Knight.

Stone, Gregory P. "American Sports: Play and Display," in Dunning.

——. "Wrestling: The Great American Passion Play," in Dunning.

————, ed. *Games, Sports and Power*. New Brunswick, N.J.: *transaction*, 1972.

Stone, Sue S. "Bowling," in Slovenko and Knight.

Stuhldreher, Mary. *Many a Saturday Afternoon*. New York: McKay, 1964.

Sutton-Smith, Brian, and Roberts, John M. "The Cross-Cultural and Psychological Study of Games," in Lüschen.

Talamini, John T. "School Athletics: Public Policy versus Practice," in Talamini and Page.

————, and Page, Charles H., eds. *Sport and Society: An Anthology*. Boston: Little, Brown, 1973.

Tarbeaux, Frank. *The Autobiography of Frank Tarbeaux*. New York: Vanguard, 1930.

Taylor, Ian. " 'Football Mad': A Speculative Sociology of Football Hooliganism," in Dunning.

Tennyson, Charles. "They Taught the World to Play." *Victorian Studies*, March 1959.

Thomas, Lewis. *The Lives of a Cell: Notes of a Biology Watcher*. New York: Viking, 1975.

Thorp, Margaret F. *Charles Kingsley*. Princeton: Princeton Univ. Press, 1937.

Thurber, James. "University Days," from *My Life and Hard Times*, in *The Thurber Carnival*. New York: Harper, 1945.

Underwood, John. "The College Game Is Best." *Sports Illustrated*, 20 Sept. 1965.

————. "Look Who's Up and About." *Sports Illustrated*, 8 Sept. 1975.

Updike, John. *Picked-Up Pieces*. New York: Knopf, 1975.

Vaille, F.O., and Clark, H.A., eds. *The Harvard Book. A Series of Historical, Biographical, and Descriptive Sketches*. 2 vols. Cambridge: Harvard Univ. Press, 1875.

VanderZwaag, Harold J. *Toward a Philosophy of Sport*. Reading, Mass.: Addison-Wesley, 1972.

Van Dyne, Larry. *Chronicle of Higher Education*. 17 Feb. 1976.

Vanek, Miroslav, and Cratty, Bryant J., eds. *Psychology and the Superior Athlete*. New York: Macmillan, 1970.

Vare, Robert. *Buckeye: A Study of Coach Woody Hayes and the Ohio State Football Machine*. New York: Harper, 1974.

Veblen, Thorstein. *The Theory of the Leisure Class*. New York, 1899.

Ward, Gene, and Hyman, Dick. *Football Wit and Humor*. New York: Grosset, 1970.

Ward, Stephen D. "The Superior Athlete," in Slovenko and Knight.

Weinberg, S. Kirson, and Arond, Henry. "The Occupational Culture of the Boxer," in Loy and Kenyon.

Weiss, Paul. *Sport: A Philosophic Inquiry*. Carbondale: Southern Illinois Univ. Press, 1971.

Wertenbaker, Thomas J. *Princeton: 1746-1896*. Princeton: Princeton Univ. Press, 1946.

Wheelwright, Philip. *The Burning Fountain: A Study in the Language of Symbolism*. Bloomington: Indiana Univ. Press, 1954.

Whiting, H.T.A. "Psychology of Competition," in Whiting.

———, ed. *Readings in Sports Psychology*. London: Kimpton, 1972.

Whitman, Walt. *Democratic Vistas*. New York, 1871.

Wilson, Kenneth L., and Brondfield, Jerry. *The Big Ten*. Englewood Cliffs, N.J.: Prentice-Hall, 1967.

Yellen, Samuel. "How Football Died," in Newcombe.

Zeegers, Machiel. "The Swindler as a Player," in Slovenko and Knight.

Zurcher, Louis A., Jr., and Meadow, Arnold. "On Bullfights and Baseball: An Example of Interaction of Social Institutions," in Lüschen.

Index